# INTRODUCTION

## First A Preface

First and foremost, this is a story because it is mine. It may not be "real" in the usual perceptive limits of many but nevertheless, it is part of what we individually perceive as reality.

In particular, it is my reality and my truth because it was my Soul that assisted me in seeking out the evidence for this version of truth... after I learned to listen to it.

Would it have made a big difference in my life it I had listened earlier? As far as this STRAWMAN story is concerned, it would have changed the energy engagement and under the law of Cause and Effect brought forward a much different life less filled with conflict and anger. Why? Because when you learn to listen to your Higher Inner Self, the Lower Self does not get away with its ego dominated desires and habits; and a whole new way of living emerges. This type of information that is as upsetting as it is bizarre, would not have been received the same way. It would have been tempered by the Soul from a higher plateau. The perception of your truth, once it emerges as negative - like fraud or deception - is there for you to forgive those who created the untruth, and move on.

So there are four lessons brought about by this story of the mythical STRAWMAN:

1. Listen to your own Soul speaking to your Lower Mind about this type of "truth" sooner than later, and,
2. Accept this story as a story that you can improve on in some way that does not create conflict and anger, and,
3. Listen to your Soul that knows only truth and guides you to live a life of bliss and joy based upon peace, harmony and love.
4. Although there may many stories and perceptions that are in conflict with your own "truths" they reflect the laws and culture at the present time. To rebel or conflict with these is best undertaken in a peaceful way because the truth can set you free but it can also put you in jail.

So read it, enjoy the story, ask your own Soul about it and get some advice, then move on to improvement and perfection. Spare yourself the conflict and negative energy that the word "fraud" brings to your ego.

## We Live In A Corporate World

Once king's conquered and maintained control by physical riches to hire military might. Now conquest is executed through debt money and commerce. Once kings took possession of lands and continents by piracy and the laws of the Sea. Now it is done by bankruptcy, takeovers, Title acquisitions and Code of Law under the laws of the sea. Once kings created dynasties and kingdoms. Now they create corporations. Once kings had slaves and serfs to do the bidding. Now they are called employees.

The UNITED STATES OF AMERICA is a registered corporation since the Act of 1871 which established the District of Columbia, we have been living under the UNITED STATES CORPORATION which is owned by certain international bankers and aristocracy of Europe

# The Soul's STORY of the STRAWMAN

**Ed Rychkun**

www.edrychkun.com

## ISBN 978-1-927066-09-6

There is no copyright to this book as it is a compilation of many other's research and opinions on this topic. It is not provided to offer advice on any commercial or tax strategy. It is for the purpose of presenting a different historical story of commerce and the Soul's evolution on Earth.

www.edrychkun.com.

# CONTENTS

**INTRODUCTION** — 5
    First A Preface — 5
    We Live In A Corporate World — 6
    Enter The STRAWMAN — 10

**1 ONCE UPON A TIME** — 15

**2 REMEMBER WHO YOU ARE** — 26
    Above All Remember Higher or Inner Self — 30

**3 THE BERTH OF THE EARTHLING** — 36
    Preparing For The Berthing — 36
    The Physical Berth On Earth — 38
    Creation of The STRAWMAN — 40

**4 THE EARLY CHILDHOOD** — 43
    Registering Human Capital — 44
    Registering Human Banking Assets — 47
    Bond Trading On World Markets — 51

**5 THE AGE OF MATURITY** — 53
    The Schooling Years — 53
    Application Of Social Insurance Number — 54
    Issuance of SIN Number — 56
    Rollover Of Estate Executor — 56
    Probating The Estate — 58
    Income Taxes And Working Off The Debt — 59
    Banking And Loans — 60
    Final Death Of The STRAWMAN — 61

**6 RESURRECTION OF THE SOUL** — 63
    The Awakening Begins — 65
    The New Earth Revelations — 66

**7 INTRODUCING CORPORATION PLANET EARTH** — 71
    The Corporate Empires — 73
    And Then There is PLANET EARTH — 81

**8 THE THREADS THAT BIND EARTH** — 82
    The Religious Pyramids — 85
    The Vatican Empire — 87
    The Pyramid Of Debt — 92
    The Corporate Pyramids — 94

| | |
|---|---:|
| The Corporate Model Of Sumeria | **97** |
| Corporation PLANET EARTH | **101** |
| The Hierarchy Of Earthlings | **107** |
| **9 THE GLOBAL RULERS: THE"gods"** | **109** |
| Bloodlines Of The Global Rulers | **111** |
| The 13 Royal Bloodlines | **115** |
| A Word About gods | **120** |
| **10 THE STORY OF BANKRUPT AMERICA** | **122** |
| America Is Bankrupt Again | **124** |
| Money Banking Systems: The Real Power | **134** |
| **11 THE STORY OF CODE OF LAW** | **139** |
| Evolution Of The Code Of Law | **139** |
| The New Subjects Under "The Law" | **160** |
| The Establishment Of Human Capital | **167** |
| **12 COMMERCE AND MONEY CHAINS OF CONTROL** | **171** |
| The Money Kingdoms | **172** |
| A Story Of Money | **174** |
| Local Banks And The Process Of Money Creation | **179** |
| A Short History Of Banking Evolution In America | **183** |
| The Federal Government And The National Debt | **200** |
| The Elegant Corporate Structure | **208** |
| "Money" Is A Record Of Debt | **211** |
| Relevance To Canada And Other Nations | **218** |
| Moving Higher In The Corporate Pyramid | **220** |
| **13 THE FINAL CORPORATE OVERLAY: EARTHLINGS** | **237** |
| Corporate Legal Fictions Overlay Real People | **238** |
| History Review Of The STRAWMAN | **241** |
| The Relation To The Constitution | **245** |
| The Creation Of Three Trusts | **249** |
| The Administrators Of The STRAWMAN Fictions | **251** |
| The Detailed Story of The STRAWMAN | **255** |
| All STRAWMEN Are Make-Believe Ships At Sea | **268** |
| Who Became The Administrators Of The Trusts? | **271** |
| **14 MARITIME LAWS OF THE SEA** | **274** |
| UNITED STATES Corporation | **274** |
| What Is Maritime Law? | **275** |
| All Corporate Bodies Are Ships At Sea | **276** |

| | |
|---|---|
| Admiralty And Maritime Law | **279** |
| The Flag Shows Substantive Law Of Admiralty | **283** |
| How Admiralty Happened | **287** |
| Plausible Deniability: The Background Plan | **289** |
| **15 THE LAWS OF THE LAND** | **293** |
| The Uniform Commercial Code Laws | **293** |
| Uniform Commercial Code: Law Of The Land | **296** |
| Everything Is Commerce | **309** |
| Precepts and Maxims Of Commercial Law | **311** |
| The Ten Commandments | **317** |
| **16 THE TRUST AS A PRIME CORPORATE VEHICLE** | **321** |
| The History Of Trusts | **322** |
| Setting Up A Trust: The Mechanics | **325** |
| Vatican & State Cestui Que Trusts | **328** |
| Cestui Que As A Method Of Fraud | **329** |
| Cestui Que A Medieval Invention | **331** |
| Significance Of The Cestui Que Vie Trust | **335** |
| A Final Word Of Advice | **339** |

and Britain. The President of the UNITED STATES is the Chief Executive Officer (CEO) of this corporation. Under Maritime Admiralty law the corporation, not the constitutional entity, is in control.

Canada is a registered corporation as a subsidiary of the UK Registered in the USA. CANADA'S Corporate registered number is 0000230098 CANADA DC SIC: 8880 American Depositary Receipt. It's Business Address is the Canadian Embassy 1746 Massachusetts Ave., NW, Washington, DC 20036..."

Most everything we know of has a name that represents the real thing. The word Canada may to us represent the physical country, but in commerce, the word CANADA is what is registered as the commercial entity that represents the physical thing. Commerce is now conducted by trading titles-pieces of paper that represent the real thing. A Title deed for property represents the property but is not the actual property. The Title has restrictions which, when you assume is the same as the property, applies to the one holding the Title. In fact any word is just a word that represents the physical real thing. Even the densest individual will admit the word itself is not the real thing.

This has become a corporate world and this simple distinction is made to create a fictional web of commerce that overlays the real thing and simulates the kingdoms and dynasties. Now, when that fictional entity is registered, it is done so in capital letters, like CANADA and the UNITED STATES OF AMERICA.

The most obvious overlay of this fiction is represented by a very common corporate structure called a Sole Proprietor. A **sole proprietorship**, also known as the **sole trader** or simply a **proprietorship**, is a type of business entity that is owned and run by one individual or one legal person (e.g. corporation, LLC) and in which there is no legal distinction between the owner and the business. The owner receives all profits (subject to taxation specific to the business) and has unlimited responsibility for all losses and debts. Every asset of the business is owned by the proprietor and all debts of the business are the proprietor's. A sole proprietor may use a trade name or business name other than his, her or its legal name. Thus your name can be the corporation but it is not the physical you... you take responsibility for the laws governing it.

The corporate world operates in commerce through money, corporate charters, regulations, and missions created by the owners. There are literally millions of corporations that fall under two classes. Privately-held companies are - no surprise here - privately held. This means that, in most cases, the company is owned by the company's founders, management or a group of private investors. A public company, on the other hand, is a company that has sold a portion of itself to the public via an initial public offering of some of its stock, meaning shareholders have claim to part of the company's assets and profits.

One of the biggest differences between the two types of companies deals with public disclosure. If it's a public U.S. company, which means it is trading on a U.S. stock exchange, it is typically required to file quarterly earnings reports (among other things) with the Securities and Exchange Commission (SEC). This information is also made available to shareholders and the public. Private companies, however, are not required to disclose their financial information to anyone since they do not trade stock on a stock exchange.

The main advantage public companies have is their ability to tap the financial markets by selling stock (equity) or bonds (debt) to raise capital (i.e. cash) for expansion and projects. The main advantage to private companies is that management doesn't have to answer to stockholders and isn't required to file disclosure statements with the SEC. However, a private company can't dip into the public capital markets and must therefore turn to private funding, which can boost the cost of capital and may limit expansion. It has been said often that private companies seek to minimize the tax bite, while public companies seek to increase profits for shareholders. In short, private companies have lower quality – and most likely less detailed – financial information than public companies.

The popular misconception is that privately-held companies are small and of little interest. In fact, there are many big-name companies that are also privately held - check out the Forbes.com list of the largest private companies in 2006.

Corporations have grown to be accepted worldwide because they allow the few to control the many. It is simple; the pyramid structure allows the CEO to control the rest and it allows the board of Directors to control the CEO. Corporations allow engagement in commerce and provide a means to satisfy needs of ego and profit. They can have rules and regulations attached to them that cannot be attached to humans; but by working for a corporation, a human can then take on the rules applied to the corporations. They can hold assets. They can be built into great pyramids of power - into dynasties. and they can be created in secret.

The most secret corporation is the brotherhood, the blood vows, the handshakes, the cults, the bloodlines, the quiet unregistered agreements to conduct affairs a specific commercial way.

Corporations are a wondrous creation of man that were invented all the way back in Sumeria. But they can also serve a more devious purpose.

Even we as humans are registered corporations.

# Enter The STRAWMAN

People also have a fictitious corporate overlay like the Sole Proprietor that they are apparently not aware of. It is like a Trust that is designed to hold assets. Because this appears to have purposes of commerce that is unknown to the real thing it overlays, it has been given the name STRAWMAN. It, like a private corporation, is designed to engage in commerce under the laws of formation. The difference here is that it is another prolific commercial structure called a Trust.

The literal meaning provided by most dictionaries is, of course, "A bundle of straw made into the likeness of a man and often used as a scarecrow" Here are some popular definitions:

### *AMERICAN HERITAGE DICTIONARY*
1) A person who is set up as cover or a front for a questionable enterprise.
2) An argument or opponent set up so as to be easily refuted or defeated.

### RANDOM HOUSE WEBSTER'S UNABRIDGED DICTIONARY defines STRAWMAN as:
A person whose importance or function is only nominal, as to cover another's activities; front.

A fabricated or conveniently weak or innocuous person, object, matter, etc., used as a seeming adversary or argument: *The issue she railed about was no more than a straw man.* [the word 'scapegoat' sort, but not exactly, comes to mind here].

### MERRIAM-WEBSTER'S UNABRIDGED DICTIONARY
An imaginary argument of no substance advanced in order to be easily confuted or an imaginary adversary advancing such an argument.

A person usually without means or position who is vested with some nominal or fictitious post or responsibility as a cover in proceedings of doubtful legality or to shield the real author of an action: front, dummy. A person set up to serve as a cover for a usually questionable transaction.

**MAN OF STRAW; STRAW MAN**: A **man of straw** would certainly be one without a heart or conscience, so that this expression is apt for "an unscrupulous person who will do anything for gain." However, the words may refer to real "**straw men**," who in the past loitered near English courts with a straw in one of their shoes—this indicating that they would be willing to give false testimony or swear to anything in court for enough money.

*MAN OF STRAW*: An (often imaginary) person, object, or abstract entity set up for the purpose of being knocked down; a front, a diversionary tactic, a red herring; a nonentity, an ineffectual person, a cipher. The common denominator of these various meanings of the term is the sense of *straw* as a thing of little worth, substance, or solidity, a sense current in the language since the time of Chaucer. Apparently the original *man of straw* was a man of little substance or means in the monetary sense, i.e., poor. Such were wont to sell their services as witnesses, willing to act as perjurers to obtain money. Supposedly the sign of their availability was a straw in their shoe. Thus *man of straw* or the equally common *straw man* came to mean one who let himself be used for other's purposes. It is this latter sense which survives today, though the *man of straw* so exploited may be imaginary or fictitious. The phrase first appeared in print in the late 16th century. Thomas DeQuincey used it in its current sense in 1840.

This book, which is the **Soul's Story of The Strawman** is what would be called pseudo-fiction. It is a fiction based upon a lot of research into this topic of how this fake entity is deployed in practice. It has not, as yet, become a true accepted non-fiction because the system and cultural does not yet accept this as truth. However, this is changing rapidly as more and more people seek out the evidence on this topic and become aware of it.

Much like a corporation that is not human and is a fictional creation designed to hold assets and to conduct financial affairs, the STRAWMAN is also like a corporation designed to hold assets and conduct financial affairs in commerce. The difference is that it is as the definition implies - a fake because it has been created under fraudulent conditions that are contrary to the laws that we are used to about fraud. The big difference is that these financial affairs of commerce are still hidden from the real entity that it overlays.

The other big difference is that most do not believe it.

What you do believe is this:

- When you board a ship, Admiralty Law applies and the Captain is the law
- When you fly a flag, the law of the sea (ship) applies
- When you conquer someone, you set the rues
- When you go bankrupt, the Trustees sets the rules
- When you go bankruptcy, you pay the Receiver
- When you are a criminal, you have no rights
- When you die, your executor is in charge
- When you salvage something from the sea, salvage laws apply
- When you create a trust, trust laws apply to it
- When you create a corporation, the laws of incorporation apply to it

As you follow the story of the mythical STRAWMAN you will come to see how these relate to the birth, death and purpose of this fake creation.

This book is about the birth and death of a human and a STRAWMAN. It starts under another premise that has yet to be proven; that we all have a Soul that comes to Earth to inhabit a body.

But first, let us start with a short story about a cage of five monkeys. Inside, we hang bananas and place stairs under them. When a monkey attempts to climb the stairs, we spray the other four with cold water. They do not like cold water. If you repeat this when any monkey tries to climb to the bananas, soon the monkeys will prevent others from climbing. They kick up a fuss and even beat it. Now let us put the water away and replace one monkey. When the new one tries to climb, he gets attacked. So let us remove another original monkey and bring in another new one. It will get attacked if it tries climbing. If you do this until all five original monkeys are replaced, guess what? The monkeys that are beating the most recent one have no idea why they should not climb or why they should beat the others. After five are replaced, there is no water, no one is sprayed, yet no one climbs. Why? They know that's the way it has always been done.

Also, for extensive research on this topic, please refer to the books by Ed Rychkun:
**PLANET EARTH INC: Empire of the gods Exposed**
**PLANET EARTH INC: Empire of The gods Deposed**
found on www.amazon.com and
www.edrychkun.com

Now, let us begin with another story about a Light Being who decides to "set sail" through the cosmic sea to come into being as an Earthling.

In time, even this "fictional" story may come forward as more than just a Once Upon A Time account of the Soul and the humanoid background. For many, this story has already become closer to reality than fiction.

Regardless, as the story unfolds, we shall see that once the Earthling lands on Earth, a whole new story begins, regardless of where the Soul came from. As the chapters unfold, more and more information will be presented to support what may seem to be the strange birth of the fictional entity - the mythical STRAWMAN.

# 1

# ONCE UPON A TIME

Once upon a time, a long, long time ago in another dimension of the cosmos, there were many Light Beings enjoying life in a blissful and timeless existence of higher realms. They knew nothing else but joy as they were an aspect of the Creator and the epitome of Light itself.

In their world, lower energy and polarity between good and evil could not exist. In their states of pure light energy of Source, they would enjoy a paradise of co-existence with their total consciousness with the world of infinite possibilities. Here is where their higher minds could create their holograms of virtual reality for participation in joyful expression and experiences.

They could create and meld with other forms by virtue of their thoughts; they could be what their reality brought forward into their consciousness. They shared energies with all forms and things as they were one with spirit and all that was, and could be. All their wisdom and experiences were stored in their consciousness.

At a particular moment in their existence they were summoned to appear before a very large, magnificent entity purposely manifested to reflect Source Creation.

Because they were everywhere in the quantum soup of creation, they could simply be somewhere that their telepathic attention shifted to. This entity was looking for volunteers for a very important cosmic mission. The entity began to speak to the Light Beings.

"Within that which is the Cosmos, we have this small but very special planet out at the edge of the galaxy called Earth. It is quite unique like a beautiful paradise teeming with hundreds of thousands of different life forms. It has been something of an experimental station of spiritual and lower density evolution in the galaxy and it has a most interesting humanoid life form that incorporates the very highest and lowest frequencies known in the cosmos. It is in fact the very epitome of dualism which has come to be accepted as dark and light ."

"On the one hand it is an incredibly beautiful life form and is capable of carrying the highest frequencies of love, light and joy known throughout the whole Universe, as you all do. On the other hand it is capable of carrying the densest and darkest frequencies the cosmos has ever experienced - frequencies which the rest of creation evolved beyond eons ago. Here is the current situation. Within the domain of time, this planet goes through periodic cosmic cycles. It is now coming to the end of two major cycles - a two thousand year long age of Pisces and the twenty-five thousand year long cosmic cycle in its journey around the galaxy. It will be moving into the Age of Aquarius around the Earth year 2000."

"With the completion of this cycle, many things are coming to an end and many new things will begin. But most importantly, the planet will be experiencing an infusion of light that is dramatically increasing its frequency. Like any other major time of transition, there will be a certain amount of turbulence. Some of this will be geological, for Earth herself is a living planet and is also evolving. But much of it also involves the humanoid species that dominates the planet."

*"This will not be a particularly easy time for the species – especially for those who are sleeping and those who are vibrating at the lowest frequencies. As the frequency changes, it will create insecurity which in turn will create fear."*

*"The first era of evolution on this planet was the physical era and the crucial element was survival. The second era, which is now ending, was the mental era and the basic force here was logic and ego. The third era, which will begin at this time is the era of the heart and the key word will be love. Love as you all know, is the highest frequency. It is within this era that a new form of humanoid which is silicon based will evolve. Unlike the carbon based humanoid, the new crystalline essence will allow the evolution of a higher vibrational vessel, more resilient and able to sustain many of the higher properties that you all have, allowing both spirit and Soul to be free in lower vibrational and diverse environments. This New Earth will be a showpiece in the cosmos."*

*"There is however a challenge for those who incarnate here in that they forget their true self when they drop into the density, as will you if you go there. You will potentially trap yourself into a physical body and mind that has been controlled by those who have taken dominion over the planet. It is not that you truly forget in that all is retained as a Soul that retains total consciousness; it is that the Higher Mind of the Soul becomes over-ridden by the Lower Mind that is less concerned with spiritual matters. As so it loses communication and the higher powers of the Soul wane with no means of expression. This can be a challenge even when you do remember."*

*"Also, the beings in control have contrived many means to keep the truth and higher knowing in this state of lower vibration. There are the darkest beings who have learned to control others thus living in the dark shadows*

*and higher dimensions. They have chosen to experiment with the illusions of separation, fear, darkness, isolation, conquering, enslavement, pain, suffering, torture, and the likes to the strongest degree possible, thus controlling the Rulers of the planet. In doing so, they have completely cut themselves off from the nourishing Light of Being that supports life in the universe. The result is that they must energetically nourish themselves by feeding on low-frequency energies that resonate with their chosen mode of expression. These beings are highly developed Draconian and Grays who do not incarnate on Earth but they control those who are the Rulers of Earth."*

*"The beings that believe they have control on Earth have many names calling themselves illuminated Ones and Archons which means Rulers or Lords because they see themselves as the rulers of humanity, expressing what they believe to be as the 'enlightened ones'. They are of the Annunaki origins of Nibiru who have also evolved to the dark side for personal gains. Unfortunately, they also have developed higher capabilities which are focused on dominion over those not of their bloodlines. But even so they are unknowingly controlled by the Draconians skilled in energetic manipulations, mind control and 4th dimensional technologies. The irony of this is that while these unseen Draconian being's cleverly manipulate the Ruler Bloodline's process of physical and mental enslavement, the Rulers believe they are free to cleverly manipulate and enslave humanity the same way at a less technological level. Over many eons, this has been quite successful up until the coming shift of ages. It is the divine plan to dismantle this in the next cycle."*

*"Although the humanoids who go there have thoughts that have power – much more than they realize, this has been long forgotten and lost through the presence of fear and power. Thus words and titles have power because they frame thoughts into a certain set of beliefs without even realizing it. This framework of words has been programmed into humanity consciousness creating a cultural behavior thus calling others more 'powerful' a*

*'royal' human, 'Your Highness' thus automatically placing them above others in their minds. Thus the humanoid has given away their power to become subservient and fearful."*

*"Like the Draconian's control of the Rulers, these 'Rulers' of humanity also hide in the shadows of humanoid's minds, sending impulses of low-frequency emotion and thought to the ego and emotional bodies in order to elicit a low-frequency emotional energy that they can consume. Whereas the Draconians actually feed on the energies, the Rulers feed on the energetic process of greed, dominion and power that the enslavement of humanity provides."*

*"You may recall that once upon a time, on this very planet in the far distant past, human beings were infinitely more impressive than they are under this dominion. They were fully telepathic, multi-dimensional beings that could simultaneously perceive and navigate many dimensions at once. They built vast cities with technology that worked in harmony with Earth's energetic fields. They were in full alignment with their Divine Inner Self while expressing in physicality in a wide variety of life-affirming ways. This unlimited expression of Divine Selfhood was viewed by the rulers as a threat to their very existence, because the $3^{rd}$ density had been dominated by them for a very long time on other worlds.*

*In order to fulfill this, they set themselves up as gods with superior powers of dominion with cold vengeful consequences to those not abiding by their laws. To assist this they created religions and manipulated DNA to create a need for worship to deities such as them. To have a $3^{rd}$ density world completely free from their manipulations and feeding was something that they could not allow without a fight. The problem for them was that Earth humans were potentially so powerful they could literally brush them off with a thought. These beings only have power over others who they have manipulated and put into fear. A fully aware human who* *knows their Inner Divine Self cannot be dominated by these parasitic beings in any way"*

*"And so positioned as gods, they devised a plan to very carefully manipulate a few humans in positions of power into making an innocent mistake with terrible, cataclysmic repercussions. These humans were experimenting with new methods of harnessing and transmitting energy in vast quantities. The experiments were unprecedented and very ambitious — too ambitious because the rulers were secretly influencing some of these humans through their ego mind to push the envelope of what was thought to be possible."*

*"When an advanced phase of testing at the north pole of the planet went disastrously wrong, this large, extremely powerful device exploded with such force that it caused tremendous cataclysms on the planet, rapidly melting huge swaths of ice and creating a flood that destroyed nearly every coastal area on the planet within a day. The vast amount of death and destruction was unimaginable, and only a remnant of the many billions of humans survived. Heavily traumatized, grief stricken at the loss of their loved ones and focused only on physical survival, they fled to safe locations to try and rebuild their once great civilization. This story sounds much like what we know of as the Fall of Atlantis but it actually occurred long prior to the civilization of Atlantis, even though it too perished in a similar manner many centuries later."*

*"The incredible trauma of this experience caused a loss of perception in the survivors, making them less aware of the other dimensions that are always mingling with $3^{rd}$ density. They simply couldn't take the time to focus on any other density but this one, because their physical survival depended on being fully focused on the physical realm. At the same time, the human's deep emotional pain, grief and wounding gave the Rulers a tremendous amount of low-frequency energy that they could consume, allowing them to feast on the suffering of the surviving humans and grow more powerful."*

*"Like the Draconians, the Rulers found that as long as they stayed carefully hidden that they could send a small thought-form into the minds of the traumatized humans reminding them of all that they had lost. This would create a cascade of painful thoughts and emotions in the humanoids that would generate more energetic food for Rulers and their blood families. As each subsequent generation of humanity was born, the Rulers became more bold and instituted a program of direct interference into human consciousness. They subliminally programmed humans to be blind to their presence, allowing them to more directly influence a person's thoughts. They also programmed human consciousness to recoil away from any mention of these Rulers or their dark influence over humans, so that when confronted with such information, the immediate response would be disbelief, ridicule and mockery."*

*"Finally, in their most brilliantly sinister move, they reprogrammed the human ego to resemble their own ego, and encouraged the ego consciousness to dominate all other levels of being. They essentially reprogrammed humans to be like them: fearful, jealous, petty, dishonest, brutal, enslaving, murderous, unforgiving, punishing, etc. This insured that humans would be easy to manage as an energetic food source for thousands and thousands of years. These layers of programming have been in place in the human thought system ever since, perpetuating the discordant misadventures that we know as human history."*

*"Over time, the rulers built an energy-feeding structure surrounding the entire planet which allows them to automatically gather human-generated low-frequency energy and send fearful or other low-frequency messages into human consciousness to keep people generating energetic food. This structure exists in a higher density than the one that is evident to the oblivious humanoid, so it can only be perceived psychically or when out of body.".*

"It was the same process that the Draconians used on these Rulers. And so the galactic hierarchy was born as they took control.

"This structure is like a dark web of energy surrounding the planet that is heavy and oppressive. It serves to block energies coming to the Earth from the galactic core and other parts of the galaxy, but it cannot stop them completely. The grid is programmed with negative feedback that sends subtle signals into the sub-conscious and ego mind to keep humanoids focused on low-frequency beliefs and thought patterns."

"This dark control grid is programmed with an artificial intelligence to self-repair and notify rulers biters when it is damaged. The grid supports the Ruler's 'collectors', which are beings that connect to nearly every person on the planet, soaking up all of the low-frequency energies that we give off in our daily lives. They travel through this grid to attend to problems or directly oppress a person who's energy frequency is getting too lofty for the dark agenda. The Rulers and their bloodline in the hierarchy are heartless and unemotional about humanoids who are outside of their bloodlines."

"These Rulers have leveraged their advantages over humans to completely corrupt what we think of as human nature so familiar to you all. In the last 100 years, as the population grew exponentially over the planet, the Rulers needed to create a new strategy of control and dominion. In addition to the human nature being under the dark control grid creating a nature to lie, cheat, steal, rape, enslave and murder as a false program installed into the human mind, they learned to program the lust for power and dominion in the human nature to eliminate the true human nature of being compassionate, caring, sensitive, loving, forgiving, cooperative, empathic, creative, energetic, joyful, inquisitive, irrepressible, non-conformist, uplifting and DIVINE.

*"Their plan of total dominion, which has matured in the last 50 years was to satisfy the spiritual curiosity of true human nature by creating religions which now bind the majority of humankind into a non spiritual life that subdues their divine powers. In order to satisfy the other part of the created ego desires, they took control of commerce, money that would allow them the control nations and humanity alike. The most elegant and evil tactic was to create a monetary vehicle of power called a corporation which would allow the individuals to engage in dominion, power, profit, and satisfy a lust of ego for the darker energies programmed into them through DNA and the dark grid."*

*"The means of corporate power would not only reflect the kingship and rulers and lords but also create the illusion of power. This mechanism of Corporation, a fabricated fictional entity for commerce was then used as a means of creating a fictional mirror of the human to engage in commerce, creating the illusion it was real. This vehicle of control has been imposed upon people, nations, cities, districts, and the like to create a hierarchical structure controlled by the rulers though commerce."*

*"This vehicle is referred to as the Strawman. It is this that you will be subjected to when you incarnate on Earth. It is this vehicle that is under the control of the Rulers but at the same time you will be born into a culture that accepts the falsity of the Strawman as truth, and it will be difficult for you to rise above this and remember who you are because the lower mind and form may not listen."*

*"You will understand that the way the Rulers have conquered nations has been through what is the law of the Sea or Admiralty Law as a creation of their own to support order and control. Under this, through history, parts of the planet have been conquered by force or by the laws of salvage of the seas. Under this, a land or vessel, is claimed into ownership, and the laws of the Sea as in Admiralty and commerce preside; such as*

*when the captain of the ship as a humanoid steps onto it dictates the rules and laws. So it is that nations, lands, and other vessels have been conquered and subjected to Admirably law of piracy."*

*"So have been the tools of conquest, to impose the regulations upon that conquered by the Rulers, to become the Captains of the ships of continents, nations, and corporate dynasties.. The secondary conquest has been though monetary dominion, of seizure through bankruptcy or inability to contend against the pirates, thereby imposing the admiralty regulations upon the vessel so seized by the pirates."*

*"As Souls, not physical humans, many of Earth inhabitants descended from higher realms and higher states of consciousness during an involution into matter. As they separated from the higher realms, they gradually lost consciousness of themselves, focusing increasingly on this physical dimension. But many realized that we were heading into a more limiting condition, so they recorded important stories and information that would help them rise again to the glory that was theirs before the physical world was. Some of you may have done this."*

*"Many of you as Souls have been impregnated with the messages and meanings of that life. And as this is reawakened deep within you through silence and love, the soul-self within will emerge and so recall as you will attune with memories that have been locked in your hearts for a very long time. The is like a regression process that humanoids use to recall past lives and event. This is one of the great aspects of this new era we are entering, an awakening like a Near Death Experience without death - an awakening like none other, where whole groups of souls rise to a more universal, eternal view of life, past and future."*

*"Several of you prior to now were pure minds living in direct connection with the Universal Mind on this planet.*

*Thus many of you already know about this process of vibrational decension. First many projected into thought-forms at first, then immersed themselves in matter with their consciousness to the point that they became incarnate. Since they were now acting and experiencing independently of the Creator, less conscious of the Creator and less connected to the Life Force, they began to feel alone and separated. This caused fear and fear led to great mistakes. During these early periods on Earth, some of them completely lost touch with their true celestial nature and the Creative Forces. Others retained much or some of their connectedness. These latter ones were considered gods, yet they were also subject to the many problems and challenges that affected all who touched this realm. You will understand that throughout the ancient Egyptian teachings and records, the gods were both divine and human, powerful and vulnerable. It is many of these gods that have turned to darkness and deployed means of dominion over others, acting as the Rulers. And as has been said, this was then overtaken by even darker Lords of Darkness who orchestrate matters on Earth and other planets as well."*

# 2

# REMEMBER WHO YOU ARE

---

*"This is the current situation of Earth. The reason I am here is to seek volunteers who would be willing to incarnate in this special humanoid form on the planet at this time to help make this an easy and smooth transition. It is also an opportunity to participate n an evolution of a new life form of silica based humanoid that has not yet been tried in the cosmos. We have sent prophets and teachers in the past but they were often brutally persecuted or killed. In other instances they were set up as gods to be worshiped and these life forms built elaborate religions and rituals around them. They then used these religions to control each other. They did everything except follow the simple teachings that were offered."*

*"This time involves a different approach. No more prophets, saviours and avatars that can create religions. This time we are sending in hundreds of thousands of ordinary light beings with only two assignments. Each will incarnate into the humanoid density as a Soul and contain the essence of Spirit which we all have. As light beings and Soul those who choose to assist must stay in*

*their heart, regardless of what happens. Second, they must remember who they are, why they are there and what this is all about."*

*"Now that seems easy enough, right? Unfortunately, No! As I have said, duality has reached its peak on this planet. This species has perfected the illusion of good and evil. The greatest challenge you will experience is to remember who you really are, why you are there and what the mission is really all about. When you remember, you will be able to stay in your heart, regardless of external events. So how will you know when you are forgetting? It is easy. Watch your judgments. The moment you notice that you are in a place of judgment you will know that you have forgotten who you really are, why you are there and what this is really all about. That will be your signal."*

*"Now here is the challenge. Because of what I have told you of the Rulers on this planet you will require a great deal of discernment - wise evaluation of what is true, what is appropriate, and what is for the highest good, both for you and for the planet. In many ways, discernment is similar to judgment. However, you will know when you are in judgment and when you have moved out of your heart when you are in a place of blame."*

*"We know how challenging this planet can be. We know how very real the illusions on this planet appear to be. We understand the incredible density of this dimension and the pressure you will face. But if you survive this mission - and it is a voluntary one - you will evolve at hyper speed and assist in the evolution of a true heaven and biological-crystalline miracle humanoid. We also should say that we know that some of you who will go to this planet as star seeds, will never germinate - never awaken to the remembrance of who you really are. Some of you will awaken and begin to shine, only to be choked down by the opinions and prevailing thought forms around you. Others will awaken and remain awake*

*and your light will become a source of inspiration and remembrance for many. At the heart of this is the power of fear that will prevent your truth and your spirit from awakening."*

*"You will incarnate all over the planet; in every culture, every race, every country, and every religion. But you will be different. You will never quite fit in. As you awaken you will realize that your true family isn't those of your own race, culture, religion, country or even your biological family. It is your cosmic family - those who have come as you have come – on assignment to assist in ways large and small in the current transition."*

*"True brotherhood and joy in its highest form will come only in remembering who you really are, why you are here and what this is really all about. It will come as you rise above judgement and fear to return to the true temple of Divine Presence, your heart, where this remembrance takes place and from which you are called to serve the world and the cause of evolution towards a new form of humanoid which can hold the higher frequency of Spirit."*

*"Because of the density, you can't operate in that dimension without a this special humanoid form. This is a biological form that actually changes and ages over time. You should understand there will be a danger that if you forget who you really are, you may think you ARE your biological form instead of the fact that it is simply your vehicle in that dimension. Once there, you will notice that there is an infinite variety of forms and a great deal of attention given to these. However, in spite of the infinite variety, because this is a planet of duality, they all fall into two basic categories called 'genders'. You will find your relationship with your own form to be most instructive and interesting."*

*"The one big challenge is that to operate in that dimension, you will receive a 'personality with an ego'. This, as I mentioned before was encoded thousands of*

*Earth years ago by the Rulers that shifted DNA... This is like an identity imprint that, along with your form, will essentially make you different from everyone else and impose different needs for your ego. This will allow you to participate in the hologram there - something they call conscious reality. Once again, there will be a real danger that you will become so engrossed in the holographic personality dramas that you will forget who you really are and actually think that you ARE your personality. But for you, it will allow you to experience a different dimension than the joy you are used to. Situations on the planet and the interaction between these forms will create situations that accentuate the difference between joy and a state you are not used to called depression. It will test you to see if you know who you really are."*

"*But you also need to remember that we are going to surround this planet with a force that can disable the ego - if you find the way to turn on the switch which is the heart where your Soul will reside. At the same time, the ultimate plan is enfold the planet with the higher frequencies that will assist in rendering the Ruler Control measures more and more ineffective so that the spirit can be liberated and the Soul freed from the lower reality of ego. However, as all have free will and choice, each must choose on their own accord. This ultimate plan together with your efforts to reveal truth can help disable the ego that likes to keep the vibrations low. You can remember and accelerate into higher vibrations as you can assist in showing others the truth of who they are. But there is no need to be concerned if you fail in all this, because your form will eventually die you will return as a little light being back to where you began.*"

"*It will be like a different type of experience that can heighten your state of joy as you can experience a dramatic contrast from what you are used to. There is so much more we could tell you by way of orientation, but we think you can learn the rest experientially on site. The only thing that is important is to remember who you really are, why you are here and what this is really all about. If you can do that, everything else will work out fine."*

*"But before you decide, I will tell you how you will best remember who you are."*

## Above All Remember Higher or Inner Self

*"Understand that the restoration of your awareness that you are Divine is primary and you must gently dissolve the false layers of illusions that will be placed into your consciousness both by the lowering of density and the processes contrived by the Rulers. It is important that you re-discover your Higher Self which is your Soul, as aspect of the Creator which is actually your Inner Divine Self. You will need to train yourself to be fully seated within the heart center of your physical bodies. Then as authority figures, media, peers, the dark control grid, and the world at large convince a child that they are NOT divine, this inner divine energy leaves the body and sits above a person, waiting patiently to be reintegrated back into the heart center once again. Because this divine energy is seemingly "above" us, it gets termed the Higher Self, as opposed to the Lower self that is resident in the ego."*

*"So should you decide to participate, from this point forward, whenever you hear Higher Self substitute Inner Divine Self and notice the subtle but powerful shift in your awareness that arises from this change. Instead of seeing your Divine Self's light above you, see it emanating from your heart center where it belongs. Instead of bringing an aspect of your divine nature into you, you are going to be expanding it from deep within you. It may seem like a small thing, but this difference is very powerful, I assure you. Within your inner consciousness, this will be your own divine trigger that can be activated to re-remember who you are and to rise*

*above the mortal game that you will play out in this lower reality."*

*"Once your Divine Inner Light is expanded from your heart and surrounds your entire body, you can send a beam of loving energy to the core of the planet interact with it energetically. All of this can be done without drawing too much attention to yourself, so stick to this when you need a smooth, easy, uplifting energy experience with minimal push back from the control grid."*

*"One of the dark control grid's functions is to block energy coming to Earth from the galactic core. This grid will be weakened, and it will develop holes in it allowing the galactic energy to come through in ever increasing amounts. The Rulers know that their time is almost up, and they are desperately doing everything that they can to keep human consciousness in a low-frequency state. One result of their increasing desperation is that they are aggressively interfering with anyone who is raising their consciousness and frequency rate."*

*"Your challenge is to re-remember to become fully aware that you are tapping into your own Inner Divine Power and unleashing it. Always remember that you are the Power that these Rulers covet and feed from. They pretend to be strong, but their strength comes from you. They have nothing within them that is anywhere near as powerful as a single human being with full awareness of their True Divine Nature. That is why their dominion is based on keeping the humanoids in lower vibration of religion and feeding the ego through commerce via want for power and fear of not having it."*

*"Once your Inner Divine Light is expanded and you are connected to the Earth's core, imagine that you are projecting a beam of light from your Divine Inner Core straight up and into the core of the galaxy. Your light beam will pierce the Dark Control Grid and arrive at the galactic core almost instantly. Then say to the Galactic Core, 'I am ready to be a Galactic Conduit' at which*

*point you will receive a Cosmic Flush of galactic energy. This is an important distinction because it reinforces the notion that YOU are the Power that is initiating the cosmic flush. You're not a weak little person asking for help from the galactic core, but rather you are a powerful, incredibly important player in this cosmic game of chess that is nearing the endgame. Without YOU volunteering to be a Galactic Conduit, it would be much more difficult to dissolve the dark control grid when the time is right."*

*"Imagine hundreds and thousands of people all over the planet piercing the dark control grid and conducting a Cosmic Flush directly into the planet's core, and that light spreading to everyone who can receive it. Imagine the Rulers dashing around frantically trying to repair the holes in the control grid while the people stand strong as Galactic Conduits in spite of their attempts to get them to stop and think fearful or sad thoughts instead."*

*"The fact remains that they through the programming and creation of the culture will interfere with anyone who is actively raising their frequency of consciousness, and the Rulers have done so throughout human history. Their favorite technique is to send in a reminder about things that are wrong in your life, especially if they can distract you into blaming someone else for that problem that is suddenly on your mind induced as judgment or through fear. The use of distractions to do something fun or something you need to do as determined by ego has the consequence of stopping the embodiment of a high frequency energy state."*

*"Thus, when you notice negative energies trying to interfere with your thoughts, emotions or energy, immediately start expanding your Divine Inner Light from your heart until it surrounds your body."*

*"Command from your Divine Core that the Rulers present be captured in containment orbs, which are energetic spheres of light that keep them from running away and hiding. Then do an energy refund to send their*

*tubes and any other connections they have formed in your consciousness back to them. Staying totally calm and forgiving should be your ultimate goal. It is important not to engage in a constant state of anger, as that anger energy will actually give life to them and that energy which will return to you."*

*"Once they are contained, imagine that you are grabbing them and squeezing them to get them to let go of YOUR energy that they have been draining from you. See that low-frequency energy pooling in front of you, then hit it with a blast of light from your heart to purify and transmute it back to a state of pure energy, and reclaim that energy back into your being."*

*"I suggest that you laugh at them and remind them that they were never given permission to take your energy or enslave humanity and forgive them. This means that it is preferable to offer them the option to begin healing and gradually coming back to the light."*

*"Offering them the chance to heal and return to the light is an important point to focus on. Ultimately, everything in the universe comes from a single Divine Consciousness, even the darkest of the Rulers. This means they will eventually re-align themselves with the light and begin their journey of returning to Source, so we are simply acting as Divine Conduits to assist this process to unfold more rapidly. The Rulers won't see this as a good thing due to their lack of empathy, and they may even try to make you feel like you are violating their free will. However, humanity's free will has been repeatedly violated by these beings who are also on a path of higher evolution. and total free will. The only choices remaining to them are to heal and return to the light, or to remain as they are and eventually be recycled back and prevented from harming anyone else."*

*"The Rulers are not going to give up easily, and they will be fighting back with everything they have. This is the time you will move into. Their increased frequency and intensity of attacks on lightworkers and casual*

*meditators alike reveals their desperation. They will be weakened by the generally rising consciousness on the planet and they will be very dangerous, like an animal backed into a corner."*

*"In order for the plan to remove their influence from human consciousness to work, many Lightworkers like you will become by re-remembering and expanding their Inner Divine Light and acting as Galactic Conduits, piercing the dark control grid full of holes that allow tremendous light to stream into the earth. If you can do your part here on the ground in the lower vibratory humanoid form, the non-incarnated members of the Forces of Light will be able to make the final move and strip away the dark control grid from this planet, resulting in an instant uplifting of all life on Earth."*

*"I cannot emphasize strongly enough how important this step is in our planetary ascension. This dark control grid has been corrupting and stifling human consciousness for many, many millennia. When it is removed along with the control measures that have been embedded into the cultures, behaviors and DNA, it will be like an instant consciousness expansion for every person on the planet. Imagine everyone suddenly being free of the dark side of human nature so that the true glory of loving human consciousness can expand within the hearts and minds of everyone on Earth. And then, in an extraordinary evolution, the humanoid form can evolve into the silicon-crystalline base to hold the same light that you all hold in your present form."*

*"And so dear ones, this will be your mission, to be part of a galactic event to further the purpose of Source Creation."*

*"In order to prepare, you will need to choose by way of the male and female humanoid process of birthing, the time, place and parents that will bring you into the lower Earth Plane reality, to be born, grow and express yourself through the vessel of the physical humanoid.*

*"Finally, your Soul and Higher Mind will always be there to communicate. It is all seeing and knows only love and truth as you do. From your heart center of the humanoid form and its bio-electrical system of chakra energetics, it will communicate with your Lower Mind and the ego/intellect that will attempt to rule your earthly affairs. You will need to re-remember this and learn to listen, to differentiate from the negative web of polarity that which is prominent, unless of course you by choice decide otherwise so as to engage in it. You will within your DNA encoding that creates the form, look to seeking your purposes, your Source and the inner stillness of your Inner and Higher Self. You will always be drawn to your spiritual self."*

*"Are you ready?"*

# 3

# THE BERTH OF THE EARTHLING

## Preparing For The Berthing

And so it came to be that many of the Light Beings prepared for the entry to the Earth plane as an incarnation of Soul into a humanoid form. After selecting a time and a mother and father, the scene was set to create a home upon Earth.

And so to prepare, the parents under the laws as set forth by the Rulers of the culture became registered into the illusionary world of commerce. Under this process, the Light Being as a Soul would become housed first into the physical vessel of body of the mother then to be birthed into a vessel of its own human form.

Thus by way of a government controlled administrative process, the prospective parents would be married by way of registration and thus the creation of a marriage trust to a create a commercial entity to hold a title to the vessel.

The Light Being, now cognizant of its prospective parents watched as the opportunity to be birthed through the union of father and mother, as was the custom in this land, drew nigh.

As the Light Being now attuned to the Earth process of birthing, it could understand that by way of the marriage and application they would create a Trust which would hold the estate of their progeny of human creations. The Soul saw only truth and could clearly see and understand the intents of other's consciousness and their processes. It would be trapped within the vessel as a Soul. And so it came to understand that it as a Light Being would be a Soul becoming the progeny as a physical vessel. Having landed upon foreign land it would become released under the title of the offspring name to the Government for their use.

And so the Light Being knew that the act of Registration coming from Latin Rex, and Regis would carry the meaning of regal. Thus housed and contained in the physical vessel, it would be "registered" to itself be captured within the vessel being under legal title handed over to the Crown, leaving the vessel so named with only equitable title – the right to use, not own. And for that use the vessel would be destined to pay a "use" tax, in the form of income, sales, and property and others as so dictated by the laws of the foreign land administration.

In this way the Light Being understood that its winding down into the lower vibrations of physicality and laws of the land were imminent as it would become constrained to the vibrational level of the lower forms and be subject to the laws placed upon the vessel.. Here the administrators would follow the letter of the administrative law, and the new vessel would become the property registered by way of a name being a title copy representation of the human vessel.

# The Physical Berth on Earth

And so it came to be that the little Light Being was ready to be birthed in the form of the Soul, and it headed for Earth to take the physical form into a vessel that would house it. After dwelling in the center of the galaxy, the seed or zero point of our universe, the soul crossed the cosmic ocean which was known as the water of Nun or *'None'* by the Egyptians to be created within the foreign waters of the mother's womb.

After the conception by the parents so as to create the new human vessel from combine DNA, it would pass the first gate in the chakra system of the root chakra, the spring from which pours out the fountain of life or living energy that vitalizes everything; the birth canal.

And so the Light Being began to shift its transformation into the Soul with its knowing and higher gifts. It would wind down its own vibrations to become a fish out of water by incarnating into the human body prepared for it. Having chosen the host, the Soul and its new biological partner weaved a human body suit of flesh and blood from DNA and the life force. The Soul now taking refuge in the body would become subject to the lower vibration plane of physicality.

As the new body became woven out of DNA, the Soul would exit through the root chakra reminding it that the humanoid born were as children of None and all matter of the earth was composed of the same cosmic waters – the cosmic matrix. But it knew that the Soul would become limited into the physical manifestation of the mother's waters much different from its Divine Matrix of the ether or the cosmic ocean that is everywhere. From the matrix, the Soul would arise phoenix like with all experience and relations coming from the new matrix.

And so it was time that the cosmic Soul and its Spirit, of which it was a part were now ready to enter the new environment in a more material sense on Earth. This would be as a new entity; as the vessel of humanoid physical form harboring the soul.

As the Soul now prepared for emergence, it could understand it would become subject to a new system which would be like a ship, its cargo, and under maritime law – the laws and statutes under which it must abide.

The Soul, now a new vessel like a ship with cargo now born, became docked with the cargo out of water. The mother's water now broken, the cargo descended the birth canal, and the new born baby or soul Ark, like the Argo, a boat, instantly came under maritime law, the manufactured law of the sea. Suddenly, the Soul became aware that the process is now very different from Nature's law or Spiritual law of the cosmic matrix that it abided by naturally.

As the birthing of the new human vessel in the form of cargo, or **'argo',** occurred in the delivery room or **'berth'**, the Soul watched as a state licensed doctor, or **'dock'** examined the new being to certify a live birth. A certificate of live birth, or **'manifest'** was written itemizing details of the birth, or **'docking'**.

In its new form, the Soul realized it was actually like the **Ark or Vessel**, given an Identification number like a **sailing ship**. It was a birth registration number used to track the soul as it sails the **waters** of its Earth life. Now the Soul realized clearly that from the moment of birth to the end of the life on Earth, the manifestation of the human vessel would be regulated on Earth. The Soul now trapped within the vessel would be given liberty to go ashore but it would not have total freedom as had been known to it. Now freedom would be a choice within a boxed environment of choices limited by the laws of the land and sea as administered by Governments of the land, as dictated by the Rulers of conquest. Now the Soul understood that from now henceforth if the Soul would try to take freedoms outside of this box, it would find the human vessel thus captured in a court standing on the dock.

As such, like pirates at sea, the laws of salvage were applied to claim title to the biological machine that could be considered a chattel, property, and asset in a vast production machine. It was so done so the government could regulate all substances or energy imputed into the five primary sensors of the Soul's new vessel to control the mechanism of its output.

And so the vessel and cargo through the registration process of birth would now open an account in commerce, later to be registered through a social security number to tally the anticipated consumption of resources and production of goods and services. Here the potential would be calculated along with the cumulative tax, like a **dockage** fee for use of the dock that it would pay as its value on the open market. This lump sum would be mortgaged, and pledged as collateral by the Ruler's representatives to borrow money from financial interests; the International Monetary Fund.

## Creation Of The STRAWMAN

And so, it was the year 1942, March 14 that the vessel and cargo landed at the dock in British Columbia, Canada, ready to engage in the activities of the human experience and its senses, the Soul could now see how it being in a foreign land would be subjected to the laws and statutes.

Yet another realization became apparent. It was not clear how all the knowing of the Light Being would be transmitted through the Soul and through the vessel? Now the Soul understood its destiny and challenge as the words of the Creator rang clear.

As the yet fully conscious Soul watched, it came to see a **MAN OF STRAW** a imaginary person, object, or abstract entity would unknowingly be set up by the administrative process for the purpose of commerce. This it realized would be a front, a diversionary tactic, a red herring; a nonentity, an ineffectual person, a cipher that would support the monetary purposes. In a sense it could understand the common denominator of these various meanings of the term is the sense of *straw* as a thing of little worth, substance, or solidity. In the original *man of straw* was a man of little substance or means in the monetary sense, i.e., poor. Such were wont to sell their services as witnesses, willing to act as perjurers to obtain money. Supposedly the sign of their availability was a straw in their shoe. Thus *man of straw* or the equally common *straw man* came to mean one who let himself be used for other's purposes.

Now as the Soul watched through the heightened senses of the baby vessel, with the physical birth of the sentient human in a local hospital this would automatically place it as the prime capital asset into the Marriage Trust so named under the surname of the marriage thus holding equitable title. The parents had given the vessel of body a Name as a surname and given names that are accepted and taught as an Upper and Lower case name.

As the Soul watched, a **Certificate of Manifest** was created as the vessel (Mother) and its cargo would now be registered upon landing (born). A **Registration of Birth** was created and the Mother sign the **Birth Certification** as Trustee of under the new vessel given name. This name, like a corporation would be the name of a Trust identified by the name in capital letters, date of birth and Birth Certificate number, which would hold equitable title to the prime capital asset of newborn sentient human.

And so the new vehicle of fictitious commercial purpose became the STRAWMAN overlay upon the sentient human also encompassing the Soul and holding the Light Being within its lower vibrational sensory systems.

An estate was therefore created for the vessel's use and benefit so that it became the GRANTOR of this estate as the new human would be placing items of value within it. The parents were the creators of the estate as they created the new sentient human.

The Soul understood that the Birth Certificate referred to mother as an 'informant'. This process was as in America and Canada like many other nations under the kingdom of GREAT BRITAIN. Upon giving birth a mother would be compelled, without full disclosure, to apply for the creation of the first Cestui Que Vie trust, creating a $14^{th}$ Amendment paper citizen of the United States, a fictional structure originating from centuries ago.

Upon receipt of the mother's application the Trustees established a trust under the error of assumptions that the child had elected to accept the benefits bequeathed by the will, "under the will". The Trustees further assumed that the child was incompetent, a bankrupt and lost at sea and would be presumed dead until the child re-appeared and re-established a living status, challenged the assumption of acceptance of the benefits 'under the will' as being one of free choice and with full knowledge of the facts and redeemed the estate.

Under the assumption that the child was a $14^{th}$ Amendment citizen, the child's footprint was placed on the birth certificate by the hospital creating a slave bond that is sold to the federal reserve, who converts the certificate into a negotiable instrument and establishes a second Cestui Que Vie trust. The child's parents would be compelled to later apply for a social security number for the child, unwittingly testifying that the child was a $14^{th}$ Amendment paper citizen of the United States, not a party in interest to the trust or the trust res, and assumed to be dead after 7 years, when the federal reserve could not seize the child, they would file for the issue of the salvage bond and the child would be presumed dead.

# 4

# THE EARLY CHILDHOOD

---

It was now that the early years of childhood were upon the Vessel. The Soul could now experience the learning process of developing the human form as it began to exist within and adapt to the physical environment. Now the Soul could experience the nourishment and protection of parents while at the same time experience the new sensory systems.

As the Soul, in its wisdom as retained from the state of Light Being, could still use it higher functions, it remained in total awareness of its new environment. Now however, a change was occurring as it was losing its means of communication to other beings and its lower mind. Yet it remained connected to its Source and its Higher Self as a Light Being.

But this was shifting. Now the human form and mind were beginning to take precedence as the Lower Mind, falling to its instinctual need of ego preservation and nourishment, dominated. It began to clearly understand how the winding down into the lower form was slowly changing its ability to express and utilize the higher functions of its true being.

As the Soul watched its new process of evolution as a child, it so experienced the time when customs would dictate the next step of baptism. It could understand clearly the intent for when it as a child was baptized by the church, the Baptismal certificate was forwarded to the Vatican who would convert the certificate into a negotiable instrument and create a third Cestui Que Vie trust. By the process of baptism, the parents of the vessel then agreed to have the body fall under the code of the VATICAN Bible as written by them.

It was here that the Soul understood that these three trusts would finally represent the possession process of the property, body and soul of the humanoid vessel and child. It understood that the civil administration of CANADA and UNITED STATES operated under this triple crown of capture based on the error of assumptions that the sentient human was a $14^{th}$ Amendment citizen of the United States.

Its vessel now registered and controlled indirectly controlling the Soul the three Cestui Que Vie Trusts represented the triple crown of possession and three claims against property, body and soul by the Roman Church and State for the purpose of dominion over the people in the denial of all of rights beyond the Laws an statutes set forth against the STRAWMAN Trust and Corporation.

## Registering Human Capital

As the Soul now evolved through its form, it so learned what was polarity of right and wrong as dictated by the Father and the Mother. It began to understand the new concept of fear and love. It began to feel the helplessness of it powers and its truths as a Light Being. As the vessel of the body now limited its functionality to a new set of senses and its lower mobility, the Higher

Self consciousness of the Soul was now without influence upon the actions of the lower mind of the child. In addition, now the limitations of being a lower vibrational physical vessel in ownership through the process of trusts and corporations with rules and regulations further limited its freedom.

The Soul now felt trapped, its knowing incommunicable to this new vessel of human form, with the lower mind evolving and learning rapidly the new environment. It wondered about the purpose of the possession.

And so the Soul came to learn new lower physical and mental functionality of the vessel and its senses. In the next stage it sensed this would bring more new limits and constraints. Now the birth registration would be entered into the Provincial Treasury and actual birth of vessel and the STRAWMAN corporation in the Provincial Treasury thereby formally registering the Birth of the new cargo (child) to create an entry into the registry thus creating a Certificate of Birth in the NAME of the STRAWMAN as a fictional dead corporation which would simulate a copy of the Name and body of the vessel.

As the Government administrative process created this fictional entity, it also owned it, the number of the Birth Certificate becoming a reference in the Provincial Treasury to be like a certificate of Incorporation. It would also be a descendant of the sentient human. The Soul knew that man or a woman is "born", whereas STRAWMEN are *"wholly brought into separate existence."* Each event would thus qualify as a "birth". The birth certificate documents created a muddied mixture of the two events that allowed the system to both claim that it is the vessels birth certificate yet also claim to hold title to (not ownership of) the corporately colored STRAWMAN.

In order to properly register the process of ownership, the Soul saw the delivery of the birth certificate to the origins of parent and Ministry of Finance. For after creating the Birth Certificate on bank note paper, the Soul saw that in USA the bank note paper came from the American Bank Note Company, whereas in Canada it came from the CANADIAN BANK NOTE COMPANY LIMITED).

And so, a Certified Original Copy of The Birth Certificate was sent back to the parents who were Trustee for the sentient human they created. The original was retained by the Ministry of Finance on behalf of the provincial Treasury. This copy was an acknowledgement that the sentient human was born in the jurisdiction as landed cargo in Canada or US and would now be a capital asset belonging to the Municipality where the cargo was given birth to.

The Soul clearly understood that unknown to the administration of the Municipality, the Government at the Municipal level claimed an interest in every child within its jurisdiction as a valuable asset as a human resource which if properly trained, could contribute valuable assets provided by its labor for many years. As the human vessel it would therefore be pledged as a human capital resource that would contribute to the welfare of the Municipality of origin every year. On the back of the formal birth certificate was written: **Revenue Receipt: For Treasury Use Only.**

In a process, unbeknown to government employees the assets of the trusts were now registered as human capital in the provincial human resources registry.

And so it would be that this formal registration process placed the human vessel containing the Soul as a 'ward of the Government'. It was so presented as a safeguard for the child and the parents, thus allowing the creation and registration of a commercial entity used for the purpose of exploitation.

In the next phase, the Soul saw that there was a registration of the STRAWMAN as an entity with the

Federal Ministry Of Finance and the Secretary Treasurer of the nation. The NAME of the STRAWMAN was now representing a new asset of the sentient human and would be registered in the Individual Master File as a Foreigner from a foreign jurisdiction being a Criminal with multiple criminal charges. This the Soul understood that as a alien, resident of Puerto Rico, having a criminal record, the STRAWMAN would have no rights and would be guilty before proving innocence as it would now fall under Maritime Law.

And so, the Soul had come to understand that yet another criminal limitation was imposed upon the STRAWMAN. And by the acceptance of the Corporation and the human vessel being the same, the laws and the record would be assumed by it, trapped in the body, now trapped in the corporation. The soul clearly knew the difference between the STRAWMAN name in capital letters and the given first names added to the family surname in upper and lower case letters. But this was simply part of its journey and it had no way to communicate to the parents or child.

This process, the Soul was now awakened to, was opposite to the way it would allow freedom under common law where the real human is innocent until proven guilty. The registration number would be the Birth Certificate number and as the Government owned this entity it could attach criminal violations or whatever history it deemed necessary to keep the STRAWMAN in penal position under the Admiralty, not Common laws.

As the Soul assimilated the process, it saw that the STRAWMAN Trust/Corporation was assigned a Municipal bond number by the Federal Ministry of Finance creating a negotiable instrument, a registered security, a stock certificate of the corporation against which the sentient human would be the surety of this bond: a pedigree chattel document establishing the existence of the STRAWMAN in the name of STRAWMAN and giving authority to Provincial department to issue a Birth

Certificate to the parents on the Soul and vessel's behalf.

And so this number as the Treasury Direct number on the Birth Certificate in Canada where the Vessel had landed was assigned a bond value set at over 1 million dollars. The Birth Certificate would be registered as a warehouse receipt for the sentient body, a delivery receipt, an industrial bond between the sentient human and the Trust/Corporation (STRAWMAN) owned by the Government. The Soul noted that on the issued Certificate received by the parents, as was on the marriage certificate, placed in red numbers was stated *"Revenue Receipt XXXxXX for Treasury Use only"* thereby being a security instrument to set the means for the owners to obtain loans from its creditor under which it, the Nation, was bankrupt.

And the Soul now clearly understood that this account so opened was one which on behalf of the sentient human the Rulers now had a pledge of all its assets for life.

Now, as the Soul assimilated deeper into this claim, it understood that when the government process unknowingly pledged the sentient human's assets for life, it was because the country went bankrupt and was in a state of receivership. Thus, each nation falling under this would have receivers of revenue created for the purpose of receiving the revenues for those whom they were indebted to. The Soul understood that governments were so deeply in debt that they had nothing left to pledge. So they had to pledge the sentient human, its assets and future labor to pay back the debt.

The Soul noted that there were five different levels of capitalization used in names of *'persons'* that were seldom questioned. It was an evolution of the cultural beliefs so imposed upon all. The sentient human being was john doe. The Natural human was John Doe. The quasi natural/artificial person was John DOE. The corporation/artificial-person was JOHN DOE and finally, the Nomme de Guerre was DOE, JOHN.

The Soul understood that each of these had different rights. The sentient human being had all the unalienable rights and freedoms as provided by God. The Natural human had the rights and freedoms as provided by man with the Magna Charta and Canadian Bill of Rights, often referred to as the Common law. The quasi natural/artificial person had lost some rights, but not all rights. The corporation/artificial-person had limited rights and freedoms as provided by the creator of the corporation. The Nomme de Guerre had no rights and freedoms and was a complete slave to the Admiral of a ship.

The Soul understood that this military connection occurred as Court cases would be conducted in Admiralty law the law of the ship. Here the Soul knew that once its human vessel set foot on it or the courts, it would be subject to the laws of the Admiral running the ship so represented as the Judge.

## Registering Human Banking Assets

In the next stage of the administrative process, the Soul saw the registration of the trust and the assets with the international banking system. First was the Bank of Canada and then the Federal Reserve Bank, and the International Monetary Fund as controlled by the Rulers. This was because the USA/CA had been bankrupt for decades, having no substance such as gold and silver to back it. The only asset it had were the men and woman and their labour which was pledged to the IMF, a private commercial entity that the bankruptcy/receivership deal was made with. The pledge of labor was registered as the collateral for the interest on the loan of the World Bank which the private banking entity associated with the IMF. Each Capital Asset allowed the treasury to issue the birth certificate and the bond which was registered within the Canadian and US banking systems. The Bond was registered with the World Bank and the Bank of Canada. This information, the Soul saw, was found along the lower left-hand edge of the note.

And so for one holding a certified copy of the bank note in the sentient human name it would have some set value of well over $1,000,000. The number in red ink would represent a bond number or a bond tracking number. The Bank of Canada or the Federal Reserve Banks would then issue debt instruments as paper which would be assumed to be money as a draw against the IMF line of credit - all to be paid off by the efforts of the sentient human and its pledge.

As the Soul followed the process, it saw the further international registration where the bond was assigned an international CUSIP 9 character number through CGS. Here the Municipal Issuer access was through an authorized representative such as The Canadian Depository for Securities to cover a wide range of global financial instruments, including extensive equity and debt issues, derivatives, syndicated loans and U.S. listed equity options. This was done through CGS, CUSIP GLOBAL SERVICES and DDTC New York, and MSRB Municipal Securities Rulemaking Board in Virginia.

The Soul understood the process; treasury issued a bond on the birth certificate and the bond was sold at a securities exchange and bought by the Federal Reserve Bank/Bank of Canada which then used it as collateral to issue bank notes. The bond was held in trust for the Federal government at the Depository Trust Corporation. And so the Soul and its vessel would be the sureties on these bonds so the labour/energy would then payable at some future date. In commercial terms, the vessel would become the "transmitting utility" for the transmission of energy.

The birth certificate created a FICTION (the name of the baby in upper case letters). The state/province sold the birth certificate to the Commerce Department of the corporations of USA/CA, which in turn placed a bond on the birth certificate thereby making it a negotiable instrument, and placing the fictional STRAWMAN, into the warehouse of the corporation of USA/CA. Representation for the created fiction was given to the BAR (British Accredited Registry/Regency), owned and operated by the Crown, for the purpose of contracting the fiction into a third party action.

## Bond Trading On World Markets

And so, with a new asset at hand, bond trading on world markets through the World Bank and Fidelity Trust would now provide an opportunity to reap investment returns on the human capital asset. The World Bank, on behalf of the Ministry of Finance and the Bank of Canada would lodge the bond with Fidelity Trust offshore in the Caribbean or other trading securities institutions for the purpose of trading it and deriving interest or profit from the activity.

It would be brokered as a security and traded on the exchanges such as New York Stock Exchange, each vessel and its efforts being the collateral for the interest on the loan of the World Bank. The bond would be sold at a securities exchange and bought by the FRB/BoC, (Federal Reserve Bank/Bank of Canada) which would then uses it as collateral to issue bank notes. Under the fractional reserve banking regulations, the original securities would be leveraged to create 10 such securities. As a result if the original bond value was 1 million, the value of securities to be traded on the worlds market would be $1 million.

As the Soul continued to understand the process, now the Rulers would attain monetary enrichment held in trust. The bond being a claim of capital would be held in trust for the Bank of Canada at the Depository Trust Corporation. The sentient human as the surety for this bond would be the one who would have the penal municipal bond against it and would be the guarantee for the payment of it. It would be through the sentient human's labour/energy payable at some future date to be held in trust.

Hence the sentient human would be the 'transmitting utility' for the transmission of energy. The bond held in trust for the Government at the Depository Trust Corporation or DTC in New York owned by the IMF as private agency. The sentient humans thus would be the unknowing sureties on the bonds where labour/energy is then payable at some future date. The bond would become part of the estate of the sentient human. At the same time the DTC in collaboration with the World Bank would be free to use the original financial instrument provided as the Birth Certificate to trade on the market, so as to derive interest and enrichment as lodged into the DTC account under the Birth Registration number.

Thus, until the age of maturity the vessel would build an estate over time through its worldly efforts, with the bonds as assets being registered in the name of the Commercial Enterprise of the STRAWMAN. So all commerce would be transacted under this STRAWMAN NAME where the bond or any other assets that may have come into existence during the early life would be registered against. The municipal bonds would continue to generate revenue every year.

# 5

# THE AGE OF MATURITY

## The Schooling Years

As the earth years passed, the Soul now became aware of another process of education that would further limit its communication links with the human vessel. Through the childhood years, as the human vessel became more physically adept, the influence of the Soul's higher Mind and higher functions became less and less important. Now it was 1948 in the Earth time and the lower mind as well as the body were gaining prominence in the affairs of behavior.

The family beliefs and culture had dictated the learned behavior of the lower mind but still the Higher Mind of the Soul could communicate. And as the Soul had realized, unbeknown to parents and vessel, the scene of commercial behavior had been set. What the Soul realized was that it had no direct influence over the vessel anymore, as by choice, the lower mind was being trained and educated into the 3D lower vibrational culture and senses governed by the ego.

But now, it was time to train and educate the human mind and form into a new process of formal education, so dictated by the laws and culture of the land, as set forth through the Rulers.

As the Soul now watched over the years of 1950 to 1960, the educational process centered on training the lower mind so as to earn a living and to enter the world of commerce as set forth by the system and culture so dictated by the Rulers.

Here, the lower mind would become immersed in the polarity of the world system, into the corporate world and become addicted to the money system that would feed the ego of the lower mind. As so, the Higher Mind now became further and further removed from the communication to the lower mind. And so it was that the vessel, now prepared to reach the age of maturity would be trained in body and mind to begin its payback obligation through the STRAWMAN.

The Soul now fully understood how the winding down process under the influence of the Rulers had captured it and had worked to remove its Higher Mind influence from the mortal life of the Vessel that housed it.

## Application Of Social Insurance Number

It was now the year 1960, and the human vessel's lower mind was fully trained to enter the world of commerce. Now a new phase would occur. As was the custom in the land, upon the age of maturity, the sentient human would undergo the application of the Social Insurance Number (SIN or SSN) as a formal process. As the Soul followed this administrative process the human application would provides evidence of birth and claim to be a United States or Canadian citizen, a party with no vested interest in a freehold, the trust or the trust res. This action, the Soul understood, would create a declaration that the free born vessel would be technically or commercially deceased; the decedent retaining no interest in the property and that the vessel in its dual capacity as a legal fiction citizen would become the Executor of the estate so created in the name of the STRAWMAN.

This would also be the formalization of the pledge of future commercial output and consent to be taxed on that effort. As the application would be done under the Crown/State owned STRAWMAN name, the name found on the birth certificate, and with that certificate being the pledged document to the bankruptcy creditor, that would mean that the now adult human, by attachment through application for registration, would become synonymous with it and become a ward owned by the corporate Crown of the City of London, and thus to the Vatican.

Thus, all of the property, including the adult vessel's labour (100%) would be claimed by the Rulers and the owner of the STRAWMAN Corporation. From that point on, the Soul could see that all things purchased, possessed, and wages earned were in the Crown/State owned name. The wages or earnings that would be kept for the vessel's use and enjoyment would become a 'benefit' so allowed from the Rulers through the administrative process.

And so, the Soul understood, as it always saw truth, that unknown to the lower mind of the vessel, through the application of SIN or SSN this would signal the equivalent wind up, cessation or death of the vessel as the real sentient being. The STRAWMAN corporation and Estate so contained would then become available to provide the Government with the means to hold the estate to be probated like a will.

## Issuance Of The SIN Number

Now the Soul further watched the administrative process behind what the mortal lower mind could see. The issuance of the SIN/SSN was followed by the registration with the tax and finance authorities of the land, Such issuance would be equivalent to a Certificate of Cessation, or Winding-Up of the company, or appropriately, a Death Certificate for the sentient human vessel. The certification of the death provided the Government owned STRAWMAN the means to create the Estate of that STRAWMAN in that name of that registered foreigner.

At this age of maturity, the Soul could understand that with the ability to work and engage in commerce to earn a living such application was a Government requirement to account for the income created by the vessel's efforts, all accumulated into the estate. It would be registered with the Tax authority such as the CRA or IRS that would remit this to the Receiver who acted as the receiver in bankruptcy for the IMF against all bankrupt treasuries and municipalities through the Federal Ministry of Finance then the Bank of Canada.

The Soul could see that residual revenues after tax would be the benefit to live a life and to use for the survival of the vessel. But the taxes would form part of the Federal Transfer payments. The federal government and the Bank of Canada would be authorized to send these to the provincial government every year--back to the local municipal level. The Federal Minister of Finance would act as a fiduciary over that revenue and bond. Those funds would technically belong to the Vessel **as** supported by the secret pledge.

## Rollover Of The Estate Executor

With the SIN or SSN completed, there was a rollover of the estate excecutorship through the Ministry of Finance.

With the technical cessation of the sentient human, only the shadow overlay of the criminal STRAWMAN registered in the IMF alien files then existed. The Soul noted another unknown deceptive practice accepted by the lower mind. As the sentient human and its Father never claimed that the sentient human had not deceased, because neither were aware, the sentient human now fulfilled automatically and became the Executor in the Executor Office. The sentient human would now be an earthly estate walking around creating what it was to be beneficiary of.

The Certificate of Birth or Live Birth Certificate would be the Public Record of the Estate and that the Estate would be Probated. The Soul understood that under the laws of the land, a trust could only exist if there was already an Estate in existence. The address of the estate would be the file number on the birth certificate and the estate would reside at the file number. Restricted to the file number it could not move anywhere else.

Unknowingly the sentient human nor its Father would not step forward to claim the vessel as being alive for the positions as Beneficiary and Grantor and hence the Government would step in through a change of Fiduciary (Form 56) to have the role of executor for the foreigner's created estate assumed by the sentient human who by default abandoned it. The trustees would become the Beneficiaries and the sentient human would effectively be as Grantor, judged incompetent at the age of maturity. Until the sentient human would step up and correct this situation all judges would treat the sentient human as a criminal since it was the sentient human who assumed the role of the DEAD MAN criminal, as registered in the IMF file. As that overlay, the sentient criminal would have no rights, and would be incompetent to engage in the executor role.

## Probating The Estate

The Soul understood that at the point of probate, a living Executor would be required. The sentient human could then becomes the legitimate Executor authorized to occupy the Executor Office because when it was born, the Executor Office (the Birth Certificate) was sent and then only 3 people could get a copy of the Birth Certificate – sentient human, mom and dad. Once the sentient human reached the age of maturity (21), it would become the only one authorized until it came of age.

The Soul understood that the father had the authority to occupy the Executor Office of the Estate bearing STRAWMAN provided he was aware. Upon attaining the age of majority (21), the sentient human could step into and assume the proper capacity in the Executor Office of Estate. As the grantor of the estate, the sentient human would be the only one who could appoint the Executor or assign its duties to someone else. The Executor could appoint trustees but could not authorize fictional entities to administrate the estate. By definition the *Executor is the authority that grants the power and duties and liabilities to each of the trustees, and to any beneficiaries. A "grantor", is not equivalent to an Executor, and does not have or enjoy the Executor's powers, rights, or immunities. Through the process when the sentient human was declared diseased, a New Executor then assigned the STRAWMAN as trustee who has no claim of right. The executor must be a live human and that become the sentient human thus allowing the government to be the beneficiaries.*

Now at the age of maturity, the soul as trapped in a technically deceased body is free to provide labor and effort under the laws and statutes which govern the STRAWMAN.

# Income Taxes And Working Off The Debt

And so it would be that the Lower Mind and conditionally trained vessel would abide by the laws of the land and culture.

The Vessel would marry and have children as their parents did before them, living a life of polarity, working for a living, and growing further and further away from the Soul's Higher Mind.

Now totally trapped in the systems and laws and cultures so created and influenced by the Rulers of Dominion, the Lower Mind would engage in the corporate world of commerce and pyramid structures, addicted to the worship of the Rulers religions, kingship and money to feed the ego of desires, protection and propagation.

Sometimes, the Soul's whisperings to the lower mind would be heard but never to be followed, for the system to allow the lower ego mind to flourish would outweigh the need for the Soul's spiritual knowing.

As the Soul watched and learned, it saw how part of the debt obligation was administered through income taxes and working off the debt. As the vessel now worked, the efforts were recorded against the SIN and taxes were paid to the IRS and CRA private corporations administered and policed by taxation laws. As the STRAWMAN belonged to the Government and they were the Executors of the estate, the tax proceeds would be remitted towards the debt of the country, through CRA, the Ministry of Finance and the Bank of Canada to be deposited in the World Bank for the account of the IMF. This was the payback that the vessel pledged unknowingly and the transfer payments would be paid by the world bank as debt to the bankrupt operating company CANADA. The administrative process of accounting within this receivership would be the purpose of the Agencies created within the Country, such as the Bank of Canada, Federal Reserve Banks, and the CRA. The Ministries of the Country would be there to administer and account for the payment and receipt of debt money.

## Banking And Loans

In further understanding the system of banking and loans through the local federal reserve banks and Bank of Canada, the Soul saw more truths. As the sentient human vessel applied for loans, credit and mortgages, it became the sole means of creating real money, providing the authorization in the form of loan agreements, and promissory notes on behalf of the STRAWMAN/TRUST that pledged payments back. All bank documents, without exception would show the STRAWMAN name. Similar to becoming the surety on the bonds created by them, the sentients would provide the signatures for banks to create "money" for which each vessel would become the surety to pay it to them. The banks that could not create money could create entries that would simulate money being loaned to the sentient who would pay them the amount and interest while they used these instruments to trade on the open market.

The banks would then be able to combine these instruments into bonds of 100 million or greater and trade this to their benefit through the DTC CUSIP through the World Bank in association with the Bank of Canada who had the fiduciary duty of creation and monitoring this as a product of supporting the bankrupt nation. The amounts would be registered in the DTC as they would be accounted for within the registry. The Soul understood that there were 20 Federal Reserve Banks listed in Canada including Montreal, Alberta Treasury, Scotia, HSBC, Credential Securities, CIBC and Bank of Canada as the Authority reporting to the Federal Reserve. The Bank of Canada, like the US Federal Reserve Bank were Central Banks.

The sentient only signed these contracts for SSN/SIN numbers, registrations and other licenses because it was led to believe this artificial CORPORATION was the sentient and was obliged to sign. It was not told that by signing these contracts it was signing away lawful *rights* and *freedoms* and giving the government total control of sentient life, property and labour. It was clear that the World Bank would not want anyone to find out that these contracts would be *fraudulent* under their own laws. And that because of that fact sentients always retained all lawful *rights* and *freedoms*. Although this was so the sentients had been deceived into being bound by rules, statutes and "laws" that simply did not apply to human beings, it was nevertheless is the way it was   accepted.

## Final Death Of The STRAWMAN

As the Soul looked forward to understand how this all ended, it clearly understood the final chapter of death when the Soul was freed and the Vessel died of its living Spirit. This would occur when the final death of the STRAWMAN would be recorded through the VITAL STATISTICS AGENCY or like Government Agency in the local jurisdiction where the sentient human had been acting on behalf of the Executor.

Once the death was registered, the information would travel back to all the entities up the line to the IMF. At the point of the death the sentient human would have accumulated three estates. One was the Constructive Trust that was abandoned, and the other would contain the possessions accumulated under private affairs, except where the sentient human has registered into the commercial system under the name of the STRAWMAN.

The other would be the divine trust with the Vatican. In this case, while the sentient was "alive", it was the title of the asset that would be held for the sentient's right to use it, but it would not hold the asset itself. This process would be common throughout the system as was the case in a real estate transaction. That title would entitle the sentient to live in, make repairs, and reside as if the physical property was owned outright. This the Soul noted, was truth as in reality it is simply a tenancy with certain rights that are possible. This would be deemed the sentient human's benefit of tenancy under alleged ownership also allowing the sentient to trade and sell the use of what is not physically owned in a way that it would so appear as the real thing. Thus it would all belong to the Government which was in turn owned by the IMF under the commercial laws of Bankruptcy. The true power behind this process was that it would be the true owners that could 'legally' confiscate the real property should so desire.

The Soul understood that when the sentient human does actually die, a Registration of Death would be issued through the same Vital Statistics agency and the STRAWMAN along with the sentient human cease to exist in actuality. The hidden estate of the STRAWMAN would then be the property of the IMF as the supporter of the nation's bankruptcy. The gravestone and Death Certificate would mark the termination of the STRAWMAN and the sentient as one and the same. The birth certificate bonds and securities created would cease to be of value as would other assets within the STRAWMAN TRUST. However, this would not prevent the World Bank to do as they wished with it and the proceeds of enrichments. On the national level, the STRAWMAN fiction and the human would cease to exist and would not contribute revenues and services. From the National warehouse of the corporation of USA/CA, the entries would then be deleted.

As this final death process involves the physical death of the vessel housing the Soul, the Soul would then be freed to leave back to whence it came.

# 6

# RESURRECTION OF THE SOUL

---

And so the Soul, through the vessel of the Earthling and the overlay of the STRAWMAN engaged in life with occasional communications between its Higher Mind and the Lower Mind.

Together, they worked and played, engaging in the customs of the culture and following the rules set down by the laws attached to the corporate worlds, countries, nations, and jurisdictions within which they chose to live.

It was so that the Soul whispered its Higher thoughts and wisdom to the Earthling. A few times, it would be heard but most times the nigglings from the heart were lost in the lower density priorities of survival and struggle for money.

It was 1998 when the Soul's relation to the Lower Mind began to shift. It was here that something experienced through the life of the Vessel began to bring new thoughts and actions into the expressive role of the Earthling.

It was like the spirit and the Soul were emerging.

It was the time of great change that the Soul had been told about that was coming nigh. It was the time of the Harmonic Convergence.

It was now that a communication channel was opening and the Lower Mind was hearing a new story of evolution on the planet. Even in the midst of chaos from mass consciousness polarity of conflict, doom and destruction, as portrayed by the bibles and the Book of Revelations, there was a new story emerging.

## The Awakening Begins

Now there was a new consciousness occurring as a time which was referred to as the Harmonic Convergence. Like a new "buzz" it was a process of change in consciousness. More and more people were beginning to "think" differently about the material world, about the meaning of life, about the world around them. It's was like Morpheus in the Matrix who said: "*...there is a feeling something is not right. It is about how we relate to each other and how we relate to the Earth we live on. It's about all these gods and those kings and queens and high government officials that people gave their trust to. Something is not right.*

It was time for the Soul and Higher Mind to attempt its emergence. Underneath more and more of thinking time was a deep stir, a wave of desire for a better earth of peace and love. It was the evolution of a different conscious awareness. It was about a peaceful cohabitation and it began as something in the back of the Lower Mind—a sort of gut feeling from the heart that there was a different truth than programmed into the Lower Mind reality. It was the Soul and the Higher Mind now emerging into consciousness. It could now project a heart feeling that the sentient was chasing the wrong dreams and perhaps there was more to life than living in a materialistic ego centered life, under the spell of the

Rulers who loved taxes, obedience, rules, and loved to hoard for their own kind.

Dawning was what many referred to in this new feeling as the New Age, some the Unity Consciousness, some just the End Times. There were many names for this and as many ideas on this. But one thing that was sure was this new consciousness of self incorporated was that it was not an organized religion or a group. There were no leaders, no real dogma. It was some evolving awareness that had a common spiritual denominator, and it was based upon love of all things, a peaceful world of harmony that was marked by a transition time. It was a strange felling of the unified Souls that something better was available. It was the Soul finally speaking through the heart in a way that could not be overridden by the Lower Mind.

The Soul was speaking now. It did not matter whether there were saviors, great mystics, healers and wonderful products, coming forward; the bottom line was that they were focused on the same dream—one of a New Earth and a new human that could be more than it was led to believe. It was a new story of Revelations of rapture, revelation and resurrection.

Now the Soul was bringing a truth out that told the difference between religious and spiritual, best exemplified by the dominant groups. In simple terms it was clear that religion dealt with a mortal human who lived a life to serve god and the Rulers under the training of the Lower Mind. That Earthling would die beholding to the gods for his salvation into eternity. But the new story was about the emergence of the an immortal being here for the expression through temporary form of human body to express and expand love to attain joy, as an aspect of God, the Creator himself. Now the Soul could communicate that religion was about serving god as the Rulers, but Spirituality was about being God.

Now the Soul was speaking loud and clear as the Light Being recalled what had been communicated from the Creator about the Divine Plan. It was unfolding now and before all who could recognize it and it had never happened before. This End Time was to begin between the turn of the century and 2012, and as the Light Being had been told, it would have to do with various cosmic forces and planetary alignments that would happen once in 26,000 years. These were the forces that were influencing the liberation of consciousness, and hence behavior allowing the captured Soul a voice.

The Vessel and Lower Mind now knew it was a knowing of the truth and that everyone had a choice as to whether they let this new consciousness into their awareness to create new behavior. It was still free will that would allow the Soul to be heard.

It was the shift into the new 26,000 year cycle—called the Age of Aquarius—that was evolving into a commonality to certain things that were going to happen It showered a new "knowing" into the consciousness of humanity as many Souls raised their voices in unison.

And so it was that the Vessel and Lower mind began the quest into this new world. A quest for truth about what was, what it was and what would enter the consciousness of the Lower Mind. Now it was time to be the Scribe that the Light Being had come to Earth to be. To reveal the truth in the light of what it was.

So it was written a new a New Earth story.

## The New Earth Revelations

The Soul now revealed to the Lower Mind that Revelation was indeed the revealing or disclosing, or making something obvious through active or passive communication with supernatural and divine entities. This time, the **Revelation** originated directly from the Source and the Light Being's Home directly to all who could listen and into their personal consciousness, not through anyone else. It was because all as Souls from Source were all God, as Christ had taught. So it would be all Souls implementing this new plan. There would be no middle men to tell anyone what the Word of God was because each would begin to understand that it was each so awakened to the truth of their Souls that would be the "chosen ones" already privy to the truth of God.

But it was not going to be disclosed by Jesus himself. It all being awakened that would go through a **Resurrection** and all who so chose to believe this would resurrect themselves coming back to a re-life as the Second Coming of Christ. It would not be one prophet, it would be all! It would not be a plan executed by the Rulers. It would be a second coming of all who chose.

The Soul explained. There would not be chosen ones after a big meeting deciding to remove all Christians from the Earth, to protect them. This **Rapture** would is simply be our own choice when each understood that each was something else than what each have been told to believe as a mortal human. So Jesus would not "snatch us" out of harm's way if we had been good. It is each that simply decided a new way. For under this story good and bad were judgments and love cannot and does not judge. Thus, there would be no judgment. It's would be like a mother who truly loved her child; regardless of what it did, she loved him and did not judge. It would no longer be the other people who judge and force her to action—the consciousness of others prevails.

Then the Soul revealed that through **Revelation** it would indeed be the revealing or disclosing, through active or passive communication of who we really were—an aspect of God, an eternal Light Being borrowing a body to experience a time slice on Earth at a very special time. And this would be where a common denominator of vibration would fit in as each would begin to vibrate higher and higher, releasing many of those miraculous abilities that Jesus the Christ himself had—especially the healing. It would be a mass revealing of the truth of teachings of Jesus the Christ through the consciousness shift. But it would *not* be Jesus suddenly appearing. It would be the Time of Revelation when the *knowing* of this, and in many cases, the *showing* of this (as he did), would be revealed. It would be about attaining a higher expression of God through each as a piece of God which is everything as One, living laughing and loving in thought, word and deed.

So now it was clear that this Revelation would be the revealing of Jesus Christ as being each of us and that the message would come directly from God the Father as a wakeup call of rapture, not through the self proclaimed gods of the Rulers. And it would be a revealing that there is no sin and that the heaven we seek is already within us as immortal, eternal aspects of God. So would be a call not to serve gods, or listen to other's interpretations of God's Word, but to BE God and know for each self what is its Soul's truth.  The revealing would be each do not need gurus, bishops, meditators or the likes to tell them the secrets of heaven, being eternal and how to have a better life. It would be simply the acceptance of who each truly was as a Light Being that is already living a life as a Spiritual entity borrowing a body to be within rather than a body looking for spirit outside of itself.

And it came clear that for those poor souls that would not want to believe or accept this, it would be **Armageddon.** But this was not the biblical one. It would be the one that each is in now; the one that creates fear, conflict, with a drive of ego to survive and dominate. It would manifest a world of separation from who awakened to the truth.  So for those that have not chosen to believe who they are, it would be the acceleration of the Law of Cause and Effect, being left in their own harm's way. They would continue to pay their karma of sins of hatred and separation and conflict and fear as each is doing right now. Under the Revelations, there would be a major difference; it would become clear to all the understanding of how each in Armageddon attract that which they created. It would be clear that this was not God's will; it wasn't God that did this, it was each who would choose to continue their own hell. It was each that would attract it by the energy it chose to create; the big difference being that energy in the Old Earth could not be inflicted upon anyone else like it had been for thousands of years. by the Rulers. And through this time, this manifestation of reality would manifest itself to return faster and faster until it would becomes instant. And so the one so choosing to adhere to old ways would deal with their own karma and simply die and leave as mortals to never again incarnate upon Earth.

That would be the true Armageddon where each would create their own Hell at their own choosing, and of their own intensity. And so the fight with that which was taught as polarity and the Devil and Hell, holding on to the old ways of deception and greed so inflict on others would become a fight with each Lower Self as the Devil is within.

And the Soul now revealed that rapture would not be people that would be snatched out of their own devils (harm's way). It would a process of rapture for the ones that would choose to understand who they were—and the snatching would be of their own accord.

There would not be a big battle between Satan and the kings of the Earth as the end of the world dawned. It would be a battle of each in their own mind, of who each is and the battle between the Lower and Higher minds. It would be about each Vessel's own conscious awareness and belief that each would do battle with. It is about the knowing that each would inflict upon their mortal being to create their own life. The battle of Armageddon would be a battle of belief in each self. That would be the choice between lower and higher.

And then the Soul revealed another old over-used term of **Crucifixion.** In these shifting times of End Times it would be the process of crucifying what is Hell by leaving it behind and choosing Heaven. It would be the death of the old in choice of the new. Like before, everyone had a choice of how (bad or good) they perceived any situation. And when they learn that what they perceive as they think, speak feel and act upon brings upon them like energy, they will pay more attention to what they think and do. That is what the choice will be all about.

So the story now revealed by the Soul was clear, as it would become clear to many more. It would not be a story written by God in an autographed hard cover. And it would not be written by the Rulers from the words of the gods. And there would not be leaders. It would be an unfolding all around everyone at the same time if each would have the eyes, ears and heart to open to this revelation.

And so the Soul revealed, it was now time for the Soul to come forward and to open to a new life as so guided by the Higher Mind. It was why this Light Being was in the Vessel and that ways of old polarity had no more significance. It was the time when *"... and the meek shall inherit the earth".*

Read on...

# 7

# INTRODUCING CORPORATION PLANET EARTH

Is this a true story? Does it really matter?

The truth is that once the Soul is born into a body of a family and culture, that body and mind are simply subjected to that culture and whatever it deems to be important as its 'laws'. Whether this is family, a race, a kingdom, a species, a culture, a nation, a religion, a corporation, whatever, Earthlings tend to create their code of law that governs behavior.

As such, one can have a fruitful life, or choose a stressful life depending upon the choice of how one accepts or rejects these rules. Thus if one believes they have had a fruitful life, the STRAWMAN and the dominion of the Illuminated Ones is irrelevant. The story is thus a very interesting synopsis of something that shows a different point of view and an administrative process Earthlings have accepted as being part of the evolution of Earth and the experience of the Soul while in the body.

If on the other hand, the Soul while in the body, is looking for a different expression, and is bombarded with a stressful life, the Earthling has a choice to leave into a different culture, become more entangled and stressful, or take an action to change that culture.

In retrospect, many cultures have evolved under the Rulers or Illuminated Ones that has served to create a better world of expression. The pathway is littered with billions of casualties of conquest, conflict and unhappy people but it is nevertheless in many countries a better place.

If one accepts the STRAWMAN as a means to this, cares not about a deception, uses the debt system as it is given, doesn't hold real assets and has title to them to use them and enjoy his life, and care little about elevating the spiritual side of the Soul, then even in a chaotic environment where everything is not right, one can have a fruitful life.

However, there are many that do indeed feel that there is more to a fruitful life, and that things can be less stressful in their families and cultures and governments and there can be more freedom from fear and stress too have abundance and prosperity and health.

In addition, here is the real issue. If this is a deception that according to the laws of these Rulers, there exists an enormous estate for every STRAWMAN that accounts for the true credit and effort created by the sentient human counterpart it would seem appropriate that those who have deceived must pay back that which they have stolen by substitution. Debt is replaced by what has been taken (gold, money, and real assets). Would that be a worthwhile mission?

Thus, as this feeling grows and truths emerge, so does the consciousness of the mass, and thus change is made. Like the rise and demise of kingdoms, cultures, races, corporations, and people, so does the ebb and flow of good and bad shift upon the evolution of species. The shift cannot occur for the better until the people know the truth of what it is that has to change.

That is why this story is important, for it can be the catalyst that precipitates a better shift.

So the story now brings new evidence into play on the premise that if we understand how and why this STRAWMAN story occurred, and why; then perhaps we can shift that which we do not like into something that is better for all. In the past, this decision has been in the control of the Rulers who run PLANET EARTH INC. the ultimate kingdom. They have determined what is best for Earthlings and what is important.

However, judging from the record, the history is filled with wars, death, poverty, disease, and manipulation for the purpose of power and dominion. So now the question is: can this be managed better? At this particular time in the evolution of the Earthling, there are enormous tsunamis of change; to governments, to spiritual attention, to a need for transparency, honesty and controls. Why? Because much of what has evolved in this leadership has come about through greed, deception, and ego desires for power. Thus the consciousness is already shifted but new solutions are not at hand and the fear of loss for those Rulers of PLANET EARTH creates more havoc.

## The Corporate Empires

The current generation has grown accustomed to Corporations. They are a fiction vehicle created by their founders under government regulations and the founding articles of incorporation. A corporation has no heart or conscience. It is directed and run by sentient humans and is designed to hold assets and conduct business. The pyramid structures allow the founders power over others labor and the option to create great profit (or loss) so as to create a personal kingdom to satisfy personal needs and goals

Thus, these fabrications called corporation are everywhere all designed to engage in some form of business and commerce. For this phenomenon has grown to change people to be heartless and ruthless in order create profit for their owners. So many of the people have taken on the qualities of the dead fictional corporation. It is obvious that there are private corporations (that do not abide by any rules) and there are private corporations that abide by private rules. And there are public corporations that abide by public rules. They can be enormous and they can be small. There are 30 million corporations in the USA

Reports published on Forbes say there are 147 companies that control "everything".In a published report from Swiss research they discovered that global corporate control has a distinct bow-tie shape, with a dominant core of 147 firms radiating out from the middle. Each of these 147 own interlocking stakes of one another and together they control 40% of the wealth in the network. A total of 737 control 80% of it all. The top 20 are at the bottom of the post. This is, say the paper's authors, the first map of the structure of global corporate control.

**The Top Fifty Corporate Owners**

1. Barclays plc
2. Capital Group Companies Inc
3. FMR Corporation
4. AXA
5. State Street Corporation
6. JP Morgan Chase & Co
7. Legal & General Group plc
8. Vanguard Group Inc
9. UBS AG
10. Merrill Lynch & Co Inc
11. Wellington Management Co LLP
12. Deutsche Bank AG
13. Franklin Resources Inc

14. Credit Suisse Group
15. Walton Enterprises LLC (holding company for Wal-Mart heirs)
16. Bank of New York Mellon Corp
17. Natixis
18. Goldman Sachs Group Inc
19. T Rowe Price Group Inc
20. Legg Mason Inc

According to the 2011 annual factbook from the Investment Company Institute, there is $24.7 trillion in all the mutual funds in the world (a little less than half from the US). Based on data from the ICI, $1.24 trillion of this is directly invested in index funds, plus another $992 billion in assets beyond that $24.7 trillion in Exchange Traded Funds, which aren't mutual funds but are index funds. That means the bulk of that money is in "active" managed funds or fund of funds.

The funny thing is that this is all based on shares, bonds, and funds of 24.7 trillion. These are just paper instruments to represent money. So where is the real money?

Another report published by Forbes That means the real power to control the world lies with only four companies:

**McGraw-Hill**, which owns Standard & Poor's,

**Northwestern Mutual**, which owns Russell Investments, the index arm of which runs the benchmark Russell 1,000 and Russell 3,000,

**CME Group** which owns 90% of Dow Jones Indexes,

**Barclay's**, which took over Lehman Brothers and its Lehman Aggregate Bond Index, the dominant world bond fund index. Together, these four firms dominate the world of indexing. And in turn, that means they hold real sway over the world's money.

There are 60-100 million multinationals. There could be millions of trusts. According to the study, which will be published shortly in the scientific journal *PLoS One*, there is a core group of 1,318 multinational companies that sit at the centre of global commerce. They own a majority of shares in 60 per cent of the world's large businesses and manufacturers.

Within that group, the researchers identified a "super-entity" of 147 companies that control 40 per cent of the wealth within the multinational commerce network. According to the researchers, each of the 147 companies is owned by other companies within the "super-entity," essentially creating a self-contained network of wealth.
A majority of the companies listed in the network are financial institutions, with British bank Barclays at the top of the list. Asset managers Capital Group Companies and Fidelity Investments are in second and third, while insurer AXA and State Street Corporation round off the top five.

Interestingly, the bogeyman of financial reform champions, Goldman Sachs, placed only 18th on the list. The researchers say their work is evidence the world may need global anti-trust regulations -- rules designed to keep companies from becoming too large in their sector, or from developing de facto agreements to cooperate with competitors.

Complex systems experts note the tendency for wealth to concentrate in a small number of hands is natural. "The Occupy Wall Street claim that one per cent of people have most of the wealth reflects a logical phase of the self-organizing economy," Dan Braha of the New England Complex Systems Institute told *NewScientist*. Critics of the study say the researchers were measuring the wrong things, and therefore providing an incorrect image of global wealth.

As one commenter argued on the Forbes website, looking at the ownership structure of multinational corporations doesn't give you an idea of who controls the wealth, because many of the companies on the study's list are managers of wealth, not owners of it.

The list also doesn't measure "pension plans, corporate [retirement] plans and individual funds [that] manage trillions in assets ultimately belonging to individuals who are predominantly not in the one per cent, the commenter wrote. "*There are a number of 'custodian banks' in the list... Again, they do not own the assets, or even really control the assets -- they merely house the assets. A better list would be the actual asset OWNERS, rather than the vendors who manage, house and clear said assets.*"

**Here are the 5 companies at the top of the Swiss researchers' rankings**

**5 State street:** This 209-year-old, Boston-based company ranks in fifth place on Vitali et al's Network of Global Corporate Control. The company manages more than $2 trillion in assets, has assets itself of around $160 billion, and employs just short of 30,000 people

**4 AXA Insurance**: Paris-based AXA manages more than $1.1 trillion of other people's money, has $730 billion in assets and employs more than 100,000 people around the world. AXA CEO Henri de Castries is shown here in 2008.

**3: Fidelity Investments Fidelity Investments** is primarily a brokerage and mutual fund manager. The company has seen significant job reductions, with its staff falling from 47,000 in 2007 to 38,000 in 2009 -- a sign that even companies near the centre of global power aren't immune from downsizing

**2: Capital Group** Founded by self-made financier Jonathan Bell Lovelace in 1931, Capital Group Companies today manages more than $1 trillion of assets with a surprisingly small staff, around 7,500 people. The Los Angeles-based investment management firm likes to keep a low profile, and counts Fidelity Investments among its largest competitors.

**1: Barclays** The 321-year-old British bank Barclays plc has been a mover and shaker in the world of finance since before anyone had conjured up the word "capitalism." In the 1990s, the bank's prominence in the UK made it a target of "Mardis Gras Bomber" Edgar Pearce. In 2008, Barclays bought the investment banking and trading divisions of Lehman Brothers, the Wall Street financial firm whose bankruptcy triggered the financial crisis

The Swiss Federal Institute (SFI) in Zurich released a study entitled "The Network of Global Corporate Control" that proves a small consortiums of corporations – mainly banks – run the world. A mere 147 corporations which form a "super entity" have control 40% of the world's wealth; which is the real economy. These mega-corporations are at the center of the global economy. The banks found to be most influential include:
• Barclays
• Goldman Sachs
• JPMorgan Chase & Co
• Vanguard Group
• UBS
• Deutsche Bank

- Bank of New York Mellon Corp
- Morgan Stanley
- Bank of America Corp
- Société Générale

Consider that ten mega corporations control the output of almost everything you buy; from household products to pet food to jeans.

According to a chart via Reddit, called "The Illusion of Choice," these corporations create a chain that begins at one of 10 super companies. You've heard of the biggest names, but it's amazing to see what these giants own or influence.

(*Note*: The chart shows a mix of networks. Parent companies may own, own shares of, or may simply partner with their branch networks. For example, Coca-Cola does not own Monster, but distributes the energy drink. Another note: it has not been updated to reflect P&G's sale of Pringles to Kellogg's.

Here are just a few examples: Yum Brands owns KFC and Taco Bell. The company was a spin-off of Pepsi. All Yum Brands restaurants sell only Pepsi products because of a special partnership with the soda-maker.

### $84 billion-company Proctor & Gamble
Is the largest advertiser in the U.S. It is paired with a number of diverse brands that produce everything from medicine to toothpaste to high-end fashion. All tallied, P&G reportedly serves a whopping 4.8 billion people around the world through this network.

### $200 billion-corporation Nestle
**Is** famous for chocolate, but which is the biggest food company in the world — owns nearly 8,000 different

brands worldwide, and takes stake in or is partnered with a swath of others. Included in this network is shampoo company L'Oreal, baby food giant Gerber, clothing brand Diesel, and pet food makers Purina and Friskies.

**Unilever**
Of soap fame, reportedly serves 2 billion people around the world, controlling a network that produces everything from Q-tips to Skippy peanut butter.

And it's not just the products you buy and consume, either. In recent decades, the very news and information that you get has bundled together: 90% of the media is now controlled by just six companies, down from 50 in 1983, according to a Frugal Dad infographic.

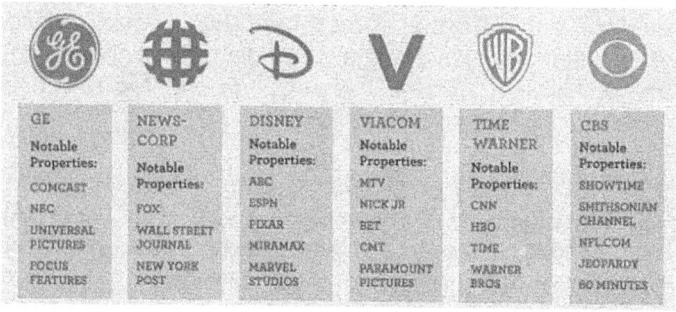

It gets even more macro. 37 banks have merged to become just four —JPMorgan Chase, Bank of America, Wells Fargo and CitiGroup in a little over two decades, according to a Federal Reserve map

The nation's 10 largest financial institutionshold54% of our total financial assets; in 1990, they held 20%. As *MotherJones* reports, the number of banks has dropped from more than 12,500 to about 8,000.

The numbers are stark showing this mind-bending reality of mega corps. This is the corporate world we live in.

## And Then There Is PLANET EARTH INC

It is not difficult to understand that like the four public companies reported to control the 147 companies that control everything (everything being the funny shares and bond type money world), there is a private system that also controls the debt or what is perceived to "real" money; like all major banks are private corporations.

It is not difficult to understand that corporation are nothing but a fictitious representation that require real people to run them and give them purpose and profit for the owners.

These examples given here are not to show this is bad or good. It just is this way as the empires have become larger and larger. But most of this is "reported" through public entities, so it is a bit of a diversion from the real control which is through private corporations and trusts.

These examples simply show that there are enormous fictions structures based upon "assets". But of interest is to carry this further to see what fictitious entity is running the big empire of Planet Earth.

For this, we must introduce PLANET EARTH INC. This has been a topic of two books:
PLANET EARTH INC: The Empire of gods exposed
PLANET EARTH INC: The Empire of the gods deposed
These books were written by consolidating man researcher' information on the Rulers and how they got there. It can be found at Amazon.com or www.edrychkun.com.

In this short book, I will bring forward some of the key elements detailed in these books. This has to do with the process of who is in control of the kingdom and Empire of PLANET EARTH INC and how that control was implemented.

The keys tools of the king's conquest and dominion are:

- **Law**
- **Commerce**
- **Money**
- **Corporations and Trusts**

We will also look at some different history from what has been taught. We will see how these key tools have been used to create the monolithic kingdom of corporation PLANET EARTH INC as run by the Rulers, and how they have derived this from their roles as gods.

# 8

# THE THREADS THAT BIND EARTH: RELIGION AND COMMERCE

There are two major forces on Planet Earth that have been the root to the greatest strife in the history of mankind. The purpose of this STRAWMAN follow-up chapter is not to paint a dismal picture of what has happened and brand it as deception or conspiracy; it is to simply inform from a different point of view. We as Earthlings have in majority simply received what we have asked for and sometimes it takes a wakeup call to look back to see what is wrong in order to determine what is right. Some love to engage in the energies of what is wrong. Others prefer to engage in what is right as determined from what seems wrong. Within this, we all choose our ways and our paths very much influenced by the experiences in two major forces of commerce and religion. It is pretty difficult to go somewhere on the planet and ignore these two forces. That is why Soul's come here repeatedly; to experience the polarity.

It has been so for a long time. Historical research shows these two forces have been active and evolving over thousands of years, originating in Babylonia and Sumeria and even earlier. Over the last thousands of years, these human tendencies to seek freedom, prosperity and spirit have become more and influenced by the religious orders and the international bankers. At least this is the way it has evolved. There have always been those who have sought dominion over others and there have always been those that have sought sovereignty of spirit, peace and harmony. There have always been gods, kings and queens. There have always been those who had special powers and resources to control armies so as to advance their personal goals. And there have always been gods, either mythical, in the minds, and perhaps even in reality that have been kind and vengeful, peaceful and warlike to serve their own purposes. And it seems that there have always been the religious orders and higher priests that have proclaimed themselves to be conveyors and administrators of these god's desires. Some of these have been from the dark side, while others of the light side.

It does not come as a surprise that those who have taken a heartless path of dominion can easily control those who are more heart full. It is not that this is wrong or right, it is simply the way humanity has chosen it to be. It appears to be humanity's constitution that is conscious of fear; of dying, of being hurt, of not being able to attain their personal desires. It is not surprising that this fear if packaged right becomes a universally marketable product and an effective means of dominating others. Earthlings are afraid of death and they are afraid of pain. They are fearful of not surviving the way they believe they should. Such a paranoia, whether instinctual or egoistic based is a recipe for control by those who know how to administer it.

What the religions have done is to create an authority of representatives who step in as the ones who interpret what the gods say and impose beliefs preferred by them thus converting a perfectly wonderful system of spirituality into religion. On the other side, the financial gods have slowly stepped in to convert a perfectly wonderful system of money into a system of debt. Although within each there are still wondrous parts, these by humanity's own reception have dwindled the light, and much of the truth much like a corporation will bend the truth for profit and marketing purposes. Why? Because humanity accepts what religious leaders tell them and they also accept the way in which debt controls their financial affairs. What humanity has achieved with great zeal is to compromise their sovereignty of both spirit and commerce.

So let us open with a picture of where we have come to in our evolution.

## The Religious Pyramids

What is religion? It is defined as a set of beliefs concerning the cause, nature, and purpose of the universe, especially when considered as the creation of a superhuman agency or agencies, usually involving devotional and ritual observances, and often containing a moral code governing the conduct of human affairs. The greatest religions began before Christ. This table was created as of 2005.

| RELIGION | FOLLOWERS | TOTAL | % |
|---|---|---|---|
| 1. Christianity | 2,100,000,000 | 2,100,000,000 | 30.58% |
| 2. Islam | 1,500,000,000 | 3,600,000,000 | 52.42% |
| 3. Nonreligious | 1,100,000,000 | 4,700,000,000 | 68.44% |
| 4. Hinduism | 900,000,000 | 5,600,000,000 | 81.54% |
| 5. Chinese | 394,000,000 | 5,994,000,000 | 87.28% |
| 6. Buddhism | 376,000,000 | 6,370,000,000 | 92.75% |
| 7. Primal-indigenous | 300,000,000 | 6,670,000,000 | 97.12% |
| 8. African Traditional | 100,000,000 | 6,770,000,000 | 98.58% |
| 9. Sikhism | 23,000,000 | 6,793,000,000 | 98.91% |
| 10. Juche | 19,000,000 | 6,812,000,000 | 99.19% |
| 11. Spiritism | 15,000,000 | 6,827,000,000 | 99.41% |

| | | | |
|---|---:|---:|---:|
| 12. Judaism | 14,000,000 | 6,841,000,000 | 99.61% |
| 13. Baha'i | 7,000,000 | 6,848,000,000 | 99.71% |
| 14. Jainism | 4,200,000 | 6,852,200,000 | 99.77% |
| 15. Shinto | 4,000,000 | 6,856,200,000 | 99.83% |
| 16. Cao Dai | 4,000,000 | 6,860,200,000 | 99.89% |
| 17. Zoroastrianism | 2,600,000 | 6,862,800,000 | 99.93% |
| 18. Tenrikyo | 2,000,000 | 6,864,800,000 | 99.96% |
| 19. Neo-Paganism | 1,000,000 | 6,865,800,000 | 99.97% |
| 20. UnitUniversalism | 800,000 | 6,866,600,000 | 99.98% |
| 21. Rastafarianism | 600,000 | 6,867,200,000 | 99.99% |
| 22. Scientology | 500,000 | 6,867,700,000 | 100.00% |
| **Current during census** | **6,867,700,000** | | |
| **Current in 2012** | **7,028,260,000** | | |

At the time of this census, the lion's share of 98% includes 6.8 billion (now 7 billion) followers that abide by the beliefs of the world's top 7 religions. All, except 1.1 billion "nonreligious" believe in a higher deity, gods or a God. In fact there are thousands of religions that have or believe in some gods as their deity or supreme force, being, or power. These gods mostly reside in the imaginations of the Earthling, or in the mythical writings. Yet these all have a tremendous impact upon the way Earthlings conduct their earthly affairs. This has evolved to create a tremendous difference in beliefs and it has resulted in a difference of opinion as to what is the truth about their gods or one God. Difference of opinion leads to conflict and anger. This has taken shape as wars and conflict. So while there may be a fundamental belief somewhere within the scriptures and beliefs of love, peace and harmony, the historical evidence of deeds do not follow the thinking and words, as starkly exemplified by the number of deaths that have resulted from these diverse religious orders.

But notice there is a new religion (kid) on the block called nonreligious. This number is increasing exponentially and if you looked at it 10 years ago, you would see dramatic changes. In 2004, it was reported to be increasing at 15%. It must about the Soul's story?

The top 10 religions have grown into tremendous pyramids of organizational structures and power that have dominated the beliefs of the many. What is coming to light more and more is that this hierarchy is built to have the many serve the few. And these few, the monolithic religious structure such as the Vatican dictate what god says. In trust and faith, 30% of the world populations follow their beliefs.

In order to fully understand the evolution of the largest empire of Christianity, it is necessary to look at the pyramidal structure of the headquarters--the Vatican.

## The Vatican Empire

The Vatican empire does not need introduction in relation to its power and influence over many people. The history of good and evil, and how they have preached this through sin and righteousness is stark with the ungodly methods used to enforce their beliefs. Yet they are forgiven because they are the chosen ones of God. The religious and financial empire they have created has been simply "smart corporate business" which can be identified in their declarations:

Consider the 1455 Papal Bull **Romanus Pontifex**. It is the *1st* Testamentary Deed & Will & 1st Crown over Land. This is the First **Trust** ever written, and although you may believe because it was written so long ago, it is not relevant, think again. As you ponder the chapters that follow, you will find that what is in force today goes back a lot further than that. It is just that most simply don't look at history that way. Consider this Source: **http://one-evil.org/texts_papal_bulls/papal_bull.htm** where the Vatican is not shy about their power:

*"The Roman pontiff, successor of the key-bearer of the heavenly kingdom and vicar of Jesus Christ, contemplating with a father's mind all the several climes*

*of the world and the characteristics of all the nations dwelling in them and seeking and desiring the salvation of all, wholesomely ordains and disposes upon careful deliberation those things which he sees will be agreeable to the Divine Majesty and by which he may bring the sheep entrusted to him by God into the single divine fold, and may acquire for them the reward of eternal felicity, and obtain pardon for their souls. This we believe will more certainly come to pass, through the aid of the Lord, if we bestow suitable favours and special graces on those Catholic kings and princes, who, like athletes and intrepid champions of the Christian faith, as we know by the evidence of facts, not only restrain the savage excesses of the Saracens and of other infidels, enemies of the Christian name, but also for the defence and increase of the faith vanquish them and their kingdoms and habitations, though situated in the remotest parts unknown to us, and subject them to their own temporal dominion, sparing no labour and expense, in order that those kings and princes, relieved of all obstacles, may be the more animated to the prosecution of so salutary and laudable a work."*

The full text can be found through the reference above and you may be surprised that something written back then looks like it was written by a lawyer today. In the document, the Vatican (Catholic Church) clearly declares dominion over earth territories by the process of kings and queens coming into line of the faith of Christ, exerting dominion over the soul and power to put into slavery or rid the earth of those disbelievers. It is well worth the read. Now this may at first seem as a harmless, unsupported position much like we may view the "kingdom" of the Queen. It is just theoretical you may say, symbolic. But as you will learn, the ones who created these words and "symbolic structures" take them very seriously.

What follows is neither wrong or right. It just is.

Gracing the walls of St Peter's Basilica is the Vatican-approved image of God. Here is an angry bearded man in the sky, painted by Michelangelo. Cruel and violent images of God's tortured Son, suffering, bleeding and dying with thorns gouged through his skull and nails pounded through his feet and hands are on display throughout the Vatican. These images serve as reminders that God allowed His Son to be tortured and killed to save the souls of human beings who are all born sinners.

With this image, this Vatican, a separate jurisdiction, and private corporation rules over approximately 2 billion of the world's people. The colossal wealth of the Vatican includes enormous investments with the Rothschilds in Britain, France and the USA and with giant oil and weapons corporations like Shell and General Electric. The Vatican solid gold bullion, worth billions is stored with the Rothschild controlled Bank of England and the US Federal Reserve Bank.

The Catholic Church is the biggest financial power, wealth accumulator and property owner in existence, possessing more material wealth than any bank, corporation, giant trust or government anywhere on the globe. While 2/3 of the world earns less than $2 a day, and 1/5 of the world is underfed or starving to death, the Vatican hoards the world's wealth, profits from it on the stock market and at the same time preaches about giving.

The Vatican is a business engaged in the commerce of souls and sin. It has accumulated all that wealth over the millennium by placing a price-tag on sin. Many bishops and popes actively marketed guilt, sin and fear for profit, by selling indulgences. There is even a credit system as worshipers were encouraged to pre-pay for sins they hadn't yet committed and get pardoned ahead of time. Those who didn't pay-up are threatened with eternal damnation. Another method was to get wealthy land owners to hand-over their land and fortune to the church on their death bed, in exchange for a blessing which would supposedly enable them to go to heaven. Pope Leo the fifth rebuilt St Peter's Basilica by selling tickets out of hell and tickets to heaven.

In a statement published in connection with a bond prospectus, the Boston archdiocese listed its assets at Six Hundred and Thirty-five Million ($635,891,004), which is 9.9 times its liabilities. This leaves a net worth of Five Hundred and Seventy-one million dollars ($571,704,953). It is not difficult to discover the truly astonishing wealth of the church, once we add the riches of the twenty-eight archdioceses and 122 dioceses of the U.S.A., some of which are even wealthier than that of Boston. But because many of these are private corporations, there are no audits, no accountability, no regulations that disclose these holdings.

Some idea of the real estate and other forms of wealth controlled by the Catholic church may be gathered by the remark of a member of the New York Catholic Conference, namely *"that his church probably ranks second only to the United States Government in total annual purchase."* Another statement, made by a nationally syndicated Catholic priest, perhaps is even more telling. *"The Catholic church,"* he said, *"must be the biggest corporation in the United States. We have a branch office in every neighborhood. Our assets and real estate holdings must exceed those of Standard Oil, A.T.&T., and U.S. Steel combined. And our roster of dues-paying members must be second only to the tax rolls of the United States Government."*

The Catholic Church, once all the assets have been put together, is reported to be the most formidable stockbroker in the world. The Vatican, independently of each successive pope, has been increasingly orientated towards the U.S. The Wall Street Journal said that the Vatican's financial deals in the U.S. alone were so big that very often it sold or bought gold in lots of a million or more dollars at one time. Quite obviously God has a vested interest in Planet Earth's gold.

The Vatican's treasure of solid gold has been estimated by the United Nations World Magazine to amount to several billion dollars. A large bulk of this is stored in gold ingots with the U.S. Federal Reserve Bank, while banks in England and Switzerland hold the rest. But this is just a small portion of the wealth of the Vatican, which in the U.S. alone, is greater than that of the five wealthiest giant corporations of the country. When to that is added all the real estate, property, stocks and shares abroad, then the staggering accumulation of the wealth of the Catholic church becomes so formidable as to defy any rational assessment.

The Catholic Church is the biggest financial power, wealth accumulator and property owner in existence. It is a greater possessor of material riches than any other single institution, corporation, bank, giant trust, government or state of the whole globe. The pope, as the visible ruler of this immense amassment of wealth, is consequently one of the richest individuals of the twentieth century. No one can realistically assess how much he is worth because it is all private.

If you really scrutinize their product and marketing policies, the Catholic church has become the biggest mafia on earth, with their protection-racket of selling "forgiveness for sins". The Catholic church's practice of teaching people that they can be sinful all their lives and all they need to do is pay the church for "forgiveness" is seemingly one of the chief causes of all the evil and dishonesty in the world, as people are actually taught and encouraged they can be sinful and evil rather than to purify themselves and strive to become perfect; just pay up, admit you have been bad and it's quite alright.

So it is through the most incredible marketing that many people actually buy the church's products and think that they can get away with being evil all their lives. All they have to do is seek forgiveness from a priest. During the dark ages, the Catholic Church not only hoarded the wealth they collected from the poor, but they hoarded knowledge. They kept the masses ignorant and in the dark by denying them a basic education. They also prohibited anyone from reading or even possessing a Bible, under pain of death. It is business and this business has become one of the largest private corporate pyramids on Planet Earth. It is because over 30% of the Earthlings choose to support this policy.

## The Pyramid Of Debt

Here is a measurement that is <u>not private</u>. It is another staggering evolution of what is relates to the existing pyramid of debt. This interesting table is presented to show some staggering numbers of non-wealth. The figures indicate the total external debt by country. Note these are trillions of dollars.

| Rank | Country | External US dollars |
|---|---|---|
| 1 | United States | 15,570,789,000,000 |
| 2 | United Kingdom | 8,981,000,000,000 |
| 3 | Germany | 4,713,000,000,000 |
| 4 | France | 4,698,000,000,000 |
| 5 | Japan | 2,441,000,000,000 |
| 6 | Ireland | 2,378,000,000,000 |
| 7 | Netherlands | 2,344,296,360,000 |

| 8 | Italy | 2,223,000,000,000 |
|---|---|---|
| 9 | Spain | 2,166,000,000,000 |
| 10 | Luxembourg | 1,892,000,000,000 |
| 11 | Belgium | 1,241,000,000,000 |
| 12 | Switzerland | 1,200,000,000,000 |
| 13 | Australia | 1,169,000,000,000 |
| 14 | Canada | 1,009,000,000,000 |
| 15 | Sweden | 853,300,000,000 |
| 16 | Austria | 755,000,000,000 |
| 17 | Norway | 643,000,000,000 |
| 18 | China | 635,500,000,000 |
| 19 | Denmark | 559,500,000,000 |
| 20 | Greece | 532,900,000,000 |
| 21 | Portugal | 497,800,000,000 |
| 22 | Russia | 480,200,000,000 |
| 23 | Finland | 370,800,000,000 |
| 24 | Korea, south | 370,100,000,000 |
| 25 | Brazil | 310,800,000,000 |
| 26 | Turkey | 270,700,000,000 |
| 27 | India | 267,100,000,000 |
| 28 | Poland | 252,900,000,000 |
| 29 | Mexico | 212,500,000,000 |
| 30 | Indonesia | 196,100,000,000 |
| 31 | Romania | 160,900,000,000 |
| 32 | Hungary | 148,400,000,000 |
| 33 | United Arab Emirates | 122,700,000,000 |
| 34 | Argentina | 108,900,000,000 |

Now, there are actually 200 countries in debt, not 34. However, here are the top 34 accounting for at total debt of $76,729,529,173,000. Yes 76 trillion! This is the total public and private debt (i.e. gross general government debt including both intragovernmental and sub-national public entities debts) owed to nonresidents repayable in internationally accepted currencies, goods, or services, where the public debt is the money or credit owed by any level of government, from central to local, and the private debt the money or credit owed by private households or private corporations based in the country under consideration.

Who is all this owed to? Well you may have trouble tracing this private pyramid but those who say it is owed to the top international bankers who are at the top of the heap. How has all the wealth of nations been converted to this debt? It has occurred systematically through the direction of very smart financial people. It is a system of the few controlling the many which we shall investigate in detail.

## The Corporate Pyramids

It would be a senseless argument to suggest that corporations that are made of the executives and directors, do not have a preferred vested interest in themselves. That is simply the nature of corporations. The mass of employed personnel are there to carry out the functions so as to create profit or services that benefit the top owners, directors and executives. The model is not different than any of the religious and banking models. It has simply evolved and been accepted this way.

| Employer | Employees |
|---|---|
| United States Department of Defense | 3.2 million |
| People's Liberation Army (China) | 2.3 million |
| Wal-Mart | 2.1 million |
| McDonald's | 1.9 million |
| National Health Service (England) | 1.7 million |
| China National Petroleum Corporation | 1.6 million |
| State Grid Corporation of China | 1.5 million |
| Indian Railways | 1.4 million |

| | Indian Armed Forces | 1.3 million |
| | Hon Hai Precision Industry (Foxconn) | 1.2 million |

Now have a look at private banks and a list of their assets under management.

| Rank | Bank | AUM ($bn) |
|---|---|---|
| 1. | Bank of America Merrill Lynch | $1,944,740,000,000 |
| 2. | Morgan Stanley Smith Barney | $1,628,000,000,000 |
| 3. | UBS | $1,559,900,000,000 |
| 4. | Wells Fargo | $1,398,000,000,000 |
| 5. | Credit Suisse | $865,060,000,000 |
| 6. | Royal Bank of Canada | $435,150,000,000 |
| 7. | HSBC | $390,000,000,000 |
| 8. | Deutsche Bank | $368,550,000,000 |
| 9. | BNP Paribas | $340,410,000,000 |
| 10. | JP Morgan Chase | $284,000,000,000 |
| 11. | Pictet | $267,660,000,000 |
| 12. | Goldman Sachs | $229,00,000,0000 |
| 13. | ABN AMRO | $220,060,000,000 |
| 14. | Barclays | $185,910,000,000 |
| 15. | Julius Bär | $181,680,000,000 |
| 16. | Crédit Agricole | $171,810,000,000 |
| 17. | Bank of New York Mellon | $166,000,000,000 |
| 18. | Northern Trust | $154,400,000,000 |
| 19. | Lombard Odier Darier Hentsch | $153,100,000,000 |
| 20. | Citigroup | $140,700,000,000 |

So this is where Planet Earth has come to. These are not kingdoms and dynasties under the directions of their favorite gods; they are immense corporate structures that are fictional representations--constructs created by man. Religions sell beliefs. Debt is a number on a balance sheet. Neither debt or beliefs are real. Corporations are a name. Of course these have been accepted to be translated into humanity's daily reality but are these really real? They hold assets and employees as a registered name. These are the raw statistics of our evolution which explicitly reflects what the vast majority of the population of this planet are engaged in. Nations and people are:

- Fundamentally believing what the Masters of Religions **tell them** about God, gods and moral conduct, which over the last centuries has culminated in a preponderance of death and destruction, hatred and war;
- Fundamentally drumming to the masters of Finance to work towards debt reduction, to survive in a world which can never repay it;
- Fundamentally drumming to the Masters of Corporations and Government to abide by their rules and regulations so as to allow them at the top to benefit.

Fundamentally, the people of Earth drum to an invisible creations of regulations and corporate structures. Under the purpose of commerce and commercial activities corporations are created to facilitate "business". A corporation is created under the laws of a state as a separate legal entity that has privileges and liabilities that are distinct from those of its members. Entities which carried on business and were the subjects of legal rights were found in ancient Rome, and the Maurya Empire in ancient India. In medieval Europe, churches became incorporated, as did local governments, such as the Pope and the City of London Corporation.

For thousands of years, the corporation has been used to serve the purposes of commerce and to "hold" things. In fact it is an imaginary construct that holds papers that are themselves fictional representing the true physical thing. This infatuation with corporations make up the fabric of world societies.

Humanities acceptance of corporations has become the makeup of the fiber of modern civilization. It has been accepted easily as the model of modern cultures because that's the way we work for a paycheck. And we need a paycheck to acquire something we need. But while we do work for a paycheck, we are subject to the rules of the corporation. The acceptance of these fictional structures has, in the end, resulted in every individual who works for a corporation to subject to the rules attached to the corporations as designed by the ones who created them. In this light, Earthlings have slowly become employed by the greatest invisible corporation of all  PLANET EARTH INC. without knowing.

## The Corporate Model Of Sumeria

The corporate model is so well entrenched in the evolution of Planet Earth that it seems impossible to grasp it's reach of dominion. It may not come as a surprise that it forms the fabric of modern societies. People are used to working for corporations, some private, some public. The reality of this is that corporations form a pyramid structure of control and obedience towards a mission, goal, purpose of the founders, directors, owners who engage in some form of commerce.

In delving into the history of corporations, we find that it sources back to Sumeria. In its heyday, the most prominent Sumerian building was the religious temple, built atop a stepped tower called a ziggurat. Some ziggurats were as high as 70 feet. The temple was dedicated to the patron deity of the city. The people devoted great resources and labour to building these temples and to the houses of priests. The ziggurats housed workshops for craftsmen as well as temples for worship. The ziggurats were built of clay bricks joined together with bitumen, a sticky asphalt like substance. There were artisans who sculpted, cut gems, fullers who stomped on woven wools to soften cloth, and metal workers who crafted weapons as well as artistic creations. The religious class had a great deal of power, socially, politically and economically. Religion was central to the society. In summary:

- This was the largest and most important building located in the center of each Sumerian city. Sumerians believed it was the home of the city's patron god.
- It was built on a platform called a *parraku*, designed to dominate the horizon and also to provide protection from floods. Most temples were built on the remnants of older temples that were destroyed. Each king would add on to the temple with numerous stairways leading to different levels.
- The Ziggurat of Ur was on a platform 200' long, 150' wide, and rose 70 feet above the plain and dealt with the city's population or wealth.
- In early Sumer it was made of rectangular mud bricks because they didn't have stone or timber.
- It was decorated with clay cones which were dipped into red, black or buff paint and then inserted into the plaster to form zigzags or geometric designs.
- Weep holes were square or rectangular shaped holes placed at different levels in the temple to provide drainage.
- The main purpose of the ziggurat was to have a place of respect and worship for the gods. Sumerians believed blind obedience and constant gifts and sacrifices would give them protection and success on earth.
- Inside every ziggurat was a rectangular central shrine called a *cella*, for the god's emblem or statue.
- In front of the statue was an altar, a mud brick table for offerings to the god.
- The god was served regular meals of fish, mutton, honey, beer and cake.
- The god communicated his wishes to the priests.
- The god received sacrifices.
- The temple supplied employment and was administered by the priests.

- Maintenance was conducted by musicians, singers, or *hierodules* as temple slaves.
- It served as a center for commercial activity.
- it served as food storage and distribution.
- It was a marketplace for trading of goods and celebrations.

The word "ziggurat" meant "mountain of god" or hill of heaven. Each ziggurat was made up of a series of square levels. Each level was smaller than the one below it. Stairways to the top of the colossal ziggurats were believed to be the home of the city's chief god. Only priests could enter this sacred area. Around the ziggurat were courts, the center of Sumerian life. Artisans worked there; children went to school there; farmers, artisans, and traders stored their goods there; and poor were fed there. The Sumerians believed that all forces of nature were alive. They viewed them a gods because they could not control them There were more than 3,000 Sumerian gods and goddesses.

Only priests could know the gods' will. Because of this, Sumerian priests were very powerful For example, the city's god owned all land. But the priests administered the land in the god's name Also, the priests ran schools. Schools were for the sons of the rich only. Poorer boys worked in the fields or they learned a trade. Schools were rooms off the ziggurat courtyards. They were called tablet houses because they were built to teach children how to write. The children wrote with sharp-ended reeds on clay tablets the size of a postcard. Sumerian writing was called cuneiform. It was made up of hundreds of wedge-shaped markings.

Writing in Sumerian culture developed so that people could keep track of business deals. When Sumerians lived in villages, they could keep track of everything easily. When they began living in cities, it became harder to keep track of everything in their heads. To solve this problem, they developed cuneiform.

When a pupil graduated from school, he became a scribe. The ziggurat, the palace, the government, or the army employed him. Although Sumerian women did not go to school, they did have many rights. They could buy and sell property, run businesses, and own and sell slaves. Although a woman handled the house's affairs when the man was away, the men were the head of the Sumerian household. He could divorce his wife by saying, *"You're not my wife."* If he needed money, he could sell or rent his family into slavery for up to three years. The man also arranged the marriages of his children.

Children were expected to support their parents when the parents got old. They were also expected to obey older family members. Everyone was to obey the gods and priests. At first, Sumerian priests were kings of city-states. One of the most famous priest kings was Gilgamesh of Uruk.

The Sumerian priest-kings received advice from a general assembly made up of free men. When war broke out, the assembly would choose one of its members to serve as leaders until the war was over, but often these leaders stayed in power even when peace had returned. By about 3000 B. C., they took their place as permanent kings. At the same time, kingship became heredity, and the world's first monarchies were established.

These systems were designed by and administered by the Sumerian Priests who represented the gods. Has anything really changed? On the surface yes, the temples and gods seem to have disappeared within the towns. But the corporate structures and the monarchies and kingships have perhaps become more subtle? Or have we replaced these with huge churches, government buildings and massive corporation head offices?

# Corporation PLANET EARTH

By law, a corporation is created under the laws of a state as a separate legal entity that has privileges and liabilities that are distinct from those of its members. It comes from Latin *corporātus* made into a body, from *corporāre*, from *corpus* body. There are many different forms of corporations. Many corporations are established for business purposes but public bodies, charities and clubs are often corporations as well. Corporations take many forms including: statutory corporations, trusts, corporations sole, joint-stock companies and cooperatives. At the heart of this, however, is that a corporation or whatever you may call it, is simply a recorded fictional name with a bunch of rules that are attached to it. And if you work for this fictional thing, you are subject to the rules and to the dictates of those who created it. The ones who created it are the ones who create the rules. As long as you follow the rules, you receive benefits. So whatever rules you as an Earthling abide by take secondary seat to the rules of the corporation... unless there are other rules such as the Criminal Act that you have to abide by which you have somehow agreed to.

Corporations are recognized by the law to have rights and responsibilities like real people. Corporations can exercise human rights against real individuals and the state, and they can themselves be responsible for human rights violations. But in the end, does the corporation go to jail for a violation? No, the directors and creators do, not the Titles. Corporations are conceptually immortal but they can "die" when they are "dissolved" either by statutory operation, order of court, or voluntary action on the part of shareholders. Insolvency may result in a form of corporate "death", when creditors force the liquidation and dissolution of the corporation under court order, but it most often results in a restructuring of corporate holdings. Corporations can never be convicted of criminal offenses, such as fraud and manslaughter. How can they if they can't shoot the gun? Corporations are not living entities in the way that humans are. Yet they are dependent upon humans to exist.

Early corporations were established by charter (i.e. by an *ad hoc* act granted by a monarch or passed by a parliament or legislature). Most jurisdictions now allow the creation of new corporations through registration. In addition to legal personality, registered companies tend to have limited liability, be owned by shareholders who can transfer their shares to others, and controlled by a board of directors who the shareholders appoint. But these are all State laws that are imposed on corporations and, if the directors so agree to abide by these, then they are lawfully bound to do so. Yet the Directors of IBM are not responsible for the rules of Microsoft because they did not agree to do so. It is this simple.

This fictional world of corporations has grown to encompass Planet Earth and unbeknown to many, it has by way of the charters and rights, imposed upon these dead yet eternal undying fictitious structures, conditions against real individuals. How? Real live individuals work for them. When you work for a corporation you provide a service and you derive a benefit called a paycheck. While you work there, you are subject to the codes, rules of that corporations and these are developed by the board of directors that have a purpose. Violate this and you are out. That's the simple model that everybody is very familiar with.

What is not so familiar is how the PLANET EARTH Inc. has come into being and grown to its enormous size. These are simply a pyramid under which the Vatican and the IMF of debt as subsidiaries are examples of the physical things of Planet Earth becoming invisible dead overlays called a fiction over Planet Earth. Every man, woman and child that has been registered by way of a birth certificate has become an employee of PLANET EARTH Inc. because the fictional overlay has reached down into their private life. For the purpose of this book, we will typically look at a capital letter representation of something as a corporation. Planet Earth is the real physical thing, but PLANET EARTH is a fictional representation of Planet Earth. Yes, it is the infamous STRAWMAN!

The great pyramid and how PLANET EARTH came into being and became what we believe to be the real thing is the purpose of the books PLANET EARTH INC. In this book you are reading, I will present a simplistic view. It has all unfolded this way because very intelligent and purposeful Shareholders and a Board of Directors created PLANET EARTH and launched a corporate mission to employ all people on Planet Earth for their own profits and causes. Smart business people do this. They strive to create kingdoms and empires by formulating their corporate rules (missions and business plans).

In a Fortune report, the top 10 net worth billionaires account for 4.6 trillion. Number 1 is Carlos Slim Helú of Mexico who is at $69 billion, Bill Gates, is 2nd at $61 billion, Warren Buffett is number 3 at 44 billion, Bernard Arnaught is 4th at 41 billion. Amancio Ortega, is 5th at 37.5 bill, Larry Elison is 6th at 36 billion, Eike Batista is 7th at 30 billion, Stefan Perron is 8th at 26 billion, Li Ha-shing is 9th at 25.5 billion and Karl Albrecht is 10th, is at a poultry 25.4 billion. But what do you suppose the private kingdoms, like the Queen, the Rothschilds, the Pope can tally up? Our cultures and mentality not only worship these "corporate-smart" CEO's and Leaders as gods, we strive to do the same.

They have created the rules of engagement (hiring) which may not be so obvious to most but, after all, they can make the rules. But at the very top of this pyramid of corporation PLANET EARTH are the "gods" bloodlines and families that root back to Sumeria and before. Through extensive research, there appear to be 13 key families who are the silent shareholders of PLANET EARTH, each having their representatives on the equivalent of the Board of Directors. Anyone can do this of course as we create corporations all the time and hire people to advance our missions. Is there any difference from a Winery in France that has been a profitable venture for the "family" for 300 years? The question is: Can you enforce the rules of your creation on others and make a profit for the kingdom? All empires, kingdom, dynasties, and corporations require leaders and workers that may be perceived as their "slaves" in order to exist, maintain power and flourish. This has been the history of Planet Earth. Earthlings have been there to work for dynasties and empires run by kings and queens. Their mission has been to protect their bloodlines and to maintain their empires. In mythologies and days before that has been done by muscle and might as the power of conquest. But this shifted to different tools of conquest called religion and money.

In the mission of the PLANET EARTH, the founders have encoded the laws and corporate charters upon each of the subsidiaries as participants in the pyramid in such a way as to take control of the beliefs, money, military, and commerce of Planet Earth. And so it has come to pass that humanity has indeed accepted the fictional things as real the same way we all accept the rules of the corporations we work for. But under PLANET EARTH the business plan has engaged vehicles such as the corporation of GOD with the corporate charter of The Bibles. And the corporation of IMF and UNITED NATIONS with their charter of a New World Order, a new monetary system and one god has come to the forefront. The goal is to employ all the residents of Earth, and, in the eyes of the owners, make the slaves happier

For those who are happy to be employed by the PLANET EARTH Inc. and are happy with the laws as set forth in Corporation GOD, all is wonderful. View the stories in this book as a revelation of how you came to be so lucky. But consider that perhaps PLANET EARTH is leading to a New Age of One Order, namely the real God?

For those who are unhappy to be employed, or driven by their higher spiritual needs, this book may shed some light on how to quit those jobs and not have to work for PLANET EARTH. What may be the great revelation in this case is how they came to be unknowingly employed and how to quit what may be an undesirable employment. On the next page is what PLANET EARTH may look like. In the grand scheme of things, the structure is no different than a large multinational corporation like IBM, EXXON or SONY.

And so here is the lead-in to the rest of this book. It is your choice as to how the information is brought into your daily reality. Like Morpheus in the Matrix movie said:

*"I imagine right now you feel a bit like Alice, tumbling down a rabbit hole. You have the look of a man who accepts what he sees expecting never to wake up. You're here because you know something that you can't explain, but you feel it. There is something wrong with the world. You don't know what it is, but it is there, like a splinter in your mind, driving you mad. It is this feeling that has brought you to me. Do you know what I'm talking about?"*

Neo then replies with: *"The Matrix"*. Then Morpheus goes on:

*"Do you want to know what it is? The matrix is everywhere, it is all around us. Even now in this very room. You can see it when you look out your window, or turn on your television set. You can feel it when you go*

*to work, when you go to church, when you pay your taxes. It is the wool that has been pulled over your eyes to blind you from the truth. You are a slave Neo like everyone else. You were born into a prison that you cannot see, that you cannot smell, or taste or touch. A prison for your mind. Unfortunately no one can be told what the Matrix is. You have to see it for yourself. This is your last chance. After this, there is no turning back. Take the blue pill, the story ends, you wake up in your bed and believe whatever you want to believe. Take the red pill, you will stay in wonderland, and I will show you how deep the rabbit hole goes. Remember, what I am offering is the truth, nothing more. Follow me."*

History is filled with the conquering power of military force, or as mythology would tell us, the conquering force of dark. It would seem a natural evolution of mankind to learn how the riches of old (gold silver, jewels, etc.) that would pay for armies to protect their dynasties, empires and kingdoms, would gravitate to simple total control of money. And it would make sense that those who were skilled in the mythological arts of darkness would use this to attain that power of money.

In all history there have been those that had special talents and riches to protect their bloodiness. It is really no different than the father and mother of the household who protects their bloodline as family. Even the family is a pyramid structure of power.

On the next page, is a picture of what the pyramid of the Planetary family called Earthlings would look like. And then we can look at a simple picture of the pyramid of PLANET EARTH INC. This is neither evil, nor good. It just is the way the peoples of Planet Earth have accepted it to be.

# The Hierarchy of Earthlings

# The Empire of PLANET EARTH

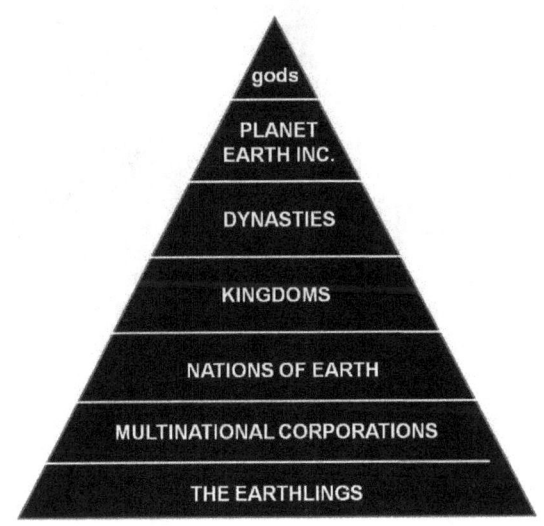

Now let us look more closely at Empire of PLANET EARTH and the gods. Let us work our way down the hierarchy relating real people and international organizations to our simple model. **Let us look at who and what really controls THE EARTHLINGS. For a full treatment of this see m two books PLANET EARTH INC 1 and 2.**

# 9

# THE GLOBAL RULERS: THE "gods"

---

In the previous chapter we were introduced to a simplistic picture of PLANET EARTH Inc. and it's structure. In the next series of chapters we will take you on historical journey as to how this happened. Of course it is difficult to inspect this and piece together the structure because they are purposely private. A **privately held company** or **close corporation** is a business company owned either by non-governmental organizations or by a relatively small number of shareholders or company members. They do not offer or trade its company stock (shares) with the general public on the stock market exchanges, but rather the company's stock is offered, owned and traded or exchanged privately. These companies are virtually invisible compared to publicly traded counterparts or **publicly held company**. In 2008, 441 of the largest private companies in the United States accounted for $1.8 trillion in revenues and employed 6.2 million people according to Forbes. Needless to say privately held companies generally have fewer or less comprehensive reporting requirements for transparency, via annual reports than do publicly traded companies. For example, privately held companies are not generally required to publish their financial statements. By not being required to disclose details about their operations and financial outlook, private companies are not forced to disclose information that may potentially be valuable to competitors and can avoid the immediate erosion of customer and stakeholder confidence in the event of financial duress. Further, private company executives may steer their ships without shareholder approval, and at the same time keep information about their operations secret, like the Federal Reserve. At the extreme end of this are private structures like societies, cults, and the likes that are not even known about or registered, held together by common blood, interests, oaths, and pacts. Thus, much of what follows is an attempt to piece together a vast puzzle of private corporations that form the people and companies of PLANET EARTH Inc.

Despite the complexity and the possible inaccuracies, the researchers on this topic have become prolific and the truth will eventually be known. The lesson here is that some such structure exists and is run by some very astute ones who have power over nations and humanity. Humanity, as we shall see, worships and follows the lead of thousands of gods. But in all these god structures, there are those who have come to be at the top of the heap. Much research has come forward on who these are and in a simplistic view, one must only look to who controls the pyramids we have already discussed; the debt (money), the beliefs (Vatican), the products (corporations) and the power (military).

The ones who are at the top of these heaps are alleged to be the gods, the Global Elite, the Rulers, The Powers

That Be, there are many names. They are our starting point and like doing some due diligence on any corporation, one must look to the alleged Founders, the Directors, the private Owners of the corporations. In following our simple model, we will look at these special people as the bloodlines of the Global Elite.

## Bloodlines Of The Global Rulers

History both myth and alleged nonfiction are founded upon the rise and fall of dynasties and kingdoms as controlled by gods, kings/queens, emperors, and dictators. It is rife with a common phenomenon where even the gods rise and fall in power. Always prevalent in this is the conflict between good and evil, between conflicts of purpose, where the means of control is through armies and greed for wealth through slaves to do the bidding of those who have some special powers of dominion over others. Mankind has been obsessed with this strange addiction to royalty, power, fame and fortune, an inherent trait of self improvement and carnal desire for power. The evolution of this phenomenon has manifested itself in corporations with pyramidal structures of the many serving the few. Prolific upon Planet Earth is the Age of Corporations that effectively allow anyone, even a slave, to become a "king" of a "dynasty".

This inherent desire for wealth and power, and the bowing to its authority has remained through time because Earthlings are trained to bow down simply because they accept it for fear of not so doing. Even now nothing has really changed as unbelievable masses flock to see the Queen, the Presidents, the Pope, or anyone who has by force or by special skill attained a position of power and authority. They are immediately the one to be admired and followed without any regard for what their real purposes are. It has always been this way both in fact and fiction and it is still prevalent today. Only the means of controlling those required to fight, to create movements against opposition, to maintain the dynasty, to retain a position of greatness, has shifted in form at the lower reaches. But while the corporate dynasties play the game of thrones, nations maintain the might with armies called the military. And so it seems that the drive to superiority, to greatness relative to others, the need to satisfy the erotic needs of the human mind and form continue like a broken record. The broken record is an unending inventory of dynasties, civilizations, and cultures; and destruction. And now it is nations, corporations, governments that have risen and fallen like the natural cycle of growth and decay of all life on the planet.

There are those who have attained special powers like the gods and the myths tell. There are those that have attained control of special information and power over others. There are those who have through heartless cold disassociation from the deed controlled through fear and death. As humanity supposedly became more "intelligent" so the gods and dynasty leaders had to adjust the techniques to continue the control and the preservation of their kingdoms. There are now countless dynasties and equivalents in kings and queens that hoarded wealth at the expense of those below them in their power hierarchy. Countless corporations, nations, kingdoms are as we have pointed out, pyramid structures of power and management have become the norm of power to satisfy those who create and run them.

It is said that the best slave is the one who believes he is free. And the apparent belief of freedom has indeed been nurtured so as to continue the means by which dynasties can retain their existence. This is neither bad nor good. As pointed out before, it is all choice and it is all just business that Earthlings accept. And it is clear that there must be, in all this evolution, those who are better at this business than the others. It is the way it is and it always seems to have been that way. The powerful become so at the expense of the powerless. And it can hardly be surprising to understand that someone controls the biggest corporation of all, PLANET EARTH INC.

Yet, in the end, if you believe you are free, then all this that is told here about slaves is meaningless for indeed one can have a decent life within the family, culture, nation, or world one is born into. It is choice.

On the other hand, many do not have much of a fruitful life, and know something is not right for them. The choices however to escape that trap which is not right seems so unattainable that all that can be done is to mumble in a beer or bury the head in the sand and attempt to disallow the issues into ones reality. For those the choice is there and the powerful information is there, but a trigger is needed to see that a choice does exist as in this book.

**gods**

**Royal Bloodlines**

**Kings and Queens**

**Rulers and Dictators**

**Earthlings**

Through various means, be it technology, special psychic powers, mysticism, occult, spiritual, knowledge, birth, or bloodlines, the gods and the global elite have managed to retain their power over others through time; and they have managed to retain their great kingdoms of wealth. Some have fallen, some have risen but there seems to be the ones that have held fast in their dominion. It is this group and their extraordinary march to the conquest of the ultimate empire of Planet Earth that is our topic. We shall now begin to unfold the pieces of history in the following chapters through the gods and those extraordinary people of power as they have worked to conquer Earth and the resident Earthling through a fictional corporate vessel we refer to as **PLANET EARTH INC.** in this book.

In a simple model, there are the gods and the bloodlines who have a plan. In a simple model, all gods, bloodlines, and humanity are evolving on a path; simply at different stages of growth and evolution. In a simple model, no one is good or bad, they are simply evolving. And so it is now of interest to look at these royal bloodlines more closely to attempt to see what their secrets of success in maintaining their dynasties may be.

Research points to 13 bloodlines that have this strong hold on Planet Earth who have become the spotlight of many researchers. This is because these people have power and wealth beyond comprehension. Up there, there are no rules. Even the corporations have so significance; bonds and undertakings for fear of death do. They have a mixture of experience and powers that go beyond understanding and have played influential roles in the world's business for centuries. And when it comes to the greatest and largest corporations on earth--particularly the ones alleged to be under the PLANET EARTH INC pyramid, the CEO's, Presidents, and Directors who run these are mere amateurs in comparison. It is just good business.

If you are a businessman or businesswoman, think about this in terms of a corporate business, having access to unlimited capital, being interested in corporate takeovers, bankrupt companies, and being able to influence the market for the products and services, how would you make out? As we develop our corporate pyramid of PLANET EARTH you will see a list of some of the largest corporations on Planet Earth that fall within the influence of these bloodlines.

# The 13 Royal Bloodlines

It is important to understand that when it comes to corporations and the affairs of commerce, there are those that are much more adept than others. From the greatest corporation to the smallest, the process of creating a financially viable and "successful" business resides with the ones that create the missions, implement the rules of conduct and direct the affairs of those hired to serve their purpose. It is no surprise that someone must be on top of the largest corporation of all we call PLANET EARTH INC because their skill set and business smarts are better than the rest of the ones working for them.

Corporation PLANET EARTH is no different. Like any corporation, it is a private fictional entity created by humans; a fictional construct to hold its treasures and to organize its purpose into reality. There are those that play this game of conquering people through conquering nations. And so we come to the part of the story where those top humans need an introduction to see who they are, what their special talents are, and have a quick look at their kingdoms.

Long ago in the dark unwritten pages of human history, powerful kings discovered how they could control other men by torture, magical practices, wars, politics, religion and interest taking. These elite families designed strategies and tactics to perpetuate their special knowings, technologies and abilities into practice. Because these people live in the private domains, and are outside of the scope of the inquisitors and peering eyes, the accumulations of fortunes has allowed them to march towards the conquering of PLANET EARTH in their own way without rules except their own.

In the last decades, many researchers have come forward to penetrate the layers upon layers of secrecy that have hidden these families from the profane masses, but many an author has touched upon their existence. Many have gotten into trouble. These researchers constantly point to thirteen families or bloodlines at the top, and five of these families are the inside core of these thirteen. These families are portrayed as the 13 layers of blocks found on the strange seal on the reverse side of the U.S. $1 bill.

The research that has been done on theses bloodlines is extensive. In order to introduce these families and their kingdoms, several sites have been used. The most extensive ones are:

The book **The Satanic Bloodlines by Fritz Springmeier** found at **www.theforbiddenknowledge.com/hardtruth/the_ satanic_bloodlines.htm** is recommended for detail, references and treatment of these bloodlines. In addition, their many websites such as
***www.thewatcherfiles.com/bloodlines/***
***www.illuminati-news.com/moriah.htm***
***www.bibliotecapleyades.net/bloodlines/.htm***

According to the research, the key bloodlines are as below:

| Royal Bloodlines | | Interconnected Bloodlines |
|---|---|---|
| 1 Astor | 8 Onassis | Disney |
| 2 Bundy | 9. Reynolds | MacDonald |
| 3 Collins | 10. Rockefeller | Krupp |
| 4 DuPont | 11. Rothschilds | |
| 5. Freeman | 12. Russell | |
| 6. Kennedy | 13. Van Dyn | |
| 7. Li | | |

These references all weave a detailed story of these people produced from an incredible amount of research. The information here is to summarize these dynasties and the information is taken from these sites, in particular the site of Fritz Springmeier. I have tried to summarize the information here but do not want to take away from the extensive work done by Fritz. For a full treatment, please go to Fritz's book noted above.

**Fritz Springmeier is an extensive researcher and if you should research him, you will find that his work has led him to some serious troubles. He is one of the foremost researchers and he is detailed in his references, details, interview. He has been asked why he researches the top 13 bloodlines:**

*"I have often been asked who are the Illuminati? Who are the people at the top of the conspiracy? Who are the generational satanic families? The Illuminati consists of 13 magical and powerful bloodlines. There are also some other powerful bloodlines that are worth naming but if they are in the Illuminati they have blood ties to one of the 13 powerful lineages. About half of the Illuminati people I know have had their parentage hidden from them. Many of the those who still know who their real parents are, still do not know what bloodline they belong to until the Illuminati chooses to reveal it to them. Most of the Illuminati have MPD. When high level Satanists do not have MPD they very often emotionally break under the stress of the horrible blood rituals that are required. Recently, a non-MPD Satanist in Chicago emotionally broke and gave his life to Christ. (I have videos available of an interview of this man exposing Satanism.) One of the important lineages has remained secret until 3 investigators named Lincoln, Leigh, and Bageant were spoon-fed leads and secrets.*

*They put this into a book called "Holy Blood, Holy Grail." I recommend the book and the two books which are its sequels, because they show how just one part of the 13 lineages has kept itself secret and has taken immense power of all forms to themselves. In Southern Belgium there is a castle. (If anyone is travelling there and wants to find the castle, I will show them on the map, and describe it.) This is the Mothers of Darkness castle. In that castle, is a cathedral and in that cathedral's basement a little baby Is sacrificed daily and Is coming to power. The pages are written almost round the clock. (This castle is also described in my Be Wise as Serpents book.) The history in that handwritten book would reveal the real facts behind the propaganda that the world's major news media give the gullible public. The history as that book reveals it would tell people about how Abraham Lincoln was a descendent of the Rothschilds.*

*Abraham Lincoln was the secret head of the Rosicrucians, a member of their 3 headed top council. (I have seen the paper trail proof to these things about Lincoln to my satisfaction that these things about Lincoln are true.) Adolf Hitler was also a secret member of the Rothschild lineage. Hitler carried out blood sacrifices to open his mind up to high level demonic spiritual control. Rockefeller sold Hitler oil during W.W. II via Spain to keep W.W. II going longer. The history in that book mentions people that the "history books" given the public don't-- like Michael Augustus Martinelli Von Braun Rheinhold, the most powerful Satanist in the world a few years ago. Michael Augustus Martinelli Von Braun Rheinhold had 66 Satanic Brides. And that Satanic book in the Mothers of Darkness castle also mentions the Rockefeller bloodline. Only insiders are supposed to know the real history of what has taken place in human history. The real decisions and the real movers and shakers have been hidden from the public's eyes.*

What the public is given is a stage show where illuminati puppets parade around and make big speeches according to their script. Each of the 13 families has their own set of Mothers of Darkness. Each of the 13 families has their own secret Satanic leadership Kings, Queens, Princesses and Princes of Darkness. For instance, the Rockefeller family has people who are selected as Kings and Princes within their own bloodline in secret rituals. The Kings and Princes, Queens and Princesses are strictly bloodline. They secretly rule over an area of the world for their own bloodline. This is *independent of the Illuminati's hierarchy which was diagrammed in the Jan 1993 newsletter. (my Newsletter from a Christian Ministry.) In the January, 1993 issue the Covens, Sisters of Light, Mothers of Darkness, and the Grande Mothers were diagrammed.*

*The illuminati pulls its various bloodlines together under several councils. The Grande Druid Council or your Council of 13 is your principle council for the Brotherhood of Death. Above the Council of 13 is a higher Council of 9, and an inner group of 3 is believed to head that Council of Nine. How do we know about these things? The power of God has reached into the very heart of Satan's empire and pulled out some of the most powerful Satanists and drawn them to Christ. There are several Satanists that were at the top which have managed to find Christ. in addition, some of the next echelon of the hierarchy, such as some of the Mothers of Darkness are also finding Christ. if someone wants to understand how and why decisions are made in world affairs and by who-- then you need to study the illuminati. The real answers do not rest with the proceedings of the Congress of the United States or with the publicly known leaders of the Communist countries. An example of what I am talking, there is a book entitled "Who Financed Hitler" by James Pool and Suzanne Pool. I am always glad to see that some people are willing to look behind the scenes. Believe me, there were people that Hitler listened to. They were the people he went to ritual with, and who put him into power."*

Each of the 13 bloodlines have created their own dynasty as a succession from the same family or bloodline. At the top are the Rulers, private in their affairs, who have worked towards conquering other rulers, kings and queen over countries and people so as to become the chief authority as Emperor over the Empire of Planet Earth. These dynasties have emerged into power in the last 250 years. It must be stated that there are many powerful dynasties on earth and it is not to say that these 13 are the only power force with a business plan.

## A Word About gods

So it is that at the top of the pyramid are the "gods" Upon earth today there are thousands of gods or deities. But who are the current "gods" who rule empire of Planet Earth?

The on-line dictionary says **God** is a being conceived as the perfect, omnipotent, omniscient originator and ruler of the universe. This has evolved to be the principal object of faith and worship in monotheistic religions. But **god** is defined as a supernatural being who is worshipped as the controller of some part of the universe or some aspect of life in the world, or is the personification of some force. It seems that God is the Big Boss and the gods are just in charge of part of the universe. They are inventions and constructs not the real thing. We state that GOD in this book is a fictional fake created for dubious purpose of commerce. God has never come down to write the rules; these have been interpreted through Earthlings who have positioned themselves as the experts and knowers of His (God) Word.

If you look around this planet, there are 19 major world religions which are subdivided into a total of 270 large religious groups, and many smaller ones. Some 34,000 separate Christian religions can be identified in the world with over half of them as independent churches that have no interest in linking with the big denominations. Since the Sumerians around 6000 years ago, historians have catalogued over 3700 supernatural beings, of which 2870 can be considered deities. In truth, the possibilities are nearly infinite. It is easy to pick something you can't understand, or pretend to understand, create a point of worship and surround it with a belief. And if you can convince others, pretty soon you have a god and a religion full of god's beliefs to follow. Thus because Earthlings love the idea of worshiping the famous and powerful, many gods exist. And therefore, it would be a natural assumption to conclude that the current gods are the ones who are at the top of the Earthling heap. Have the Sumerian gods who were alleged to understand the secrets of long life maintained their presence in these people? One thing is for sure.

No one on Earth is God.

Is there a supreme God? It depends upon your point of view and your beliefs. Some say Satan is God. Others say Christ is God. Others say God just is. Regardless, we find that consistently through history God above is defined by gods below. But, in our case here, god and gods are the ones that wish to rule the empire of Planet Earth. And so we come to getting to know these "gods" who would work towards being the emperors. In a simple corporate sense, these rulers of the dynasties would be the sole shareholders and directors of PLANET EARTH corporation.

In my Books PLANET EARTH INC 1 and 2 details of the research are presented and much, much more. For the purpose of this book, however, we are concerned with the key facts relating to the key tools of the Ruler's conquest and dominion:

- **Law**
- **Commerce**
- **Money**
- **Corporations and Trusts**

# 9

# THE STORY OF BANKRUPT AMERICA

We have covered the simple structure and some components of PLANET EARTH and the key players of an elegant business plan. Now it is of interest to see how their business strategy has been implemented, with particular attention to America because it became the focal point of the implementation. The story you are about to read may seem like fiction but the truth of it is emerging rapidly. There are at least 200 countries that are part of the huge debt pyramid of hundreds of trillions of dollars that was shown in the first Chapters. The story of each nation is different but the process by which they were conquered will be similar.

And so it was that the attention of the Rulers or Illuminati as directed by the gods shifted to America in a way that was not planned before. It was destined to become the Military Industrial Complex that would serve as the world police force eventually and also become the vehicle for capturing humanity under a corporate illusion. It would capture the united States under a set of special deals made due to irresponsible use of money and bankruptcy. Ironically, America was originally founded on sovereignty and freedom from the dominion of Britain but the bloodlines who knew well how to conquer kingdoms with money had been evolving into power over the same period. The process of setting up the district and city of Columbia led to the organizational structure of USA INC., and CANADA INC, fictional subsidiaries of the UNITED KINGDOM, the usurping of the money, and the eventual employment of USA and CANADA Earthlings.

Now it is time to look at the detailed chronology of how these powerful families marched towards taking over America and most of the other nations. As we have already seen, that plan was written and hidden in plain view in the money of the United States. The takeover returns us back tithe first chapter of the debt pyramid and how that has become the tool of dominion. This chapter is dedicated to that story.

The business plan is somewhat revealed in the US Dollar. We see one side of the US Dollar how it tells the story of the plan. It was issued in 1929. On the other side the US Dollar bill tells another story of how real money with intrinsic value back by precious metals, was shifted away from the US Treasury to take a new form. Prior to 1929, it stated **"Payable to Bearer on Demand"** as silver:

The new issue became **"This Note is Legal Tender for All Debts Public and Private"** which in simply a unit of debt. This what is known as "fiat" money" which has no intrinsic value except what people believe to be value.

## America Is Bankrupt-Again

In 1788, the United States was officially bankrupt. As a government it was in default to the crown of England to the tune of eighteen million plus interest. As a direct and proximate result the U.S. corporate government was bankrupt in their private capacity from the start of the constitution. Then, the debt had to be paid for a period of seventy years. After a period of seventy years, according to the Bible res judicata and stare decisis, God said America could come out of bankruptcy with England on December 31, 1858. But let us leave this for now as we will come back to this later.

Here is a summary of the American debt obligation. Under International Law, if a nation cannot pay its debts, its debts are forgiven every 70 years. Individual debts should be cancelled every 7 years as sabbatical time but for a nation it is ten times that. The mortgage was renewed in 1789. In We could have come out then but the debt was renewed and enlarged to pay for the beginning of the civil war. which began in 1859. We could have come out in 1929 but the nation renewed and enlarged the debt when the farmers pledged their lands to the public in exchange for public aid supposedly to save farming. F.D. Roosevelt instituted the New Deal and

Land Control under emergency war powers to overcome the depression and regulate farming. The great depression began in 1929. In 1999 we could have come out of bankruptcy but the nation renewed and enlarged the debt when it unknowingly chose to remain a military democracy instead of reverting to constitutional republic. The Clinton impeachment dealt with Public Policy as to whether or not Americans wanted to do this. We did not. One would begin to think that these events, like civil war, the great depression, and various large events were very timely?

Let us now look at the more recent history on what has happened with regards to governments and nations losing their sovereignty and control. The bankruptcy that put the nail in the sovereignty coffin was the one in 1933. Let us look into the United States Congressional Record, dated March 17, 1993. It is Volume 33, page H-1303. The Speaker is James Traficant, Jr. of Ohio addressing the House. This is what he says:

*'Mr. Speaker, we are here now in Chapter 11. Members of Congress are official trustees presiding over the greatest reorganization of any Bankrupt entity in world history, the U.S. government. We are setting forth hopefully, a blueprint for our future. There are some who say it is a coroner's report that will lead to our demise. It is an established fact that the United States federal government has been dissolved by the Emergency Banking Act, March 9, 1933, 48 Stat. 1, Public Law 89-719; declared by President Roosevelt, being bankrupt and insolvent. H.J.R. 192, 73rd Congress in session June 5, 1933 – Joint Resolution to Suspend the Gold Standard and Abrogate the Gold Clause. This dissolved the Sovereign Authority of the United States and the official capacities of all United States governmental Offices, Officers, and Departments is further evidence that the United States federal government exists today in name only.'*

*'The receivers of the United States Bankruptcy are the International Bankers, via the United Nations, the World Bank and the International Monetary Fund. All United States Offices, Officials, and Departments are now operating within a de facto status in name only under Emergency War Powers."*

*'With the Constitutional Republican form of government now dissolved, the receivers of the Bankruptcy have adopted a new form of government for the United States. This new form of government is known as a Democracy, being an established Socialist/Communist order under a new governor for America. This act was instituted and established by transferring and/or placing the Office of the Secretary of Treasury to that of the Governor of the International Monetary Fund. Public Law 94-564, page 8, Section H.R. 13955 reads in part: The U.S. Secretary of Treasury receives no compensation for representing the United States'."*

The Treasury appointed receiver in the bankruptcy was defined in Reorganization Plan, No. 26, 5 U.S.C.A. 903; Public Law 94-564; Legislative History, page 5967. The Secretary of the Treasury is the *'Governor'* of the International Monetary Fund Inc. of the U.N. If you care to look this up you can check out Public Law 94-564, supra, page 5942. There is also the U.S. government manual 1990/91, pages 480-81, and Treasury Delegation Order No 150-10.

On October 28$^{th}$, 1977, the United States as a *'Corporator'* and *'State'* declared insolvency. State banks and most other banks were put under control of the *'Governor'* of the *'Fund'*, namely the International Monetary Fund. Since March 9th, 1933, the United States has been in a state of declared national emergency. When congress declares an emergency, there is no constitution. A majority of people of the United States have lived all of their lives under emergency rule. For forty years, freedoms and governmental procedures guaranteed by the constitution have in varying degrees been abridged by laws brought into force by states of national emergency. This is right in the Senate Reports if you care to look.

Under this, the President may do a lot of nasty things. He can seize property, organize commodities, assign military forces abroad, institute Martial law, seize and control transportation and communication, regulate operation of private enterprise, restrict travel, and in a plethora of particular ways control the lives of all American citizens. This is documented in senate reports, senate resolutions, and executive order signed by President Clinton.

Bankruptcy is not a difficult thing to comprehend, for when you are bankrupt, you are not exactly in a negotiating position. The leaders gave their rights away because they had no choice. Now all the banks report to the Federal Reserve that then reports to the IMF that is part of the United Nations. So in the larger picture, the U.S. is just like any bankrupt company, obligated by contract to pay the debts. All the powers they have are internal and these powers must make sure they abide by the wishes of the IMF, the ultimate creditor.

This is why on U.S. money it says *'This note is legal Tender for all debts, public and private'* and on the Canadian notes state *'This note is legal Tender?'* It used to say *'Will pay the bearer on demand'*. Today we have people's labour being exchanged for checks as payment for the labour pre-given, making it pre-paid. You have to work first to get paid second. Although there is technically an exchange of labour for paper, the perception of the value of money is misunderstood by almost everyone but the top bankers. The only reason money is in existence and or in your pocket, purse, bank account where ever, is because you had to work to get it, steal it or win the lottery. In other words, the money called legal tender is backed by the labour of the people or it simply would not exist, and it could not exist any other way. It's not the money they want you to pay back that is important to them. It is the assets you create at the wholesale manufacturing price level that they have or hold title to in the end that is of interest to the banks. The asset has far greater value than the piece of paper you get paid with.

Money is now backed by nothing but our faith in it and the goods we exchange it for. Someone else has put labour energy into producing it to satisfy the requirements of the buyers and consumers. Since money is backed by labour only, it could be said then that people are assets. In fact, have you ever heard a company say its employees are its biggest assets? If a company has no employees it can't have any assets. People come before material assets because people make the material assets. The truth of the matter is people are the only energy assets, which brings us to the cause of all our problems in life today. This is even more so today than ever as the debts of countries increase at an unstoppable rate. The result is that less purchasing power and more work is required for a losing gain, which is an oxymoron but true. The national bankruptcies in U.S.A and Canada made it impossible to pay any debt with real sustenance as money, and legal tender became valueless. It was the only way to pay. This act made it impossible for anyone to pay off a debt, and no debt has been extinguished since. The bankruptcy was declared because there were no more assets available to make the interest payments that the banks would accept. To compensate for this lack of valuable assets, the governments agreed to pledge the future labour of the people, knowing full well that the assets created by the people would be exchanged happily for debt money paper.

In Canada, the Bank of Canada Act that bank ceased honoring dominion notes on March 11 1935. There are orders in council wherein gold was removed temporarily in 1934, 1933 and 1932, and led to the Bank of Canada non redemption of notes in 1935. You cannot find a Canadian quote similar to the H.J. Roosevelt bankruptcy in the U.S.A. But in March 1935, money was declared no longer redeemable, which means the bank was no longer responsible for buying it back and never has been since. The very place that issues the money doesn't even want the stuff. The bank knows it has no value, and that it represents the labour you gave in exchange for it.

In reality, both U.S. and Canada went bankrupt. The factual bankruptcy of the U.S. took place in 1931 and in Canada it was 1933 with the Act of Westminster. The Bank of Canada is the watchdog here and they are controlled from outside so the bankruptcy was implemented through the banking system universally throughout North America. And this all changed from a gold backed money system to just paper. Gold and silver were such powerful money during the founding of America that the founding fathers declared only gold or silver coins could be money in America. Since gold and silver coinage was heavy and inconvenient for a lot of transactions, they were stored in banks and a claim check was issued as a money substitute. People traded their coupons as money, or currency. Currency is not money, but a money substitute. Redeemable currency must promise to pay a dollar equivalent in gold or silver money. That was the old system. But as you have already noted, Federal Reserve Notes or FRN's, make no such promises, and are not real money. A Federal Reserve Note is a debt obligation of the federal United States government, not money. The federal United States government and the U.S. Congress were not, and have never been authorized by the constitution for the United States of America to issue real currency.

It is essential that we comprehend the distinction between real money and a paper money substitute. One cannot get rich by accumulating money substitutes. One can only get deeper into debt. '*We the people'* no longer have any money. Most Americans have not been paid any money for a very long time, perhaps not in their entire life. Now do you comprehend why you feel broke? You are really bankrupt, along with the rest of the country paying off a legacy of debt? We are simply using what we believe to be real money and accept it in exchange for goods.

Federal Reserve Notes are unsigned checks written on a closed account. These FRN's are an inflatable paper system designed to create debt through inflation. This is the same as devaluation of currency. Whenever there is an increase of the supply of a money substitute in the economy without a corresponding increase in the gold and silver backing, inflation occurs. Inflation is an invisible form of taxation that irresponsible governments inflict on their citizens. The Federal Reserve Bank that controls the supply and movement of FRN's, has access to an unlimited supply, paying only for the printing costs of what they need. FRN's are nothing more than promissory notes for U.S. Treasury Securities or T-Bills. These are just a promise to pay the debt to the Federal Reserve Bank.

One must also understand that there is a fundamental difference between paying and discharging a debt. To pay a debt, you must pay with value or substance such as gold, silver, barter, or a commodity such as labour. With FRN's, you can only discharge a debt. You cannot pay a debt with a debt currency system. You cannot service a debt with a currency that has no backing in value or substance. No contract in Common law is valid unless it involves an exchange of '*good and valuable consideration*'. So in the system it is like an endless cycle of debt.

You have to go back to the purpose here. Remember the U.S., like Canada, is broke and in receivership. The banking system in North America reports to the Federal Reserve that is a private system with ownership outside of the U.S.. They obviously did not have any choice. The Federal Reserve System is based on the Canon law and the principles of sovereignty protected in the constitution and the Bill of Rights. In fact, the international bankers used something called a '*Canon Law Trust*' as their model, adding stock and naming it a *'Joint Stock Trust'*. The US congress had passed a law making it illegal for any legal person to duplicate a Joint Stock Trust in 1873. The Federal Reserve Act was legislated post-facto to 1870, although post-facto laws are strictly forbidden by the constitution.

This was part of the deal like being subject to rules of a ship once you get on. The Federal Reserve System is a sovereign power structure separate and distinct from the federal United States government. The Federal Reserve is a maritime lender, and/or maritime insurance underwriter to the federal United States operating exclusively under Admiralty/Maritime law. The lender or underwriter bears the risks. The Maritime law compelling specific performance in paying the interest or premiums is the same.

This becomes the reality of the Matrix. Now here is where we start to get down to the bottom of this. Assets of the debtor can also be hypothecated as security by the lender or underwriter. That means you pledge something as a security without taking possession of it. The Federal Reserve Act stipulated that the interest on the debt was to be paid in gold. There was no stipulation in the Federal Reserve Act for ever paying the principle.

Prior to 1913, most Americans owned clear, allodial title to property, free and clear of any liens or mortgages. Then the Federal Reserve Act of 1913 came in. Subsequently all property within the federal United States was hypothecated to the Board of Governors of the Federal Reserve, in which the trustees or stockholders held legal title. The U.S. citizen or tenant, or franchisee, was then registered as a beneficiary of the trust via his/her birth certificate. In 1933, the federal United States hypothecated all of the present and future properties, assets and labour of their subjects to the Federal Reserve. That's all the citizens under the 14th Amendment.

In return, the Federal Reserve System agreed to extend the federal United States corporation all the credit 'money substitute' it needed. So they could print more debt anytime they liked; what a deal! It opened an equivalent of a big line of credit. Like any other debtor, the federal United States government had to assign collateral and security to their creditors as a condition of the loan. Since the federal United States didn't have any assets, they assigned the private property of their economic slaves, the US citizens as collateral against the un-payable federal debt. They also pledged the unincorporated federal territories, national parks, forests, birth certificates, and non-profit organizations, as collateral against the federal debt. All has already been transferred as payment to the international bankers.

Unwittingly, America has returned to its pre-American Revolution, feudal roots whereby all land is held by a sovereign and the common people had no rights to hold real, you call it allodial title, to property. This sounds like we are just tenants renting our own property from the Federal Reserve Bank and this has been going on for over eighty years without the informed knowledge of the American people, without a voice protesting loud enough. That's why you buy and hold titles, not the real thing. Now it's easy to grasp why America is fundamentally bankrupt.

We are reaping what has been sown by our leaders, and the results of our harvest is a painful bankruptcy. This includes a foreclosure on American property, precious liberties, and a way of life built on paper. Few of our elected representatives here or in Washington, D.C. have dared to tell the truth or are even aware of it. The federal United States is bankrupt. Our children will also inherit this un-payable debt as we have.

Now, who is the real creditor that holds the debt? Who holds the countries to ransom? There has been much speculation about who owns the Federal Reserve. It has been one of the great secrets of the century because the Federal Reserve Act of 1913 provided that the names of the owner banks be kept secret. However, R. E. McMaster, publisher of the newsletter *'The Reaper'*, asked his Swiss banking contacts which banks hold the controlling stock in the Federal Reserve. The federal system is, by the way, a private corporation #62 domiciled in Puerto Rico. The answer to who owns the Fed and by proxy the entire U.S.A. is the Rothschild Banks of London and Berlin, the Lazard brothers Bank of Paris, the Israel Moses Sieff Banks of Italy, the Warburg Bank of Hamburg and Amsterdam, the Lehman Brothers Bank of New York, the Kuhn Loeb Bank of New York, the Chase Manhattan Bank of New York, and the Goldman Sachs Bank of New York, the biggest banks on the planet.

In **The Secrets Of The Federal Reserve**, **Eustace Mullins** indicates that because the Federal Reserve bank of New York sets interest rates and controls the daily supply and price of currency throughout the U.S., the owners of that bank are the real directors of the entire system. Mullins states that *"The shareholders of these banks which own the stock of the Federal Reserve bank of New York are the people who have controlled our political and economic destinies since 1914. They are the Rothschilds, Lazard Freres (Eugene Mayer), Israel Sieff, Kuhn Loeb Company, Warburg Company, Lehman Brothers, Goldman Sachs, the Rockefeller family, and the J.P. Morgan interests"*.

Also consider that the IRS is not a U.S. government agency. It is an agency of the IMF. Next, the IMF is an agency of the UN. Third, the U.S. has not had a treasury since 1921, it is the IMF. In the U.S., social security numbers are issued by the UN through the IMF. The application for an SSN is the SS5 form. The Department of the Treasury, really the IMF, issues the SS5, not the U.S. Social Security administration. The new SS5 forms do not state who or what publishes them. The earlier SS5 forms state that they are Department of the

Treasury forms. You can get a copy of the SS5 you filled out by sending form SSA-L996 to the SS administration Here's another little tidbit about social security that will help. You probably didn't know that in the U.S., a social security check comes directly from the IMF. You can check this by looking at it. Written on the top left is United States Treasury.

How does this affect the individual? Take this down to where it affects you, your own property. Read the deed to the property that you think is yours. You are listed as a tenant. You basically don't own anything and there is probably very little you can do except be less accepting of what you are told is the truth about what you own.

But in forming your opinion, be aware of a few more interesting facts. Britain is owned by the Vatican. This is what the Treaty of 1213 was all about. The Pope can abolish any law in the United States, as stated in the Elements of Ecclesiastical Law Volume 1, pages 53-54. A 1040 form is for tribute paid to Britain as stated in the IRS Publication 6209. The Pope claims to own the entire planet through the laws of conquest and discovery. It looks like we are all human capital by Executive Order 13037. Just type Executive Order 13037 into Google and read for yourself. The UN has financed the operations of the United States government for over 50 years and now owns every man, women and child in America. The UN also holds all of the land in America in fee simple. Should I go on? This is the inheritance that your fathers and fore fathers bequeathed to you. The question is whether you will also bequeath it to the next generation.

## Money And Banking Systems: The Real Power

Let us go as far back as 2000 BC when Babylon flourished in the land of Sumer or Shinar. Then we will work forward to the present day following the history of banking, commerce and the evolution of law. Of particular importance is how bankers, originally known as money changers, evolved to control commerce. It is also important to see how the legal system evolved in parallel to support the threads that ended up binding most of our current civilizations into commerce. This will dovetail with what we have talked about before, particularly on the taxes, then we will look at who this is applied to the individuals.

A long way back in history, as we have already revealed, Babylon had a modern system of life with canals to irrigate their land for agriculture, indoor toilets, city sewage systems and public restrooms. They even had a city-to-city postal system with baked clay letters and envelopes. Babylon even had a judicial system where judges wore black robes, just as they do today. Then, because their idols became gold, silver and greed, they began to fall into disgrace but continued to rule until they were destroyed. They had a system of commerce that included coined money, banks, receipts, titles, seals, signing and merchant law which evolved into Roman law, then into Civil law and later became Maritime law. Bear this in mind as we travel forward to our present time. That which was created then still forms the foundation for today. Those who crafted these laws, codes, and the money system, which for lack of better description, were the "gods" who translated their ways and knowing through the high priests, lords, Kings and Queens through a preferred bloodline.

Around 1000 AD, goldsmiths that are the same as banks learned to leverage money. They took in gold as a deposit and loaned out more receipts as loans than they had gold in reserve knowing it was unlikely that everyone would want to take out their gold at once. This was the birth of fractional reserve banking. Recognizing the immense power here, Henry I, in 1100, took the money power away from the money changers and established the tally stick system which lasted nearly five hundred years. On a different evolutionary path involving people's rights and the emergence of law and order, it was around 1066 that the Normans, under William the Conqueror, subjugated the English people and established a royal dynasty, which still occupies the throne of England to this day. The Normans imposed on the English a system of Ruler's law which destroyed the rights of the people, resulted in the confiscation of much of their land, and inflicted a system of cruel oppression on the people that was virtually unendurable.

It is important to understand in this evolution of sovereign rights that there have always been those upper echelon hierarchies who prefer dominion over others, attempting to take away sovereignty and freedom for their own benefit, and there have always been those freedom fighters looking to improve their rights and sovereignties. This sea-saw evolution still goes on today most obvious in the financial equality. and it is within this context than many inroads had been made to liberate the rights of free men.

Because King John was one of the most cruel and ruthless Norman kings, the barons united their forces and compelled him to sign the famous Magna Charta under the threat of beheading him if he did not sign. By now, the Magna Charta not only returned to the people many of the rights which the conquerors had stolen away, it also acknowledged that the king himself, was subject to the law. And so the rights were instilled forever. So the Magna Charta not only refers to the rights of the barons, but also makes frequent reference to the rights of English freemen. The American founders counted themselves as freemen and invoked the Magna Charta as a covenant on the part of the king and his heirs so those rights would be respected. This initial victory in the partial recovery of their rights became a critical step in our history. So this is why the Magna Charta is part of the basis of our laws in America.

The foundations of parliamentary government began to develop around 1265. And this gradually developed into a legislative voice to represent the desires of the people.

It also provided a bargaining tool to regain some of the lost powers of the people and limit the tyrannical powers of the king. The parliament regained the right to have no taxation without the approval of the people's representatives. They also established the principle that there would be no laws imposed on the people that had not been fully approved by the parliament. Finally, the parliament secured the right to impeach the arrogant and abusive officers of the king whenever it could be shown that they had violated the law in the exercise of their high office.

On the banking side, there was a crucial point in this evolution around 1600 AD when Queen Elizabeth took control of the money supply and issued her own coin against the wishes of the money changers. Then, Oliver Cromwell, financed by the money changers, had King Charles killed. This plunged England into debt from wars and he took over the city of London. The private money changers wanted control again. The debt from the war was their opportunity. In 1688 AD, the money changers financed William of Orange of the Netherlands to overthrow the Stewart kings, and took possession of the English throne. In 1694 AD, England became monetarily exhausted after fifty years of war with France and Holland. These people had learned a long way back that financing a war was a way to get a grip on the enemy.

As part of the plan the private Bank of England was then formed and secured itself with politicians and their laws to protect the bank and the debt. But the kings needed more money to finance their wars and had to give more and more power to parliament, Yes, that means taxation. The old tally system was then attacked by the private Bank of England and it was replaced with a private money system which took away the power of the king to control money.

And the Elite group of bankers, whom you have already met within the Ruler bloodlines behind the private banks, were very cunning at financing special conflicts that resulted in huge debts. Then they were on the spot to be of service – for a heavy price of course. They had learned from the Templars. And if there are those that are smarter from a business, or commercial point of view, guess who takes control? It simply becomes a business opportunity to those smarter. In 1698 AD, the English debt then rocketed from one and a quarter million pounds to sixteen million pounds within a few short years. Then in 1748 AD, Amshel Bauer in Germany opened a goldsmith shop under the name of Red Shield. In German tongue this is pronounced Roth chield, or Rothschild, the history of which we will cover in more detail later.

# 11

# THE STORY OF CODE OF LAW

## Evolution Of Code Of Law

Now, on the law side of the story, we have another picture. During the reign of two German kings over England, namely George I and George II, between 1714 and 1760, the parliament was left on its own more than ever before. The government was run almost entirely by the king's prime minister. This meant that he and the other members of parliament serving in the prime minister's cabinet could appoint all of the officials and have a relatively free hand in running the government. This brought England to the status of a limited monarchy with a parliament system of government that allowed the legislature to exercise practically unlimited power.

With all these tyrants and taxes, many frustrated Europeans began the migration to America in order to find spiritual and social freedom. It was only in America that Englishmen acquired the advantages. America, of course, was part of the English colonies. But this was where the first opportunity for local or provincial assemblies was developed. It was where the people elected the delegates instead of the dictators. This was first inaugurated in Virginia as early as 1619. As the colonies gained in economic and political strength, they demanded the full recognition of their rights as Englishmen.

It was at this time that the colonies asserted their unalienable rights of self-government by issuing the Declaration of Independence of 1776 to the king of England. The people of America then confederated together as the United States. Their form of government was a confederated republic, where the states remained supreme. Prior to the Revolution of 1763 most commerce was done by barter and also by paper money printed by different states. All of it, however, was based on the production of goods and services created by the people. It was later after the constitution was adopted in 1789, only gold and silver coin could be used as money in the United States. This was all very good and it set the scene for creating one of the most powerful nations on the planet. So they could carve out their own freedoms uninhibited by the British rule but they still had to pay taxes to the king.

But this was also the way to get out of the grip of oppressive taxes, dictators and regulations. America, by the Declaration of Independence of 1776, declared war on England. However, most people do not realize that the primary reason for the war was not *"taxation without representation"*, but the forced payment of taxes to the King in gold not paper money. America was then flourishing by using their own fiat money system based only on their production - not a gold based system that could be manipulated by the king. The king could not control the fiat money system of the U.S. and therefore passed a law requiring them to pay taxes in gold only. As the king had most of the gold and the colonies had little, unemployment ensued. The embittered souls cried for war.

Although America did win the revolutionary war with England, there was a malfunction in the plans for America. Money powers were waiting at the gate from the beginning. To answer why, let us go back in history to a date of January 1, 1788. The United States as a government was in default to the crown of England to the tune of eighteen million plus interest. As a direct and proximate result the U.S. corporate government was bankrupt in their private capacity from the start of the constitution. Then, the debt had to be paid for a period of seventy years.

After a period of seventy years, according to the Bible res judicata and stare decisis, God said America could come out of bankruptcy with England on December 31, 1858. And let's say as an operation of law, at that time some notice was given to the nation that might have gone something like this: *"Excuse me, do you people really want to leave Babylon and have your liberty back now, or would you prefer to maintain the Crown of England as your master and serve him faithfully?"* Suppose it was something along those lines. Look at Leviticus 3:17, which says that if you love your master and your period of service is up, you can go to the judges, recite the fact that you love your master and you don't want to leave him, you can choose to serve him for the rest of your life, and you've just placed yourself into voluntary servitude. So in the year of 1858, after December 31$^{st}$, the crown of England, through its attorney agents, gave notice to the country, *"Hey, you guys want to leave Babylon and go back to original jurisdiction, or do you want to have your government remain under us?"*

Apparently, the southern states did not wish to remain under slavery and walked out of congress. Evidently what happened is the people failed to give Notice of Lawful Protest, which was their acquiescent vote to remain in Babylon under the crown of England with continuing debt plus a reorganization of government. Now you are under a new law forum because the old law forum was entitled to liberty and freedom. The south walked out, ending the public side of the constitution. The people did not protest in any manner because they were busy fighting the civil war, therefore we had to create a new law forum that all people volunteered into, to go on for another seventy years of captivity.

Although the British Empire, as a world government, lost the American revolution, the power structure behind it did not lose the war. The most visible of the power structure identities was the East India Company, owned by the bankers and the crown in London, England. This was an entirely private enterprise whose flag was adopted by Queen Elizabeth in 1600 which happened to have thirteen red and white horizontal stripes with a blue rectangle in its upper left-hand corner.

While the British government lost the war in 1776, the East India Company's owners constituted a portion of the invisible, sovereign power structure (banks) behind the British government. They were able to move right into the new U.S.A economy, together, and in close association with America's most powerful landowners. It was a matter of bribery and trickery so in fact, representatives from the commercial Elite, namely the international bankers and their representatives, came in at influential levels in the states.

As a side note there is a site **http://100777.com/myron** where the infiltration through the Masons and the Illuminati representatives is revealed by a fellow named **Myron Fagan**. Some of these he names as Thomas Jefferson, founder of the Democratic party, Alexander Hamilton, and many other prominent U.S. leaders. But the idea was to get into influential positions at the top and in both parties so it really didn't matter who got in, the private Elite had a foot in the door either way.

The leaders, after winning the war, started to craft their U.S. constitution that was adopted March 4 1789.

George Washington was then elected president in April of 1789. Six documents became the basis and guidelines in creating their constitution. It is important to know at this point that any constitution must have some prior reference to establish it. Based on this premise, any and every constitution thereafter must have an enabling clause. From this point onward, no constitution may diminish, in any manner, those rights already established in the six documents. Next, the people of the various states created the state governments for the protection of their rights. They delegated certain authority from the people powers by and through the state constitutions in order that the three branches of government could properly carry out the dictates outlined in the constitutions to protect their rights.

It was here that the states created the United States. The American constitution created a new structure of government that was established on a much higher plane than either the parliamentary system or the confederation of states. It was a people's *constitutional republic* where a certain amount of power was delegated to the confederation of states and a certain amount was delegated to the federal government. The United States, by way of the Congress of the United States, had certain powers delegated by the constitution. So far as the several states party to the constitution was concerned, the United States could not exercise power not delegated by the constitution. All power not delegated to the United States by the constitution was reserved to the confederation of states within their respective territorial borders, or to the people.

Behind the scenes, the constitution was pushed and supported by the private bankers through their associates. They had a plan for their own control over the United States of America. Had the articles of confederation been completed and adopted, instead of the constitution, the bankers would have far less control than they achieved. In fact, THE UNITED STATES, in capital letters is like the name of a corporation and it consists only of the ten miles square of Washington, District of Columbia, its territories of Guam, Samoa, Mariana Islands, and Puerto Rico. Yes, one of the god's key strongholds.

One of the powers granted in the federal constitution is to the congress in Article 1, section 8, clause 16 and 17. Clause 16 stated: *"To exercise exclusive legislation in all cases whatsoever, over such district (not exceeding ten mile square) as may, by cession of particular states, and the acceptance of congress, become the seat of government of the United States, and to exercise like authority over all places purchased, by the consent of the legislature of the state in which the same shall be, for the erection of forts, magazines, arsenals, dockyards, and the needful buildings'.* Clause 17 then stated: *'To make all laws which shall be necessary and proper for carrying into execution the foregoing powers, and all the new powers vested by this constitution in the government of the United States, or in any department or officer thereof".* This means congress has absolute; or what is described as plenary power.

This is municipal, police power, and the like. But, pay attention to this. Where does congress have such plenary power? You may be surprised to hear that this is only within the geographical area of the District of Columbia, and all forts, magazines, arsenals, dockyards, and other needful buildings within a few states. The United States is an abstraction. It exists only on paper. It is a total fiction. It exists as an idea. But it as a corporation is totally owned private subsidiary of BRITAIN INC and PLANET EARTH. The various Republic States of the Union exist in substance and reality. The United States only takes on physical reality after congress positively activates constitutionally delegated powers through statutes enacted in accordance with Article I section 7 of the constitution.

It's important to remember the US Congress does have the right to make all laws regarding Washington D.C.

within the ten miles square and territories owned by the United States. This tiny scope of legislative powers is the only authority relating to people of the various states.

Let us go back to President Washington. Here is where the story thickens. William Morris, with the help of Alexander Hamilton, an alleged *"plant of the Illuminati"* who was the Secretary of Treasury, heavily promoted the First National bank, secretly known as the Bank of England (the old Babylon reincarnated), to legislation in order to create a private bank. In 1781, Congress chartered this First National bank for a term of twenty years, to the same European bankers that were holding the debts before the war. The bankers loaned worthless, un-backed, non-secured printed money to each other to charter this first bank. So the U.S. was not really severed. They still owed money to the bankers.

After thousands of lives were lost fighting a war to get control of their own money, why did congress contract with the same bankers that started the revolutionary war in the first place? Very simple. Since the crown (Rothschild) was the creditor, they demanded a private bank to hold the securities of the United States as the pledged assets to the crown of England in order to secure the debt to which the United States had defaulted. The holder of the securities was the private bank. So under public international law, the creditor nation forced the United States to establish a private bank to hold the securities as the collateral for the loan. As throughout history, Babylon follows wherever we go.

In 1785 AD, the youngest Rothschild, Nathan, expanded his wealth to twenty thousand pounds in a fifteen year period by using other people's money. An increase of twenty-five thousand percent. Now that may not seem like much but it is the principle of money growth and interest that they used that was impressive. In 1787 Amshel Rothschild made the famous statement: *"Let me issue and control a Nations money and I care not who writes the laws.'* Thomas Jefferson stated, *'If the*

*American people ever allow the previous banks to control the issue of their currency, first by inflation then by deflation, the banks and the corporations which grow up around them will deprive the people of all property until their children wake homeless on the Continent their fathers conquered.*" We just don't think in international or global commerce where the Elite are quite comfortable, orchestrating control not on bankrupt people, but on nations. It's all the same game, just like bankruptcies and takeovers are a daily thing in business.

In 1790 (August 4), Article One of the U.S. Statutes at Large, pages 138-178, abolished the States of the Republic and created Federal Districts. In the same year, the former States of the Republic reorganized as Corporations and their legislatures wrote new State Constitutions, absent defined boundaries, which they presented to the people of each state for a vote... the new State Constitutions fraudulently made the people "Citizens" of the new Corporate States through the 14th Amendment-remember?  A Citizen is also defined as a "corporate fiction."

About this time these Elite are getting to be a pretty powerful banking force in Europe. In 1798 AD, the five Rothschild brothers expanded by opening banks in each of the major cities of Europe. These were opened in Germany, France, and Britain. Now remember the charter for the private bank in the U.S. was for only twenty years. This was until 1811. But what happened in 1812? The War of 1812. What did England attack? It was Washington, D.C. Yes, the ten miles square where they burned the White House and other buildings. Yet the attack by England on the ten miles square was not an act of war. What cause the war was the United States not extending the First National bank into the Second National bank to continue to maintain the securities on the unpaid debt. At least this so according to international law. So when the United States did an act of war by not giving the lawful creditor the securities in a peaceful manner, the only remedy open under international law to the creditor was to come in on letters of marque and seize the assets to protect their loan. Did the Second National bank get approved? Absolutely. After England attacked the nation that was in default, they saw the light and enacted the Second National bank. This power held for another twenty years, which was to expire about 1836.

By this time, the Elite are well entrenched in the international legal system. It has already been stated what the meaning of Attorney means. It means with obligation to the courts and to the public, *not to the client,* and wherever the duties of his client conflict with those he is obligated to as an officer of the court in the administration of justice, the former must yield to the later. All attorneys owe their allegiance first to the crown of England, next to the courts and then to the public and finally, to their clients. The BAR is the acronym for British Accreditation Regency. Attorneys are members of the BAR. The American Bar Association is a branch of the Bar Council, sole bar association in England. All laws, today in America, are copyrighted property of a British company, all state codes are private, commercial, British-owned '*law*'. All attorneys follow instruction from England. Attorn means to twist and turn over their clients to the private law of the bankruptcy. That is their job. That is their pledge to those whom they owe allegiance. Note also that by definition, the obligations and duties of attorneys extend to the court and the '*public*' (government) before any mere '*client*'. Clients are wards of the court and therefore persons of unsound mind. Just ask an attorney to see if they are aware of this. Attorneys are actually like an external police force making sure the external deals are honoured. Thus, laws and code written in the city of London (the tax free one) can be imposed on any other corporation within the corporate umbrella without question.

So note that the War of 1812 was waged mostly in Washington, D.C. The British burned all the repository buildings, attempting to destroy all records of the new

United States in Washington, D.C. Thus, the war of 1812 was partly waged to prevent the passage and enforcement of the new amendment. Most book repositories throughout the states were burned to the ground and all records destroyed. There's a famous painting in Washington D.C. It can be found in many books, depicting the British boarding a ship after they surrendered. The painting showed the British carrying their rifles as they mounted the gangplank. The truth is they lost a battle but a different war was won. As a result of the accumulated debt of waging that war, a new bank charter was issued for another twenty years.

But then a new kid hit the block. President Andrew Jackson put an end to this second charter in 1836. Jackson's reasoning was simple. He said the constitution does not delegate authority for congress to establish a national bank. Jackson's rationale has never been seriously challenged, and the constitution has never been amended to authorize congress to establish a national bank. Nor, for that matter, does the constitution delegate authority for the United States to establish corporations, particularly private corporations. So there was not a national bank established in America for more than 75 years, until 1913 called the Federal Reserve Bank. Andrew Jackson did an excellent job. What did congress do with Andrew Jackson? They impeached him because congress is made up mostly of attorneys and representatives of the Elite.

The attorneys have a title of nobility to the crown of England. So congress is populated by attorneys who are titles of nobility to the crown of England. It would seem logical to assume congress represents the bankers. The bankers hired an assassin to kill Andrew Jackson using two pistols. However, the plot failed as both pistols misfired. Andrew Jackson violated public international law because he denied the creditor his just lien rights on the debtor. However, the bankers did not lend value or substance so in actuality they had an unperfected lien and the law actually did not apply.

In 1845, Congress passed legislation that would ultimately allow Common Law to be usurped by Admiralty Law. The yellow fringe placed at the bottom of court flags shows this is still true. Before 1845, Americans were considered sovereign individuals who governed themselves under Common Law.

Andrew Jackson stated that: "*Controlling our currency, receiving our public money, and holding thousands of our citizens in dependence would be more formidable and dangerous than a military power of the enemy*." He knew what was going on.

In following this story, in 1860-61, the southern states walked out of congress. Abraham Lincoln was elected president. The south walked out and declared their states rights pursuant to the constitution. Slavery was only window dressing for the Civil War. The war had nothing to do with slavery. It had to do with state's rights and the national debt to the bankers. The south wanted to be redeemed from the crown in England. The north wanted to remain under their dominion and their debt. When the south walked out of congress, this ended the public side of the split constitution as far as the government was concerned. What remained of the government was the private side, the democracy under the rule of the bankers.

In 1860 Congress was adjourned Sine Die. And so Lincoln could not legally reconvene Congress.

When this new leader President Lincoln came into power, by Executive Order 1, on April 15, 1861 he proclaimed the equivalent of the first **Trading With the Enemy Act.** President Lincoln stated: "*The government should create, issue, and circulate all currency and credit needed to satisfy the spending power of the government and the buying power of consumers.'* Further, he quoted, *'The privilege of creating and issuing money is not only* *the supreme prerogative of government, but it is the governments' greatest opportunity.*" He obviously wanted to restructure the U.S. and the debt and the order to put the nation under Marshall law would lead to a new structure.

And so in 1861, President Lincoln declared a National Emergency and Martial Law, which gave the President unprecedented powers and removed it from the other branches. This has NEVER been reversed.

In 1863, Lincoln established the **The Lieber Code of April 24, 1863,** also known as Instructions for the Government of Armies of the United States in the Field, General Order No 100, or Lieber Instruction signed by President Abraham Lincoln. He knew full well what was coming and thus prepared for it. He placed our "trust" in the hands of the military as the proper authority to protect us, America, as the first Bank Act of 1863 began the road to Banksterville. However, those who were interested in gaining access to all the gold and other wealth had another plan, which directly is related to the civil war and the assassination of Abraham Lincoln.

Reading the "Lieber Code" one will learn important directly related evidence of the who, what, when, where, why and how this corruption against America was invented, and spread throughout Europe and Asia like a malignant cancer. Reference **http://unmasker4maine.files.wordpress.com/2011/05/lieber-code.pdf**)

The London bankers were quite worried about Abraham Lincoln's plan to create money. This potentially took the wind out of their private sails, losing control of money. They published an article in the **London Times – Hazard Circular** in 1865 regarding fiat money in America: "*If this mischievous financial policy, which has its origins in North America, shall become endurrated down to a fixture, then that government will furnish its* *own money without cost. It will pay off debts and be without debt. It will have all the money necessary to carry on its commerce. It will become prosperous without precedent in the history of the world. The brains, and the wealth of all the countries will go to North America. That country must be destroyed or it will destroy every Monarchy on the globe."* Check it out on ***www.xat.org/xat/usury.html.***

This certainly hit the nail on the head as to how to get out of the grip. This is exactly what the U.S. and Canada need to do now to get rid of this debt to the IMF. It was smart of Lincoln to figure that out then. They could wipe out any link to the private money guys and start on their own. But in 1865, Lincoln was murdered because he defied the bankers by printing interest free money to pay for the war efforts. In 1865, the capital was moved to Washington, D.C., a separate country – not a part of the United States of America.

This Lieber Code was established but used to the bankers advantage taking away your property and your rights. As a side note, it is quite simple to see that the courts have been employing one side of the military code against the general public, thus employing administrative rules, but did not acting within the policies, procedures and/or guidelines of those rules. And so the courts have come to employ civil rules and procedures failing to follow even those policies and procedures. The courts, police, sheriff, judges et al, were hired or appointed as Constitutional employees to act in good behavior and within the boundaries of the law, and having had taken an oath to uphold the same, but have in many instances, the judges in every instance, knowingly violated the very essence of the Constitution, breaching their own contract.

So the government operated fully under the authority of private law dictated by the creditor. In 1871 the default again loomed and bankruptcy was eminent. So in 1871, the ten miles square was incorporated in England. They used the constitution as their by-laws. Not as authority *under* the constitution but as authority *over* the constitution. They copyrighted not only the constitution but also many names such as, THE UNITED STATES, U.S. THE UNITED STATES OF AMERICA, U.S.A and many other titles as their own. This is the final blow to the original constitution. From here on out, the UNITED STATES was governed entirely by private corporate law, dictated by the banks as creditors.

From 1864-1867, several Reconstruction Acts were passed forcing the states to ratify the 14th Amendment, which made everyone slaves indirectly. For, following the Civil War, Congress submitted to the states three amendments as part of its Reconstruction program to guarantee equal civil and legal rights to black citizens. The major provision of the 14th amendment was to grant citizenship to *"All persons born or naturalized in the United States,"* thereby granting citizenship to former slaves. Another equally important provision was the statement that *"nor shall any state deprive any person of life, liberty, or property, without due process of law; nor deny to any person within its jurisdiction the equal protection of the laws."* The right to due process of law and equal protection of the law now applied to both the Federal and state governments. On June 16, 1866, the House Joint Resolution proposing the 14th amendment to the Constitution was submitted to the states. On July 28, 1868, the 14th amendment was declared, in a certificate of the Secretary of State, ratified by the necessary 28 of the 37 States, and became part of the supreme law of the land.

Congressman John A. Bingham of Ohio, the primary author of the first section of the 14th amendment, intended that the amendment also nationalize the Federal Bill of Rights by making it binding upon the states. Senator Jacob Howard of Michigan, introducing the amendment, specifically stated that the privileges and immunities clause would extend to the states *"the personal rights guaranteed and secured by the first eight amendments."* Historians disagree on how widely Bingham's and Howard's views were shared at the time in the Congress, or across the country in general. No one in Congress explicitly contradicted their view of the Amendment, but only a few members said anything at all about its meaning on this issue. For many years, the Supreme Court ruled that the Amendment did not extend the Bill of Rights to the States.

Not only did the 14th amendment fail to extend the Bill of Rights to the states; it also failed to protect the rights of black citizens. One legacy of Reconstruction was the determined struggle of black and white citizens to make the promise of the 14th amendment a reality. Citizens petitioned and initiated court cases, Congress enacted legislation, and the executive branch attempted to enforce measures that would guard all citizens' rights. While these citizens did not succeed in empowering the 14th amendment during the Reconstruction, they effectively articulated arguments and offered dissenting opinions that would be the basis for change in the 20th century.

This Amendment XIV states as follows:

*Section 1. All persons born or naturalized in the United States, and subject to the jurisdiction thereof, are citizens of the United States and of the state wherein they reside. No state shall make or enforce any law which shall abridge the privileges or immunities of citizens of the United States; nor shall any state deprive any person of life, liberty, or property, without due process of law; nor deny to any person within its jurisdiction the equal protection of the laws.*

*Section 2. Representatives shall be apportioned among the several states according to their respective numbers, counting the whole number of persons in each state, excluding Indians not taxed. But when the right to vote* at any election for the choice of electors for President and Vice President of the United States, Representatives in Congress, the executive and judicial officers of a state, or the members of the legislature thereof, is denied to any of the male inhabitants of such state, being twenty-one years of age, and citizens of the United States, or in any way abridged, except for participation in rebellion, or other crime, the basis of representation therein shall be reduced in the proportion which the number of such male citizens shall bear to the whole number of male citizens twenty-one years of age in such state.

Section 3. No person shall be a Senator or Representative in Congress, or elector of President and Vice President, or hold any office, civil or military, under the United States, or under any state, who, having previously taken an oath, as a member of Congress, or as an officer of the United States, or as a member of any state legislature, or as an executive or judicial officer of any state, to support the Constitution of the United States, shall have engaged in insurrection or rebellion against the same, or given aid or comfort to the enemies thereof. But Congress may by a vote of two-thirds of each House, remove such disability.

Section 4. The validity of the public debt of the United States, authorized by law, including debts incurred for payment of pensions and bounties for services in suppressing insurrection or rebellion, shall not be questioned. But neither the United States nor any state shall assume or pay any debt or obligation incurred in aid of insurrection or rebellion against the United States, or any claim for the loss or emancipation of any slave; but all such debts, obligations and claims shall be held illegal and void.

*Section 5. The Congress shall have power to enforce, by appropriate legislation, the provisions of this article.*

It all looks well and good but the clever trick here is that citizens and persons are not the real thing and if you believe it is, and contract accordingly, it is indeed attached to you as reality. So the bottom line: if you want the benefit of being citizen or person, by the acceptance of the benefit, you are fully employed by the UNITED STATES Inc., a subsidiary of PLANET EARTH, just like other nations.

And so in 1871, The United States became a Corporation with a new constitution and a new corporate government, and the original constitutional government was vacated to become dormant, but it was never terminated. The new constitution had to be ratified by the people according to the original constitution, but it never was. The whole process occurred behind closed doors. The people are the source of financing for this new government.

Then, in 1909, default loomed once more. The U.S. government went to the crown of England and asked for an extension of time. This extension was granted for another twenty years on several conditions. One of the conditions was that the United States allow the creditors to establish a new national bank. This was done in 1913, with the Federal Reserve Bank. This, along with the $16^{th}$ Amendment, collection of Income tax enacted February 25, 1913, and the $17^{th}$ Amendment enacted May 31, 1913, were the conditions for the extension of time. The $16^{th}$ and $17^{th}$ Amendments further reduced the states power. The UNITED STATES adopted the Babylonian system.

In 1917 the people were again drafted into the First World War. The debt accumulated so that it became impossible to pay off the debt in 1929. This was the year of the stock market crash and the beginning of The Great Depression. The stock market crash moved billions of dollars from the people to the banks. This provided an opportunity to removed cash from circulation. Hence the change in currency to debt._Those who still possessed any cash invested in high interest yielding treasury bonds driven higher by increased demand. As a result, even more cash was removed from circulation from the general public to the point where there was not enough cash left in circulation to buy the goods being produced. Production came to a halt as inventory overcrowded the market. There were more products on the market than there was cash to buy them. Prices plummeted and industries plunged into bankruptcy, throwing millions more people out of work and out of cash. Foreclosures on homes, factories, businesses and farms rose to the highest level in the history of America. A mere dime was literally salvation to many families now living on the street. Millions of people lost everything they had, keeping only the clothes on their backs.

In 1917, the Trading with the Enemy Act (TWEA) was passed. This act was implemented to deal with the countries we were at war with during World War I. It gave the President and the Alien Property Custodian the right to seize the assets of the people included in this act and if they wanted to do business in this country they could apply for a license to do so. By 1921, the Federal Reserve Bank (the trustee for the Alien Property Custodian) held over $700,000,000 in trust. Understand that this trust was based on our assets, not theirs.

All this gave the international bankers a pretty sweet opportunity. In Europe, in 1930, the International Bankers declared several nations bankrupt, not just the United States. Then in 1933, President Roosevelt was elected and took office. His first act as president was to declare, publicly, the United States bankrupt. He further went on to issue his Presidential Executive Order on March $5^{th}$, 1933 that all United States citizens must turn in all their gold in return for Federal Reserve notes. This was passed into law by congress on June $5^{th}$, 1933.

And so in 1933, 48 Stat 1, of the TWEA was amended to include the United States Person because they wanted to take people's gold away. Executive Order 6102 was created to make it illegal for a U.S. Citizen to own gold. In order for the Government to take gold away and violate Constitutional rights, we the people were reclassified as ENEMY COMBATANTS.

In 1933, there was another United States bankruptcy. In the first bankruptcy the United States collateralized all public lands. In the 1933 bankruptcy, the U.S. government collateralized the private lands of the people (a lien) – they borrowed money against private lands. They were then mortgaged. That is why we pay property taxes.

From a speech in Congress in The Bankruptcy of the United States Congressional Record, March 17, 1993, Vol. 33, page H-1303, Speaker Representative James Trafficant Jr. (Ohio) addressing the House states:

*"...It is an established fact that the United States Federal Government has been dissolved by the Emergency Banking Act, March 9, 1933, 48 Stat. 1, Public Law 89-719; declared by President Roosevelt, being bankrupt and insolvent. H.J.R. 192, 73rd Congress m session June 5, 1933 - Joint Resolution To Suspend The Gold Standard and Abrogate The Gold Clause dissolved the Sovereign Authority of the United States and the official capacities of all United States Governmental Offices, Officers, and Departments and is further evidence that the United States Federal Government exists today in name only.*

*The receivers of the United States Bankruptcy are the International Bankers, via the United Nations, the World Bank and the International Monetary Fund. All United States Offices, Officials, and Departments are now operating within a de facto status in name only under*

*Emergency War Powers. With the Constitutional Republican form of Government now dissolved, the receivers of the Bankruptcy have adopted a new form of government for the United States. This new form of government is known as a Democracy, being an established Socialist/Communist order under a new governor for America. This act was instituted and established by transferring and/or placing the Office of the Secretary of Treasury to that of the Governor of the International Monetary Fund. Public Law 94-564, page 8, Section H.R. 13955 reads in part: "The U.S. Secretary of Treasury receives no compensation for representing the United States...*

Prior to 1913, most Americans owned clear, allodial title to property, free and clear of any liens of mortgages until the Federal Reserve Act (1913) "Hypothecated" all property within the Federal United States to the Board of Governors of the Federal Reserve, in which the Trustees (stockholders) held legal title. The U.S. Citizen (tenant, franchisee) was registered as a "beneficiary" of the trust via his/her birth certificate. In 1933, the Federal United States hypothecated all of the present and future properties, assets, and labour of their "subjects," the 14th Amendment U.S. Citizen to the Federal Reserve System. In return, the Federal Reserve System agreed to extend the federal United States Corporation all of the credit "money substitute" it needed.

Like any debtor, the Federal United States government had to assign collateral and security to their creditors as a condition of the loan. Since the Federal United States didn't have any assets, they assigned the private property of their "economic slaves," the U.S. Citizens, as collateral against the federal debt. They also pledged the unincorporated federal territories, national parks, forests, birth certificates, and nonprofit organizations as collateral against the federal debt. All has already been transferred as payment to the international bankers.

Unwittingly, America has returned to its pre-American Revolution feudal roots whereby all land is held by a sovereign and the common people had no rights to hold allodial title to property. Once again, we the People are the tenants and sharecroppers renting our own property from a Sovereign in the guise of the Federal Reserve Bank. We the People had exchanged one master for another.

The people turned in all the gold at that time. Why? Were they United States citizens? No. They were still a sovereign people until that time. They just *thought* that they were required to turn in all the gold. In reality, only those people living in Washington, D.C., and the $14^{th}$ Amendment citizens were so required. People were still sovereign and were not under the jurisdiction of the United States of America that was incorporated in 1871. When the people turned in the gold, they just volunteered into the jurisdiction of the ten miles square of Washington D.C. and their laws. They became $14^{th}$ Amendment citizens. Their birth certificates and the title to their bodies were registered in the Commercial Registry. This title to bodies, all of their property and all of their future labour, was pledged to the international bankers as security for the money owed in bankruptcy. This was done under the authority of commercial law that is exactly the same as Babylonian law by and through title. The American people were not in bankruptcy. Only the corporate UNITED STATES was in bankruptcy.

And so it came to pass that it was only the politicians and the ten miles square of Washington, D.C. the UNITED STATES CORPORATION that went into bankruptcy, and not the American people.

In 1944, Washington D.C. was deeded to the International Monetary Fund (IMF) by the Breton Woods Agreement. The IMF is made up of wealthy people that own most of the banking industries of the world. It is an organized group of bankers that have taken control of most governments of the world so the bankers run the world. Congress, the IRS, and the President work for the IMF. The IRS is not a U.S. government agency. It is an agency of the IMF. (Diversified Metal Products v. IRS et al. CV-93-405E-EJE U.S.D.C.D.I., Public Law 94-564, Senate Report 94-1148 pg. 5967, Reorganization Plan No. 26, Public Law 102-391.)

This was the beginning of the states losing the remainder of their sovereignty. It was not until 1944 that the corporate states lost all their power over the corporate United States with the Buck Act. With this Act, the states became, $14^{th}$ Amendment Citizens as well. This completed the destruction of the corporate states having any power to protect against usurpation by the U.S. government. The corporate states then went under the jurisdiction of Washington, D.C.

## The New Subjects Under "The Law"

How did everyone become a '*subject*' of the artificial UNITED STATES and their Code of Law written in the city of London? The U.S. corporation has no more power over people than does the Taco Bell Corporation. It is because as citizens and persons, they themselves became corporations, as we shall reveal in the next chapter.

It must be understood that the march to a uniform commercial law system has assisted the process control through the adoption of the Uniform Commercial Code by all states in 1964 and a number of other like laws and acts were incorporated into this nation. This made the Uniform Commercial Code, the supreme law of the land. This code has prevailed for a long time, back to Babylonian times.

We can see throughout our history that Babylon, their commerce and Merchant law has followed wherever productive people go. The bankers were waiting in the wings when we founded this country. It was only two years after the constitution was enacted that the bankers threw the people into bankruptcy. The newly founded government moved over to the side under the ten square mile that congress controlled.

In 1860, the southern states walked out of congress. This officially ended the lawful side of the constitution. Then in 1871, the ten square miles and its territories, that congress controlled was incorporated in England and the constitution was adopted as the by-laws of that corporation. This ended, completely, the constitution. The people no longer had a constitution.

THE UNITED STATES, as a corporation, created in England, came under the jurisdiction of England, or more appropriately ENGLAND INC. This entitled England to create laws as England saw fit, establish those laws in THE UNITED STATES and everyone who at that time was a $14^{th}$ Amendment citizen was subject to obey those laws. This also placed the Congress of THE UNITED STATES above that portion of what we think is the constitution, not under the authority of the constitution. The only Bill of Rights left at this point in time is some amendments. That is all the courts are required to take cognizance of when you appear in their courts.

Then the merchants of Babylon were able to keep the US debt current, and the bankers, moved from the establishment of the First National bank deeper into the nation by the creation of the Federal Reserve Bank in 1913. The 1929 stock market crash and the great depression that followed placed the American people in desperation, homelessness, poverty and even starvation. The minds of the people were focused on survival. They were then in a condition to accept any handout given by the government, no matter what the cost to their freedoms.

It was then that Roosevelt treasonously placed this entire nation into socialism. Socialism is a class of ideologies favoring a socio-economic system in which property and the distribution of wealth are subject to social control. As an economic system, socialism is associated with collective ownership of the means of production. This control may be either direct — exercised through popular collectives such as workers' councils or cooperatives — or it may be indirect — exercised on behalf of the people by the state. The modern socialist movement had its origin largely in the working class movement of the late 19th century. In this period, the term socialism was first used in connection with European social critics who condemned capitalism and private property. For Karl Marx, who helped establish and define the modern socialist movement, socialism implied the abolition of money, markets, capital, and labor as a commodity.

People were drawn in as 14th Amendment citizens through the registration of their birth certificates. People were further enticed deeper into that system by volunteering for many other licenses and privileges given by the government. People were also made enemies of THE UNITED STATES. This act gave the UNITED STATES authority, under the laws of war and as a captured people, to force anything on the people they choose to create.

Thereafter, the people sank further into communism. If you read the ten planks of communism you'll discover that this nation has fulfilled every plank successfully. The Internet is full of this, but you can go to sites like ***www.libertyzone.com/Communist-Manifesto-Planks.html*** and read about how the Americans are actually following this. It may not be so obvious to you and we have already covered this earlier but in a nutshell the planks are:

1. abolition of private property and the application of all rents of land to public purposes.
2. heavy progressive or graduated income tax.
3. abolition of all rights of inheritance.
4. confiscation of the property of all emigrants and rebels.

5. centralization of credit in the hands of the state, by means of a national bank with State capital and an exclusive monopoly.
6. centralization of the means of communications and transportation in the hands of the State.
7. extension of factories and instruments of production owned by the state, the bringing into cultivation of waste lands, and the improvement of the soil generally in accordance with a common plan.
8. equal liability of all to labour. Establishment of industrial armies, especially for agriculture.
9. combination of agriculture with manufacturing industries, gradual abolition of the distinction between town and country, by a more equitable distribution of population over the country. And ten is free education for all children in public schools, with abolition of children's factory labour in its present form and a combination of education with industrial production.

It is an insidious process. And although, as you will come to understand, the physically property you believe you hold is represented by a "title" or "certificate" that is simply a piece of paper just like your dollar bill. In 1976, congress removed any semblance of justice in the court system. From this point forward, the *officers of the court* can construe and construct the laws to mean anything they chose them to mean. As $14^{th}$ Amendment citizens, people are not citizens of the America they have always thought. They are actually citizens of England, through the corporation of THE UNITED STATES.

Today, as in ancient Babylon, and the Elite, the idol of worship is money, like Federal Reserve notes. It was Rothschild who said his god was money and the Earthling has gravitated to the same belief (except those who say money is evil) There is no law today except as fiction of copyrighted statutes, to be interpreted by judges who construe and construct whatever they choose to have those statutes enforced. The banking system evolved to create a larger and larger fake money empire, while the legal system evolved along with a perception of improved human rights. They waited in the wing to use this to take over nations through the creation of corporations and fictional entities where they are attaching their own laws and acts to the bankrupt nation. Human rights have actually deteriorated because we have given these away to satisfy our greed for money. Commerce is the thread that binds us as well as nations.

In 1976, Congress took away any semblance of law or justice left within our court system. All law today is now construed, constructed and made up by the judge as it happens before your very eyes. They took away any control or authority we might have had over the court system. You can check out Senate Bill 94-204 which deals with the court system and Senate Bill 94-381 dealing with public law. This has been very well hidden from all of us. Many of us going into court often wonder why and how the courts can simply override the laws we put into our paperwork. It's very simple now that we know how they do it. They operate on the words *'construe and construct'*.

A simple word such as *'in'* changed to *'at'* as in *'at law'* or *'in law'* has a totally separate meaning. For example, if you're in the river, you are wet and you can swim. But if you're at the river, you might enjoy a refreshing picnic, play baseball or run races. See the difference a simple word can make? And, the attorneys often change this word when they answer your motions – in addition to many others. It will pay you in dividends to read the answers of attorneys to your paperwork. Compare what they say the case law says to the actual case law itself. You'll discover that they have actually changed the words therein. This is illegal you might say. No, not, according to the above Senate Bills. You see, they can now construe and construct any law or statute to mean whatever they decide it means, for their benefit. You don't know any of this. You think they are railroading you in a kangaroo court. No, they are *'legal'* in what they do. They usually follow the law to the letter; *their* law, private law, the law of contract, that you know nothing about. This law is called contract law.

If you don't understand the above and realize what law you are dealing with when you go into court, you will lose. They operate in total fiction, in la la land, in the Land of Oz. They can only recognize contracts. So, when you go into any court, be aware that it is their law, that the judge or the prosecutor can *'construe'* and *'construct'* that law in any fashion they choose. It will always mean what they choose it to mean. So, are the courts bound by the constitution? Law? Statutes? No, its contracts only and the statutes used to enforce the contracts. And when we use their statutes, constitution, Universal Commercial Code, rules and regulations, all copyrighted – without a license from the BAR, we are in violation of copyright infringement and punishment is mandatory. There is NO law in this nation – or the world for that matter – there is only contract law.

Smart commerce rules the world. Dumb ones that spend money on wars and silly things like that to protect rights just get into debt and get taken over losing their freedoms a different way. It is just good business to take advantage of the dumb ones. And the thread that binds them is commerce, now an empire of debt money controlled by the founders of PLANET EARTH.

Now we are getting to the pith at the bottom of the pyramid. First, if you were born in the United States, your birth certificate was voluntarily given by your mother to the state and then entered into the Commercial Registry for registration, within the UNITED STATES. This, in commerce, gave title to your body by way of a constructive contract. This placed everyone as a member of the Babylonian system in every manner. This process will be detailed in a subsequent chapter.

So the people of the United States accept the bankruptcy attached to the UNITED STATES, the big Strawman (As you know, a fictitious business structure explained in a separate chapter) owned by ENGLAND. The government created an artificial *"person"*, just like a *"citizen"* an organization, a fictitious entity, and what we now know as an artificial entity. By and through an adhesion contract, the government then made the real man or woman, responsible for, and fiduciary for, and surety for, that artificial entity. This is how your artificial entity secured the National debt and through it, you became a $14^{th}$ Amendment citizen of the UNITED STATES. All licenses and all existing contracts are made between the UNITED STATES or THE STATE OF whatever state or province in CANADA you live in and your artificial entity. That fictitious entity binds you to the UNITED STATES because they have, through adhesion contract, made you the real man or woman, fiduciary and responsible for that artificial entity. Of course, you voluntarily sign, and even request, all those contracts.

And all of these contracts you sign carry with it your agreement to obey and uphold all the laws, rules and regulations passed by the congress of the UNITED STATES CORPORATION and THE STATE OF whatever, and will be enforced against you. And these are enforced by the attorneys loyal to the crown.

From that day forward, people could never own any property because the state now had possession of it all. In 1964, the state obtained title to property. People can only rent their homes that they believe they own. They only have a certificate of title to the car they think they own. The state owns the true title to their homes and to their cars, to everything they thought or think they own. You married the state through your marriage license and your children became wards of the state. All of this was pledged, including all the fruits of your future labour, to the bankers as security against the national debt and was placed in the possession of the Secretary of State of each state as an agent for the trustee of the bankruptcy - The U.S. Secretary of Treasury.

To further tighten this process, when people applied for a social security number after 1935, they further volunteered to enter into a contract after the Social Security Act was signed into law. This process had many other ramifications to it as the actual corporate structure that was set up was a special trust. Similarly, many further contracts were entered into by applying for licenses – all voluntarily of course – for some perceived benefit.

## The Establishment Of Human Capital

The story does not end here. The process, as we have discussed, made the debt obligations shift to the people who were registered as human capital. The final ratification and obvious confirmation, however, was stated in 1997. In 1997, **Executive Order 1997, provided the nails in the coffins of the living man. Executive Order No. 13037 was a COMMISSION TO STUDY CAPITAL BUDGETING** Ex. Ord. No. 13037, Mar. 3, 1997, 62 F.R. 10185, as amended by Ex. Ord. No. 13066, Oct. 29, 1997, 62 F.R. 59273; Ex. Ord. No. 13108, Dec. 11, 1998, 63 F.R. 69175, provided: In it, President Clinton declared:

*By the authority vested in me as President by the Constitution and the laws of the United States of America, including the Federal Advisory Committee Act, as amended (5 U.S.C. App.), it is hereby ordered as follows:*

*Section 1. Establishment. There is established the Commission to Study Capital Budgeting ("Commission"). The Commission shall be bipartisan and shall be composed of no more than 20 members appointed by the President. The members of the Commission shall be chosen from among individuals with expertise in public and private finance, government officials, and leaders in the labour and business communities. The President shall designate two co-chairs from among the members of the Commission.*

Sec. 2. Functions. *The Commission shall report on the following:*
*(a) Capital budgeting practices in other countries, in State and local governments in this country, and in the private sector; the differences and similarities in their capital budgeting concepts and processes; and the pertinence of their capital budgeting practices for budget decision-making and accounting for actual budget outcomes by the Federal Government;*
*(b) The **appropriate definition** of capital for Federal budgeting, including: **use of capital for the Federal Government itself or the economy at large**; ownership by the Federal Government or some other entity; defense and nondefense capital; physical capital and intangible or **human capital**; distinctions among investments in and for current, future, and retired workers; distinctions between capital to increase productivity and capital to enhance the quality of life; and existing definitions of capital for budgeting;*
*(c) The role of depreciation in capital budgeting, and the concept and measurement of depreciation for purposes of a Federal capital budget; and*
*(d) The effect of a Federal capital budget on budgetary choices between capital and noncapital means of achieving public objectives; implications for macroeconomic stability; and potential mechanisms for budgetary discipline.*

Sec. 3. Report. *The Commission shall adopt its report through majority vote of its full membership. The Commission shall report to the National Economic Council by February 1, 1999.*

**Sec. 4**. *Administration.*

*(a) Members of the Commission shall serve without compensation for their work on the Commission. While engaged in the work of the Commission, members appointed from among private citizens of the United States may be allowed travel expenses, including per diem in lieu of subsistence, as authorized by law for persons serving intermittently in the Government service (5 U.S.C. 5701-5707).*

*(b) The Department of the Treasury shall provide the Commission with funding and administrative support. The Commission may have a paid staff, including detailees from Federal agencies. The Secretary of the Treasury shall perform the functions of the President under the Federal Advisory Committee Act, as amended (5 U.S.C. App.), except that of reporting to the Congress, in accordance with the guidelines and procedures established by the Administrator of General Services.*

*Sec. 5. General Provisions. The Commission shall terminate on September 30, 1999.*

*William J. Clinton*

Dear Mr. Clinton declared **capital; physical capital and intangible** or **human capital.** In reality, they already were but this put the nails in the coffins. Just like in the Matrix, where the real humans became the power energy source for the machines, living in an illusion of freedom, the human became the source of energy as capital for the Empire of PLANET EARTH.

And so it has been that the UNITED STATES and CANADA have been and still are bankrupt, as are many other nations. And so it has been that the many leaders have been pawns to the events that seem to occur at very critical decision making times. It simply seems to be good business, following a very elegant business plan. There always seems to be another reason to borrow more money right at the critical times. And if you look back to the table of nations and their debts, this has been a pattern with all the major nations of the world.

And when you control the money of nations, this is really good business!

Let us look more closely at the thing called money.

# 12

# COMMERCE AND MONEY CHAINS OF CONTROL

Now it is necessary to understand more about money, or at least what we believe is money. Money is the true insidious weapon of dominion and conquest, and through the creation of the code of law, and the corporate structures which takes on that code, it is easy to see how, when one has become irresponsibly subject to debt, one is beholding to the creditor. And when that happens, bankruptcy is the flag that is waived for assistance from those who are the "creditors". Clearly, creditors dictate their own terms. As we have said before, if you look at North American money, it does not say "*will pay the bearer on demand*" any more. It means that money is a fictitious accounting unit to measure what we believe to be money. The ones who have control of this fictional money that measures debt now create and lend it by a keystroke of the computer. Here is the story on this and how the conversion took place. But first they had to take real money out of the system.

# The Money Kingdoms

The New World Order business plan of the Rulers changed dramatically during the last bankruptcy cycle of 1929 to 1999 as we have seen. In the mythology of gods, these worshiped deities exhibited power to instill fear in humanity and so the dynasties were created. These gods, and their chosen ones had the power to create the fear in humans that kept them in control. as that control shifted, these deities super powers of mythology changed to the control of wealth to pay for armies that could take, support other dynasties. That power source has over the last thousands of years shifted to money because all civilizations recognize the power of money as it begets power. And so the business plan of PLANET EARTH shifted into the ways and means money could not only be continued to be accepted by people but it could be made out of thin air rather than having to scrounge in the earth for metals like gold to support some intrinsic value. In the last cycle, this process has been carefully orchestrated and decisively implemented so that a bank, and those in control can with the entry of a computer keystroke create money.

Let us delve into this and think back to the tables. First are the banks that have a license to create money via a keystroke.

| Rank | Bank | AUM ($bn) |
|---|---|---|
| 1. | Bank of America Merrill Lynch | $1,944,740,000,000 |
| 2. | Morgan Stanley Smith Barney | $1,628,000,000,000 |
| 3. | UBS | $1,559,900,000,000 |
| 4. | Wells Fargo | $1,398,000,000,000 |
| 5. | Credit Suisse | $865,060,000,000 |
| 6. | Royal Bank of Canada | $435,150,000,000 |
| 7. | HSBC | $390,000,000,000 |

| 8.  | Deutsche Bank | $368,550,000,000 |
| --- | --- | --- |
| 9.  | BNP Paribas | $340,410,000,000 |
| 10. | JP Morgan Chase | $284,000,000,000 |
| 11. | Pictet | $267,660,000,000 |
| 12. | Goldman Sachs | $229,00,000,0000 |
| 13. | ABN AMRO | $220,060,000,000 |
| 14. | Barclays | $185,910,000,000 |
| 15. | Julius Bär | $181,680,000,000 |
| 16. | Crédit Agricole | $171,810,000,000 |
| 17. | Bank of New York Mellon | $166,000,000,000 |
| 18. | Northern Trust | $154,400,000,000 |
| 19. | Lombard Odier Darier Hentsch | $153,100,000,000 |
| 20. | Citigroup | $140,700,000,000 |

Then there are the nations who accept that the money created by these banks all under the private world bank and IMF can create real money.

| Rank | Country | External US dollars |
| --- | --- | --- |
| 1  | United States  | 15,570,789,000,000 |
| 2  | United Kingdom | 8,981,000,000,000 |
| 3  | Germany        | 4,713,000,000,000 |
| 4  | France         | 4,698,000,000,000 |
| 5  | Japan          | 2,441,000,000,000 |
| 6  | Ireland        | 2,378,000,000,000 |
| 7  | Netherlands    | 2,344,296,360,000 |
| 8  | Italy          | 2,223,000,000,000 |
| 9  | Spain          | 2,166,000,000,000 |
| 10 | Luxembourg     | 1,892,000,000,000 |

As pointed out before, there are 200 countries listed accounting for at total debt of $76,729,529,173,000. These numbers are just numbers, and just like when you personally declare bankruptcy, what you owe is simply deleted and a new number and conditions are born. The titles to your assets are transferred but did someone pick up a truckload of money in wheel barrows? No. Over the last bankruptcy cycle the definition itself has been changed from hard money backed by intrinsic value, to soft money which is simply a piece of paper believed to have value. Yet, just as it is created by a keystroke, as in a bankruptcy or fail to pay, it can disappear with a keystroke.

## A Story Of Money

Some of this will be a repeat of what has been already presented but it is important to understand how the system of debt drops down in the hierarchy of banking down to the individual called a "person" which really the STRAWMAN. What we call money now is not money, and the only value it has is the value you and I give it. The pieces of paper you and I pass around are Federal Reserve Notes. They look like money to us because we have been told that they are money and because they spend like money, but they are not money. Money is meant to be a medium of exchanging value for value. And as long as the Earthling believes this, it will have a value represented by the commodity it buys.

Money is any object or record that is generally accepted as payment for goods and services and repayment of debts in a given socio-economic context or country. The main functions of money are distinguished as: a medium of exchange; a unit of account; a store of value; and, occasionally in the past, a standard of deferred payment. Any kind of object or secure verifiable record that fulfills these functions can serve as money. Money is historically an emergent market phenomena establishing a commodity money, but nearly all contemporary money systems are based on fiat money. Fiat money is without intrinsic use value as a physical commodity, and derives its value by being declared by a government to be legal tender; that is, it must be accepted as a form of payment within the boundaries of the country, for *"all debts, public and private*". The money supply of a country consists of currency (banknotes and coins) and bank money (the balance held in checking accounts and savings accounts). Bank money usually forms by far the largest part of the money supply. Real money is backed by intrinsic value such as gold and silver. So the medium of exchange, and the regulations surrounding the "money" has evolved from real intrinsic value (coins and gold) to bills, to a keyboard entry into a computer. To those who are authorized to make those entries, like the IMF and World Bank, this presents a wonderful control system of credit, which to those who have become bankrupt, becomes debt. Granted, as long as we can use it for the exchange of goods and services and believe it is money, everything is ok.

To understand the problem, let me explain how paper began to circulate as money: Imagine that you are in England around 1660, at a time when the only money is gold or silver coins. These are minted and put into circulation by the king. When the king is short of gold or silver and in need of something, he adulterates the money by diluting the gold with copper. The newly minted coins are the same size but with less gold. If the subjects refuse to accept these adulterated coins, no matter, the king merely has his court rule that the money is worth whatever he says it is worth. After all, he is the king.

Imagine you have worked hard and saved some money. Where will you put that money for safekeeping? In most communities there is a goldsmith who has a large iron box where he keeps his gold and silver "safe". You ask him to keep your gold and silver "safe", he agrees and you pay him a fee for his service. As proof that he has your gold and silver, he issues you a receipt. The next time you want to buy something, rather than first redeem your gold and then buy whatever you want, you use your gold receipt. It is quicker and easier. As long as the seller can go to the goldsmith and redeem the certificate for gold everything works out fine. This is probably how paper receipts began to circulate as money.

Now, place yourself in the position of the goldsmith. How long would it take you to figure out that very few people ever come at the same time to redeem their gold certificates? Maybe one day, like the king, you find yourself short of gold and silver. Could you say no to temptation, or would you tell yourself, *'I'll issue a gold receipt without any gold to back it up because, after all, who is going to check up on me. Besides, I'll have the gold in a few days to make it right'*.

You quickly learn that spending your own gold receipts causes certain unsettling questions to be asked. You come up with a new plan that gives you something for nothing but doesn't make it too noticeable: you loan gold receipts and collect interest. As long as you don't get too greedy, you can get away with this something for nothing scheme. Soon you and other goldsmith/bankers are lending four times as many paper receipts as you have in gold. This process of the goldsmith/bankers got a boost when the king of England was in need of a great deal of money to fight a war. The king turned to William Paterson.

Paterson and his friends pooled their resources and came up with £72,000 in gold and silver. But instead of lending the gold and silver directly to the king, they formed a bank and printed paper receipts equal to 16-2/3 more than their gold and silver reserves.

They lent the king £1.2 million at 8-1/3 % interest per year. Their yearly interest was £100,000. The king didn't care; he had a war to fight. After all, he would simply raise the taxes on his subjects to pay the interest. Paterson and his friends were protected. He had the foresight to lend his paper receipts to the government. Since these receipts were needed to fight a war, the king couldn't allow them to fail. He declared them legal tender. These receipts were now regarded the same as the gold for which they had stood. A new golden rule came into being: Them that have the gold rule!

Since paper money first began circulating, the situation has changed little. When the federal government wants more money, it borrows it from and through the private banking system, the Federal Reserve. The owners of the Federal Reserve are in no need of gold or silver to back up their loans to the government.

Their money is legal tender. Unlike Paterson's time, there is no gold or silver in the system. The bankers are still receiving something for nothing. And you, as a subject, give the bankers 1/3 of your time when you pay federal and social security taxes.

Most everyone knows that, at one time, our government actually had gold and silver backing our currency. Some people believe the gold and silver may still be there. Most people don't have a clue that a few, very rich individuals are in control of this country through their ownership of the privately owned Federal Reserve Banks.

To understand what is happening with our money today we need to refer to Article I, Section 8 of the U.S. Constitution which says: "*The Congress shall have Power to coin Money, regulate the Value thereof, and of foreign Coin, and fix the Standard of Weights & Measures.*" It is important to understand that the "power to coin money" is just that, coin, not print, because if you have the power to print money you end up with paper money that is worthless - just as worthless as the goldsmith/bankers in England.

To ensure that no one but Congress had control of this country's money, the founding fathers also added Article I, Section 10 which reads: "*No State shall coin Money; emit Bills of Credit; make any Thing but gold and silver coin a Tender in Payment of Debts.*" With these two articles of our Constitution in place, the founding fathers felt they had ensured the stability of the country's money supply.

In 1792 Congress passed the first Coinage Act which set the Standard Unit of Value and the ratio of gold to silver. A dollar of gold was defined as 24-8/10 grains pure 9/10 fine, and a coin dollar of silver at 371.25 grains .999 fine or 412.5 grains Standard Silver. Several times in our country's history Congress has enacted laws that have violated the Constitutional provision governing money. The last time Congress unlawfully turned over their responsibility to manage the country's money supply was with the enactment of the Federal Reserve Act in 1913. For a period of time, the Federal Reserve willingly exchanged gold and silver for paper certificates on demand. But as the depression of 1929 deepened, Congress passed a law making it unlawful to own gold, and the banks stopped redeeming paper money with gold in 1933. In 1968 all that was left supporting our money was silver, and that was removed by presidential order.

Today, there is no gold or silver backing up our money - only the full faith and credit of the United States government. The federal government has pledged you and your ability to earn money as collateral to the international bankers for over $4 trillion in loans. This is a great deal for the bankers. The bankers put up nothing, and you, as a slave, turn over to the bankers 1/3 of your income to pay your "fair share" of the federal income tax.

Your income tax does not pay for the running of the federal government. It pays the interest on the national debt - a debt that was created as a bookkeeping entry.

# Local Banks And The Process Of Money Creation

The same process used by the top banking system does not stop with the owners of the Federal Reserve. It continues through our system and includes every bank, every savings & loan and every credit card company. The process reaches into every banking transaction that you have ever been a party to. All of them, without exception, extend the control of the bankers over our lives. It is all believed to be perfectly ok, legal, believed to be very much the standard norm.

Consider this scenario. You want to buy a used car. You arrange with your bank (bank A) for a loan. The banker gives you a check made out to the car dealer for $5,000. You give the check to the car dealer. The dealer turns the car over to you and deposits the $5,000 check into his bank (bank B). It happens all the time.

Now, let's take a deeper look at the transaction. Did any money leave the bank? No. The money never left the bank because the banker didn't give you any. He gave you bank credit.

The courts have ruled that *"A check is not money"* - School Dist v. U.S. Nat'l Bank, 211 P2d 723); *"A check is an order on a bank to pay money"* - Young v. Hembree, 73 P2d 393. The courts have further ruled that "*National banks may lend their money but not their credit*" - Horton Grocery Co. v. Peoples Nat'l Bank 1928, 144 S.E. 501, 151 Va. 195, because, unlike the Federal Reserve banks, local banks are not allowed by law to create money. The nations are all bankrupt, so how could a bankrupt entity be allowed to create money. However, they believe they do it all the time.

Bank credit is the biggest fraud going because it becomes the creation of bills of credit by private corporations for their private gain. This is one of the most important issues we have to face today because 95% of the nation's money supply consists of bank credit. Bank credit, unlike Federal Reserve Notes, is not something tangible that you can see or hold. The closest you will ever get to seeing bank credit is to look at your check book or credit card. Essentially, bank credit is nothing more than the creation of numbers which are added to your checking account in a bank's bookkeeping department. When you write a check, numbers called dollars are transferred from your checking account to someone else's checking account. The creation, transfer and use of bookkeeping entries as money is what bank credit is all about. Bank credit is first created when a banker hands you a check after you take out a loan. This check is not money, but a promise from the bank to pay you money. The bank might have enough money to cash your check, as long as everyone doesn't bring their checks in at the same time.

The basis for the fraud charge is that the bank has written a check against funds which do not exist. The banker gambles that you will use your checking account in place of cash. Most of the time the banker is right, people usually deposit the check they receive in their checking account and then spend it by writing other checks against the bookkeeping entries which have been added to their account. Most people do not know that a check is not money, that bank credit is not lawful money, and that the courts have consistently ruled against the banks for lending credit.

When the car dealer deposits your check into his account, bank B then has access to $5,000 more that it can make loans against. Modern banking regulations allow banks to loan up to 90% of all money deposited. With sleight of hand and the blessing of modern bookkeeping entries, bank B can now lend an additional $4,500. A different customer at bank B wants a loan. S/he borrows the $4,500 and deposits it in bank C. Now bank C can loan 90% of the $4,500 ($4,050). All the banks (A, B & C) charge interest on each of the loans.

The process can go on indefinitely. The bank credit was created out of thin air. Most of us have several of these bank loans. Many of you have been forced into bankruptcy and forced to give up your homes because of this fraudulent system.

Suppose for a moment that you have bad or limited credit and you apply for a credit card. Given these circumstances, you would be required to put up some collateral. The bank would probably ask you to open a certificate of deposit (CD) for 125% of the credit card's credit limit. (If the credit card had a limit of $1,000, you would have to put up $1,250 in collateral).

Note that the bank has nothing to risk when you use your credit card. You have made the arrangements with the bank to lend you up to $1,000. You have promised to pay them according to the terms and conditions of the note you signed. The question is: Where does the bank get the money you borrowed?

The truth is that the PROMISSORY NOTE you signed is now an asset of the bank, and, based upon this PROMISE to pay, the bank created bank credit, which it lent to you. The bank doesn't reduce the amount of your CD as you make purchases or take out loans. As the bills come into the bank, it pays the merchant for your purchases by electronically transferring numbers in its computer. If for any reason you do not pay for your purchases, the bank has the authority to use the money in your CD to cover your credit card debt.

Look at a mortgage note. Suppose that you go to your bank to borrow money for a home. You fill out the application and the bank runs a check on you. You pass with flying colors and, next, you sign all the papers. Of course, you will have to make a deposit on your home, just like you did with the credit card. The bank will have you sign a PROMISSORY NOTE, called a mortgage, as you did with the credit card. The bank takes the title to your home as collateral, as it did with the CD. And if you default on your payments, the bank will foreclose on your home and sell it, just as they would use your CD to cover your credit card debt.

The same question arises: Where did the bank get the money it lent you for your home? Answer: It didn't lend you any money - it lent you its credit. Based on the asset of your signature on the PROMISSORY NOTE, the bank issued a check from the magic money machine which was accepted as money. What gave it value was your signature.

We know that a check is not money, but a PROMISE to pay money. That's why it needs your signature as the real guy to pay the promise. The bank lied to you. You thought you were borrowing money, and the bank lent you credit instead. In good faith, you entered into what you thought was an honest transaction, but the fact that the transaction was suspect was known only to the bank (and to the courts who have decided that it is illegal for a bank to lend its credit). In legal terms, you have been defrauded because your PROMISE to pay was backed by collateral (the title to your home), but their PROMISE to pay was backed by nothing (neither gold nor silver). In effect, the bank which risked nothing by lending you credit that it created, now has the title to your home.

So when your state is short of money, it also borrows from the banks. A state's PROMISE to pay is called a bond. These PROMISES to pay are based upon the state's ability to get you to pay. The bank accepts the bonds as an asset and does the same sleight of hand with the state that it did with you. It gives the state a check from the magic money machine. The state deposits the check back into the bank and writes more checks on the check. Again, ask yourself this: Did the bank lend your state any money in return for their PROMISE to pay? No! Once again the bank wrote a check, which is not money. And does the state actually make the promise to pay? The state is not real any more than the bank. They do it through you as they hand the responsibilities to the real people to cover the bonds they used as collateral. But a bond is just a piece of paper. The real value is back to you so somehow you have to be faked into providing that value.

Much of the money that your state collects from you in taxes goes toward paying the principal and interest on these fraudulent bank loans. You and I and our ability to pay, along with our property, homes, cars, etc., are pledged as collateral to the bankers for these loans. The bankers put up little of value. They use their magic money machine, and you and I pay.

# A Short History Of Banking Evolution In America

In a previous chapter, the Illuminati and the House of Rothschild was brought forward as to how the Rothschilds have become so influential in being architects of the current banking system. Again, it is difficult to do justice to the research and evidence presented in many websites but two stand out, namely the site ***www.redicecreations.com/specialreports/2005/08aug/redshield.html*** and **G. Edward Griffen** found at ***www.realityzone.com/creature.html***. The following story is taken from the redicecreations site above and is somewhat repetitive of the previous discussion but it is important to bring forward this story as banking is the ultimate controlling force of all nations, in particular how it evolved in America. This treatment is presented by **Johnny Silver Bea**r at ***www.Silverbearcafe.com***.

The "Illuminati" was a name used by a German sect that existed in the 15th century. They practiced the occult, and professed to possess the 'light' that Lucifer had retained when he became Satan. In an attempt to document the origins of an secret organization which has evolved into a mastodonic nightmare, successfully creating and controlling a shadow government that supersedes several national governments, and in whose hands now lay the destiny of the world, one must carefully retrace its history. The lengths to which this organization has gone to create the political machinery, and influence public sentiment to the degree necessary to propel its self-perpetuating prophecy, are, quite frankly, mind boggling. Yet the facts provide for the undeniable truth of its existence.

Amschel Bauer had a son, Meyer Amschel Bauer. At a very early age Mayer showed that he possessed immense intellectual ability, and his father spent much of his time teaching him everything he could about the money lending business and in the basic dynamics of finance. A few years after his father's death in 1755, Mayer went to work in Hannover as a clerk, in a bank, owned by the Oppenheimers. While in the employ of the Oppenheimers, he was introduced to a General von Estorff for whom he ran errands. Meyer's superior ability was quickly recognized and his advancement within the firm was swift. He was awarded a junior partnership. Von Estorff would later provide the yet-to-be formed House of Rothschild an entry into to the palace of Prince William.

His success allowed him the means to return to Frankfurt and to purchase the business his father had established in 1743. The big Red Shield was still displayed over the door. Recognizing the true significance of the Red Shield (his father had adopted it as his emblem from the Red Flag which was the emblem of the revolutionary minded Jews in Eastern Europe), Mayer Amschel Bauer changed his name to Rothschild (red shield). It was at this point that the House of Rothschild came into being.

Through his experience with the Oppenheimers, Meyer Rothschild learned that loaning money to governments and kings was much more profitable than loaning to private individuals. Not only were the loans bigger, but they were secured by the nation's taxes.

The House of Rothschild continued to buy and sell bullion and rare coins. Through their shrewd business transactions they successfully bought out or dismantled most of the competition in Europe. In 1769, Meyer became a court agent for Prince William IX of Hesse-Kassel, who was the grandson of George II of England, a cousin to George III, a nephew of the King of Denmark, and a brother- in-law to the King of Sweden. Before long, the House of Rothschild became the go between for big Frankfurt bankers like the Bethmann Brothers, and Rueppell & Harnier.

Meyer Rothschild began to realize that in order to attain the power necessary to influence and control the finances of the various monarchs in Europe, he would have to wrest this influence and power from the church, which would necessitate its destruction. To accomplish this, he enlisted the help of a Catholic priest, Adam Weishaupt, to assemble a secret Satanic order.

Adam Weishaupt was born February 6, 1748 at Ingoldstadt, Bavaria. Weishaupt, born a Jew, was educated by the Jesuits who converted him to Catholicism. He purportedly developed an intense hatred for the Jesuits. Although he became a Catholic priest, his faith had been shaken by the Jesuits and he became an atheist. Weishaupt was an ardent student of French philosopher Voltaire (1694-1778). Voltaire, a revolutionary who held liberal religious views, had written in a letter to King Frederick II, ("the Great"):

As the name implies, those individuals who are members of the Illuminati possess the 'Light of Lucifer'. As far as they are concerned, only members of the human race who possess the 'Light of Lucifer' are truly enlightened and capable of governing. Denouncing God, Weishaupt and his followers considered themselves to be the cream of the intelligentsia - the only people with the mental capacity, the knowledge, the insight and understanding necessary to govern the world and bring it peace. Their avowed purpose and goal was the establishment of a "Novus Ordo Seclorum" - a New World Order, or One World Government.

Through the network of the Illuminati membership, Meyer Rothschild's efforts were redoubled and his banking empire became firmly entrenched throughout Europe. His sons, who were made Barons of the Austrian Empire, continued to build on what their father had started and expand his financial influence.

During the American Revolution, the House of Rothschild brokered a deal between the Throne of England and Prince William of Germany. William was to provide 16,800 Hessian soldiers to help England stop the Revolution in America. Rothschild was also made responsible for the transfer of funds that were to pay the German soldiers. The transfer was never made. The soldiers were never paid, which may account for their poor showing. The Americans prevailed. At this point Meyer Rothschild set his sights on America. LCF Rothschild Group established by Edmond de Rothschild and presided over today by his son, Benjamin, is one of the most prominent organizations in the global financial sector.

Meanwhile, Benjamin Franklin, having become very familiar with the Bank of England and fractional reserve banking, (as in goldsmiths discussion), understood the dangers of a privately owned Central Bank controlling the issue of the Nation's currency and resisted the charter of a central bank until his death in 1791. That was the same year that Alexander Hamilton pushed through legislation that would provide for the charter of The First Bank of the United States. Ironically, the bank was chartered by the Bank of England to finance the war debt of the Revolutionary War. Nathan Rothschild invested heavily that first bank. He immediately set about to control all financial activity, between banks, in America.

There were a couple of problems, though. The U.S. Constitution put control of the nation's currency in the hands of Congress, and made no provisions for Congress to delegate that authority. It even established the basic currency unit, the dollar. The dollar was Constitutionally mandated to be a silver coin based on the Spanish pillar dollar and to contain 375 grains of silver.

This single provision was designed to keep the American money supply out of the hands of the banking industry. The Bank of England made several attempts to usurp control of the U.S. money supply but failed. Still, through their Illuminati agents, they continued to enlist supporters through bribery and kickbacks.

**Any proponent of a fractional reserve banking system is an economic predator.** During the next twenty years the country would fall prey to contrived financial havoc as a result of the bankers policies of creating cycles of inflation and tight money. During times of inflation the economy would boom, there would be high employment, and people would borrow money to buy houses and farms. At that point the bankers would raise interest rates and incite a depression which would, obviously, cause unemployment. People who could not pay their mortgages would have their homes and farms repossessed by the bank for a fraction of their true value. This is the essence of the Illuminati ploy, and it would recur, time and time again. In fact, it's still happening today.

By 1810, the House of Rothschild not only had a substantial stake in the Bank of the United States, they were quietly gaining control of the Bank of England. Although foreign owners were not, by law, allowed a say in the day to day operations of the Bank of the United States, there is little doubt that the American share holders and directors were, if not affiliated, complicit in the aims and goals of the Illuminati and their central bankers.

In 1811 the charter for the First Bank of America was not renewed. As a result, the House of Rothschild lost millions. This enraged Nathan Rothschild so much that he, almost single handily fomented the War of 1812. Using his formidable power and influence, he coerced the British Parliament to attempt to retake the Colonies. The first military attempt failed. The second strategy was to divide and conquer. Any serious historian will find that the Civil War was largely stirred up by Rothschild's illuminati agents in the United States.

Meyer Amschel Rothschild died on September 19, 1812. His will spelled out specific guidelines that were to be maintained by his descendants:

**1)** All important posts were to be held by only family members, and only male members were to be involved on the business end. The oldest son of the oldest son was to be the head of the family, unless otherwise agreed upon by the rest of the family, as was the case in 1812, when Nathan was appointed as the patriarch.

**2)** The family was to intermarry with their own first and second cousins, so their fortune could be kept in the family, and to maintain the appearance of a united financial empire. For example, his son James (Jacob) Mayer married the daughter of another son, Salomon Mayer. This rule became less important in later generations as they refocused family goals and married into other fortunes.

**3)** Rothschild ordered that there was never to be *"any public inventory made by the courts, or otherwise, of my estate... Also I forbid any legal action and any publication of the value of the inheritance."*

Nathan Mayer Rothschild, who, by 1820, had established a firm grip on the Bank of England stated:

*"I care not what puppet is placed upon the throne of England to rule the Empire on which the sun never sets. The man who controls Britain's money supply controls the British Empire, and I control the British money supply."*

The Second Bank of the United States, was also chartered by the Bank of England to carry the American war debt. When its charter expired in 1836, President Andrew Jackson refused to renew it, saying a central bank concentrated too much power in the hands of un elected bankers.

In 1838 Nathan made the following statement:

*"Permit me to issue and control the money of a nation, and I care not who makes its laws."*

During the first quarter of the nineteenth century the Rothschilds expanded their financial empire throughout Europe. They crisscrossed the continent with railroads, which allowed the transport of coal and steel from their newly purchases coal mines and iron works. Through a loan to the government of England, they held the first lien on the Suez Canal. They financed the Romanov dynasty in tsarist Russia, provided the funding that allowed Cecil Rhodes the opportunity to plunder and sack South Africa as well as the funding that allowed the government of France to plunder and sack North Africa.

In the years preceding the Civil War, a number of "Skull and Bones" Patriarchs were to become leaders in the Secessionist movements of various Southern States. It has been suggested that these pressures exacerbated an already tenuous situation, and set the stage for the fomentation of the Civil War. The Rothschild Banks provided financing for both the North and the South during the war. After the civil war, the more clever method was used to take over the United States. The Rothschilds financed August Belmont, Khun Loeb and the Morgan Banks. Then they financed the Harrimans (Railroads), Carnegie (Steel) and other industrial Titans. Agents like Paul Warburg, Jacob Schiff, Bernard Baruch were then sent to the United States to effect the next phase of the takeover.

By the end of the 19th. Century, the Rothschilds had controlling influence in England, U.S., France, Germany, Austria and Italy. Only Russia was left outside the financial sphere of world domination. England, through the Bank of England, ruled most of the world. Jacob Schiff, president of Khun Loeb Bank in New York was appointed by B'nai B'rith (A secret Jewish Masonic Order meaning "Bothers of the Convenant") to be the Revolutionary Leader of the Revolution in Russia. A cartel, made up of the Carnegies, Morgans , Rockefellers, and Chases would contribute to the manifestation of communism. On January 13, 1917, Leon Trotsky arrived in the United States and received a

U.S. Passport. He was frequently seen entering the palatial residence of Jacob Schiff.

Jacob Schiff, and his supporters, financed the training of Trotsky's Rebel Band, comprised mainly of Jews from New York's East Side, on Rockefeller's Standard oil Company property in New Jersey. When sufficiently trained in the techniques of guerrilla warfare and terror, Trotsky's rebel band departed with twenty million dollars worth of gold, also provided by Jacob Schiff, on the ship S.S. Kristianiafjord bound for Russia to wage the Bolshevik revolution.

After the Bolshevik Revolution and the wholesale murder of the entire Russian royal family, Standard Oil of New Jersey brought 50% of the huge Caucasus oil field even though the property had theoretically been nationalized. In 1927, Standard Oil of New York built a refinery in Russia. Then Standard Oil concluded a deal to market Soviet Oil in Europe and floated a loan of $75 million to the Bolsheviks. Jacob Schiff and Paul Warburg at the Kuhn Loeb Bank started a campaign for a central bank in the United States. They then helped the Rothschild's to manipulate the financial Panic of 1907.

Then, the panic of 1907 was used as an argument for having a central bank to prevent such occurrences. Paul Warburg told the Banking and Currency Committee: 'Let us have a national clearing house'."

The Federal Reserve Act was the brainchild of Baron Alfred Rothschild of London. The final version of the Act was decided on at a secret meeting at Jekyll Island Georgia, owned by J.P. Morgan. Present at the meeting were; A. Piatt Andrew, Assistant secretary of the Treasury, Senator Nelson Aldrich, Frank Vanderlip, President of Kuhn Loeb and Co., Henry Davidson, Senior Partner of J.P. Morgan Bank, Charles Norton, President of Morgan's First National of New York, Paul Warburg,

Partner in Khun Loeb and Co. and Benjamin Strong, President of Morgan's Bankers Trust Co.

The Federal Reserve Act of 1913, brought about the decimation of the U.S. Constitution and was the determining act of the international financiers in consolidating financial power in the United States. Pierre Jay, Initiated into the "Order of Skull and Bones" in 1892, became the first Chairman of the New York Federal Reserve Bank. A dozen members of the Federal Reserve can be linked to the same "Order."

The Rothschilds operated out of an area in the heart of London, England, the financial district, which is known as 'The City', or the 'Square Mile.' All major British banks have their main offices here, along with branch offices for 385 foreign banks, including 70 from the United States. It is here that you will find the Bank of England, the Stock Exchange, Lloyd's of London, the Baltic Exchange (shipping contracts), Fleet Street (home of publishing and newspaper interests), the London Commodity Exchange (to trade coffee, rubber, sugar and wool), and the London Metal Exchange. It is virtually the financial hub of the world.

Positioned on the north bank of the Thames River, covering an area of 677 acres or one square mile (known as the "wealthiest square mile on earth"), it has enjoyed special rights and privileges that enabled them to achieve a certain level of independence since 1191. In 1215, its citizens received a Charter from King John, granting them the right to annually elect a mayor (known as the Lord Mayor), a tradition that continues today.

Des Griffin, in his book Descent into Slavery, described 'The City' as a sovereign state (much like the Vatican), and that since the establishment of the privately owned Bank of England in 1694, this financial center has actually become the last word in England's national affairs. He contends that the country is run by powers in 'the City' and that the throne, the prime minister, and parliament are simply fronts for the real power. E. C. Knuth, in his book Empire of the City, suggests that when the queen enters 'The City,' she is subservient to the Lord Mayor (under him, is a committee of 12-14 men, known as 'The Crown'), because this privately-owned corporation is not subject to the Queen, or the Parliament. The Rothschilds have traditionally chosen the Lord mayor since 1820.

The last national election in the United States provided its citizenry with a choice between two known members of a the same Satanic cult. And even then, the outcome of this election has come under extreme scrutiny. For further exploration into the 2004 Presidential election please follow this link to ***www.heartcom.org/20reasons.htm***

And so we arrive at the point of the Federal Reserve and the fatal bankruptcy of corporate UNITED STATES. To continue this story, this is taken from ***www.silverbearcafe.com/private/natureofmoney.html*** where Johnny Silver Bear documents how we moored and drifted into the economic abyss:

In 1878, in a rare state of clarity, Congress began to redeem "greenbacks" into gold which put the United States back on the gold standard until 1933. It was well known amongst intelligent politicians, (who have, apparently, remained in the minority), that the gold standard protected citizens against the controlling tendencies of the government by offering an absolute hedge against the depreciation or devaluation of the currency. Gold provided an agent of maintenance and liquidity within and beyond national borders. Above all, it raised a mighty barrier against authoritarian interferences through the manipulation of the economic markets. Within the constraints imposed by the gold standard, America's economy remained relatively healthy until 1913.

On December 23, 1913, the U.S. Congress passed the Federal Reserve Act, placing control of this nation's money into the hands of a private corporation. This corporation was made up entirely of bankers. Calling itself the Federal Reserve, so as to seem official, it replaced the national bank system. Treasury notes were recalled and Federal Reserve notes were issued with a promise to redeem them in gold on demand. The forces behind the Federal Reserve, (American and Western European banking interests), remained tethered by the limits imposed by the gold standard, but this would soon change.

In 1920, the 66th Congress passed the Independent Treasury Act.

In 1921, the United States Congress abolished the U.S. Treasury, and, as a result, all of our country's bullion and all other instruments of value, ( i.e. moneys in trust funds and other special funds that had been kept in U.S. Treasury offices and vaults), were systematically transferred to the coffers of a private corporation!

From 1913, until 1933, under the authority of the U.S. Congress, the Federal Reserve held control of all of our country's gold. They then proceeded to loan us back our gold, at interest. We paid interest for the use of our own gold! What's wrong with this picture? What could have incited our Senators and Representatives to allow that to happen? In order to keep up with the ever rising debt service, we borrowed more of our own gold. We kept borrowing more and more of our own gold to pay more and more interest, until all the gold was gone. At that point, the country went bankrupt. as you have learned, what happened next was the bankers foreclosed on America.

On March 9, 1933, the U.S. declared bankruptcy again, as expressed in President Franklin Delano Roosevelt's Executive Orders 6073, 6102, 6111, and 6260. On April 5th, 1933, one month after his inauguration, President

Roosevelt declared a National Emergency that made it unlawful for any citizen of the United States to own gold, (see death penalty in website above), and "unconstitutionally" ordered all gold coins, gold bullion, and gold certificates to be turned into the Federal Reserve banks by May 1st under the threat of imprisonment and fines. This was technically, a national confiscation of gold and silver. This unlawful precedent set by Roosevelt would eventually lead us to the catastrophic situation we find ourselves in today.

Our bankrupt nation went into receivership and was reorganized in favor of its creditor and new owners, a private corporation of international bankers. (Since 1933, what is called the "United States Government" has been a privately owned corporation, and the property of the Federal Reserve/International Monetary Fund.)

And so, as stated before, without a word of truth to the American people, **all our good faith and credit was pledged as the surety for the debt** by the same Congressmen who created the mechanism that allowed it to occur. Those Congressmen, knew such "De Facto Transitions" were unlawful and unauthorized, but were mysteriously coerced into sanctioning, implementing, and enforcing the complete debauchment of the monetary system, and the resulting changes in all aspects of government, society, and industry in the United States of America.

From the onset of the Federal Reserve, fractional reserve bankers set out to win the war of misinformation. They did this, in part, by attempting to advance the pseudo tenets of Keynesianism, monetarism, and supply-side economics.

John Maynard Keynes, although a great friend of the bankers, was probably the most heinous influence on freedom, liberty, and the free market in the 20th century. He was a Fabian socialist and a Globalist, (is that redundant?), who provided an intellectual cover for inflationism. He is best known for authoring bogus economic theories, undermining Western values and philosophy, and providing a floor plan whereby the bankers could more easily deceive the people. It was Keynes who coined the phrase, "barbarous relic" in reference to gold. It was Keynes who desecrated the U.S. Constitution with almost every breath.

*"Lenin was certainly right. There is no subtler, no surer means of overturning the existing basis of society than to debauch the currency. The process engages all the hidden forces of economic law on the side of destruction, and does it in a manner which not one man in a million is able to diagnose."*

During the first half of the 20th century, each of four world leaders did the exact same thing within ninety days of their ascension to power. Each made it illegal for the citizens of their respective countries to own gold. Those leaders were: Mao, Stalin, Hitler, and Franklin D. Roosevelt. All four were acutely aware of the restrictions that a gold standard imposed on their abilities to wage war.

The bankers hate gold as money for the same reason. Gold as money acts as a barrier to the expansion of credit money. By pandering the lure of unlimited credit, the bankers went about recruiting politicians throughout the world. The opportunity to wage war on borrowed money turned out to be irresistible to Empire. Wars have always been very important to the banking cartels. They are very expensive. Time and time again, through loans to governments, the cartels have provided the funding for great conflicts. Imagine, being able to go to war with unlimited funds. Better yet, imagine the inability to go to war because of the lack of unlimited funds. The temptation extended to the power mongers was too great. The credit was made available with a single catch. The gist of the pitch went something like this:

*"Sure we'll loan you all the money you want, on the condition that you enact laws making all the citizens of your individual countries responsible for the interest payments, through taxation"*

One by one the leaders of every government on earth sold out, and agreed to demonetize gold, thereby allowing the continued power grab of the banking cartels through the issuance debt based currency. The result has been the methodical fleecing of the general population through the debasing of the dollar by 97%.

*Side note: In 1792 the U. S. Coinage Act (see above website) was passed by Congress.* **It invoked the death penalty for anyone debasing money** *and provided for a U.S. Mint where silver dollars were coined along with gold coins beginning in 1794. The text of Coinage Act of 1792 states: "The Dollar or Unit shall be of the value of a Spanish milled dollar as the same is now current," that is, running in the market, "to wit, three hundred and seventy-one and one-quarter grains of silver."*

On May 22nd, 1933, Congress enacted a law, against Constitutional mandate, declaring all coin and currencies then in circulation to be legal tender, dollar for dollar, as if they were gold. The President was unconstitutionally empowered to reduce the gold content to the dollar up to 50 percent.

On June 5th, 1933, Congress stabbed the gold standard out of existence by enacting a joint resolution (48 Stat. 112), that all gold clauses in contracts were outlawed and no one could legally demand gold in payment for any obligation due to him.

On January 30th, 1934, the Gold Reserve Act was passed, giving the Federal Reserve title to all the gold which had been collected. This act also changed the value/price of gold from $20.67 per ounce to $35 per ounce, which meant that all of the silver certificates the people had recently received for their gold now were worth 40 percent less.

On January 31st, 1934, after President Roosevelt fixed the dollar at 15 and 5/21 grains standard to gold. Russia and the central banks of Europe were very excited and began buying up gold in huge quantities. This planned redistribution of our country's wealth was one of the most important objectives of the Globalist's agenda. Thus a dual monetary system began which offered the gold standard for foreigners and Federal Reserve notes for Americans.

Between 1934 to 1963 all Federal Reserve notes issued had a promised to pay, or to be redeemed in "lawful money." Over a short period of time the wording on the Federal Reserve notes began to change until there was no redemption in silver promised. This was done slowly enough that the people didn't see it coming.

On November 2nd, 1963, new Federal Reserve notes with no promise to pay in "lawful money" was released. No guarantees, no value.

In 1965 silver in coins were reduced to 40 percent by President Lyndon Johnson's authorization.

President Lyndon Johnson issued a proclamation on June 24, 1968, that all Federal Reserve Silver Certificates were merely fiat legal tender and could not be redeemed in silver.

On December 31, 1970, President Richard Nixon signed into law an amendment to the Bank Holding Company Act, which, among other things, authorized the treasury to totally debase coins to a worthless value in non precious metal.

*"Single acts of tyranny may be ascribed to the accidental opinion of a day. But a series of oppressions, begun at a distinguished period, and pursued unalterably through*

*every change of ministers, too plainly proves a deliberate systematic plan of reducing us to slavery." - Thomas Jefferson.*

Since the seventies, the unfettered issuance of debt money has continued to debase our currency more rapidly than ever before. In the last three years, the debasement has accelerated exponentially.

*"The abandonment of the gold standard made it possible for the welfare statists (government bureaucrats) to use the banking system as an unlimited expansion of credit. In the absence of the gold standard, there is no way to protect savings from confiscation through inflation... Deficit spending is simply a scheme for the "hidden" confiscation of wealth. Gold stands in the way of this insidious process." -* **Alan Greenspan**

The world governments continue to babble that tired Keynesian rhetoric insisting that gold and silver have become obsolete, relics of the past. Yet in the 4th Quarter of 2006 global gold and silver demand was the highest on record, and, some of the world's largest investors are presently taking major positions in precious metals.

The cartel wants economic growth, lots of borrowers, and lots of opportunities to lend newly created funny money at interest. You can't blame them for wanting that. If I could print up all the funny money I wanted and could then lend it out at interest, I'd be happy too. That is, I would be happy to lend it if I didn't have a soul. The ravages of inflation have heretofore been thoroughly exposed and the results are blatantly apparent in our inability to successfully engineer our lives without debt. Fractional reserve banking has provided for the theft of the life blood of our nation.

Compounding the problem is the fact that the world is no longer capable of sustaining economic expansion. We are beginning to witness emerging nations, like China and

India sucking up natural resources at a rate that is way past rechargeable. We are entering a period of civilization where the keyword is sustainability, not growth.

The debasement of currency continues with abandon. The purchasing power of the dollar is quickly eroding. It is down 30% in the last three years. Conversely, the value of gold is up 30% in the last three years. Because the dollar is the reserve currency of world, every commodity, from rice to timber, from oil to precious metals, will continue to rise, priced in dollars.

The U.S.A. is currently breaking all records for the longest period of time that a nation's economy has endured after abandoning the gold standard. Our country has been foreclosed on in the past, and it's just about to be foreclosed on again. It's just a matter of time. The "endgame" is near.

*"I believe that banking institutions are more dangerous to our liberties than standing armies... If the American people ever allow private banks to control the issue of their currency, first by inflation, then by deflation, the banks and corporations that will grow up around [the banks... will deprive the people of all property until their children wake-up homeless on the continent their fathers conquered. The issuing power should be taken from the banks and restored to the people, to whom it properly belongs." -- **Thomas Jefferson** -- **The Debate Over The Re Charter Of The Bank Bill**, (1809)*

## The Federal Government And The National Debt

And so the top dogs of PLANET EARTH Inc. have played their games financing conflict and controlling the nations money.

Now, let us return to the debt. When the local bank issues you money, it is following the same process engaged in by nations. The federal government issues a bond. The bond goes to the privately owned Federal Reserve Bank. The bond is a PROMISE to pay based upon the government's ability to collect taxes from you and me. Again, the bankers issue a check from the magic money machine. And again, you pay and pay and pay.

The Constitution says that money is gold or silver, probably because they are rare, and also because they require someone's labor to bring it to us in a form that we can use. This has never changed. The Constitution also says that only Congress has the authority to coin or regulate the value of money. We got into this mess because, for the third time in history in 1913, Congress committed treason to the Constitution by illegally turning over to a group of bankers, its responsibility to coin and regulate the value of money.

Consider that these Federal Reserve Notes are made out of paper (and cotton) and cost only 2.6 cents per note to produce, regardless of denomination. You know that whoever is producing these notes is making a tremendous profit. Consider also that real money cannot be counterfeited. A pound of gold is a pound of gold, regardless of whose profile is stamped in it. The only money that can be counterfeited is the other counterfeit money (Federal Reserve Notes).

It would seem that the way out of this is for We the People to reinstate the Constitution as the Supreme Law of the Land. Until and unless we act to do so, this fraudulent money, banking and taxing system will continue to enslave us. Keep these two points in mind: first, usury, which is the requirement to pay back both the principal and the interest on a loan, is in violation of Biblical law, which demands "just weights and measures"; and second, there is always a price to be paid for dishonesty. For most of the history of this country, we operated under an honest, Constitutional system. The system could be honest again.

In Summary what the federal reserve and the government are doing at the national level, local banks are doing with us at the local level. The only difference is that instead of printing new notes, the banks are creating new checkbook money each time they make a loan.

Here's what happens when you go to the bank to get a loan for your vehicle:

- The bank has you sign a Promissory Note.
- The back of the note is then stamped, "pay to order of" or similar words.
- The note is then deposited into a transaction account in your name. Now this was not disclosed to you before you signed the note and you did not give them the authority to open a transaction account on your name.
- The bank then writes a check from your transaction account deposit that you had no knowledge of, either to you or transfers the amount to those who should be receiving it.
- The bank then sells the note to Federal Reserve or into the securities market. The proceeds of which, are used to fund the alleged loan.

Through the bank selling your note, YOU PAID FOR YOUR PURCHASE WITH THE PROMISSORY NOTE. Your note was treated by the bank as an asset that could be exchanged for cash. Anything that you can exchange for cash is an asset. What 95 % of America does not realize is that within our monetary system a Promissory Note is an asset. The moment you signed that note it became money to the bank. There was no money in existence until you signed the note. Once the bank stamped it "pay to the order of" it became a negotiable instrument. To the bank, it had **Present Value**, because they were able to sell it for cash. To you it only had **Future Value.**

What's wrong with this loan scenario? You always suspected that there was something not right when you went for a loan from the bank. Now you know what it is. Let me give you a simple illustration that will help you to understand this.

Imagine if you came to me needing a loan.
**You:** "Can you give me a loan for $10,000."
**Me:** "sure I'll loan you $10,000, but you have to give me an asset worth $10,000."
**You:** "All I've got is this diamond ring worth $10,000."
**Me:** "That will do." I then take the ring and sell it for $10,000, and come back to you with a check for $10,000.
**Me:** "Here's your $10,000 loan at 10% interest, and the payments are $200 a month for x number of years."
**You:** "xxxxxxx!" We won't even print what you would tell me to do with that loan.

In fact if you called the police I would go to jail for fraud, loan sharking, racketeering etc. BUT THIS IS EXACTLY WHAT THE BANKS ARE DOING EVERY SINGLE DAY.

**Now what is wrong with this loan?**
- It's not a loan. It's an exchange. We simply exchanged your diamond for a $10,000 check.
- It never cost me anything to make the loan. I brought nothing to the table. My assets did not decrease by $10,000, as would be the case in a true, honest loan. Therefore I had no risk.
- You provided the asset (the diamond ring). I merely sold it and gave you back your money, and then had the unmitigated gall to charge you interest on nothing.

In the same way, YOUR PROMISSORY NOTE BECAME THE FUNDING INSTRUMENT OF YOUR BANK LOAN. The bank received it as an asset, as legal tender, i.e. in the form of money and deposited in an account. According to the Uniform Commercial Code, a promissory note is a negotiable instrument, and is therefore legal tender. As such it is the funding instrument. Therefore there was no loan. It was an exchange. Your note which, could be monetized by the bank, was exchanged for the bank's check. And the bank lied and called it a loan. Banks and lending institutions only **appear** to lend money.

The "lending" techniques that are used are beyond brilliant. It took some very, very smart people to figure out how to **appear to be lending money**, but in actuality have the value supplied by the person wanting a loan. And that is what is happening.

If you are finding this rather difficult to believe, let's look at some Federal Reserve Bank publications, which actually admit that this is how bank loans work.

*"Transaction deposits are the modern counterpart of bank notes. It was a small step from printing notes to **making book entries crediting deposits of borrowers,** which the borrowers in turn could "spend" **by writing checks, thereby "printing" their own money**." (**Modern Money Mechanics, page 3, Federal Reserve Bank of Chicago**).*

*"Of course **they do not really pay out loans from the money they receive as deposits**. If they did this, no additional money would be created. **What they do when they make loans is to accept promissory notes in exchange for credits to the borrowers' transaction accounts.** Loans (assets) and deposits (liabilities) both rise by $9,000. Reserves are unchanged by the loan transactions. But the deposit credits constitute new additions to the total deposits of the banking system."* Modern Money Mechanics, page 6, Federal Reserve Bank of Chicago.

According to the Fed, it is not their policy to make loans from other depositor's money. Neither do they make loans from their own assets. They make loans by accepting promissory notes in exchange for credits to the borrower's transaction account. They even admit that it's an exchange. IF IT'S AN EXCHANGE HOW CAN IT BE A LOAN?

*"In **exchange** for the note or security, the lending institution credits the depositor's account or gives a check that can be deposited at yet another depository institution."* Two Faces of Debt, page 19 Federal Reserve Bank of Chicago.

You want more proof: **THE BANK'S OWN BOOKKEEPING ENTRIES ARE PROOF.** Let's say the bank receives a $1,000.00 check deposit. It is recorded as an asset to the bank. But in order to balance their books, on the other side of the ledger they have to record a $1,000.00 liability. The bank has an asset for $1,000.00, but it also has a liability of $1,000.00 to you, the depositor.

The bank owes you $1,000.00. You have a right to draw on that $1,000.00 whenever you choose. Now when you purchased your vehicle instead of a check you gave the bank a signed promissory note. The bank deposited it, just like a check or cash, in a transaction account in your name. Now remember that all deposits are received as assets to the bank. However, they also have a corresponding liability to the face value of your promissory note. Therefore, in reality you don't owe the bank anything. You simply exchanged your promissory note for their check, which paid for the vehicle. The account is a wash. SO WHY ARE WE PAYING MONTHLY PAYMENTS AND INTEREST FOR SOMETHING THAT, WITHIN OUR MONETARY SYSTEM, HAS ALREADY BEEN PAID FOR?

**Actually the bank owes you!** They still do not own your promissory note. They made an exchange - your promissory note (asset to the bank) was exchanged for the face value of the note. They deposited your note and then sold it remember. Therefore, on their books they still have a liability to you

Colonel Edward Mandell House is attributed with giving a very detailed outline of the plans to be implemented to enslave the American people. He stated, in a private meeting with Woodrow Wilson (President 1913 - 1921). Quote:

*"Very soon, every American will be required to register their biological property (that's you and your children) in a national system designed to keep track of the people and that will operate under the ancient system of pledging. By such methodology, we can compel people to submit to our agenda, which will affect our security as a charge back for our fiat paper currency. (property) and we will hold the security interest over them forever, by operation of the law merchant under the scheme of secured transactions. Americans, by unknowingly or unwittingly delivering the bills of lading (Birth Certificate) to us will be rendered bankrupt and insolvent, secured by their pledges.(presidency) of our dummy corporation (USA) to foment this plot against America."*
**--Colonel Edward Mandell House**

*"Every American will be forced to register or suffer being able to work and earn a living. They will be our chattels. They will be stripped of their rights and given a commercial value designed to make us a profit and they will be none the wiser, for not one man in a million could ever figure our plans and, if by accident one or two should figure it out, we have in our arsenal plausible deniability. After all, this is the only logical way to fund government, by floating liens and debts to the registrants in the form of benefits and privileges. This will inevitably reap us huge profits beyond our wildest expectations and leave every American a contributor to this fraud, which we will call "Social Insurance." Without realizing it, every American will unknowingly be our servant, however begrudgingly. The people will become helpless and without any hope for their redemption and we will employ the high office."*

The bottom line, as you have come to know, is there is no real money. The paper debt instrument has become our substitute for the real stuff. We have all just accepted that there is value in a piece of paper. And as long as the mass believes it, there is value. In reality, as long as you can trade the paper for something material, like food, shelter, and toys, everyone believes that it is the paper that has the value. At the root, it is commerce and the ability to trade things for the paper that drives this machinery of money, and it always has. Nations have progressively and cyclically moved from a gold backed money system to a paper system, then back again. In many cases, this has caused great havoc as the currencies became valueless. But nowhere in history has the magnitude of fake paper been as dramatic as in our current time. It can now be done with a simple keystroke and a ledger entry with no backing. Historically, the banking system, and those who control it have taken more and more through the banking and legal systems to lead us to the biggest monetary deception in history. This is what we live under here and now. But let us explain how this greatest illusion of all, the one that controls nations, has evolved.

At the root of the commercial box is a control mechanism we know as commerce. Commerce has been the common thread woven throughout our entire history. In a nutshell, the key components of this control mechanism includes the merchant, the money-changers or banks, the law of commerce, civil law, and maritime law. These form the glue that bound people before and it still binds people into one uniform system.

As you will come to realize, banks create money today out of thin air. Then they charge the people interest on their creation. Merchants, who produce nothing, sell products for a larger profit than is received by the producer. Thereafter, the merchants and the bankers create laws through lawmakers whom they control. These laws protect commerce and bind the people to obey through civil and Maritime law. As you may have realized, the tax system is an integral part of the process. The only reason this occurs is that we do not handle our own affairs. This same scenario has happened for more than four thousand years throughout our history. Now it is so huge and diversified into nations that it is seemingly impossible to rectify. The banking and legal systems coupled with commerce constitute the global glue so to speak. Let us delve into the history of this glue.

And the story parallels Canada and US. There is a close similarity. Of course the legal acts and events differ but the outcome is the same. Canada is just another corporation under the illusion of a free nation. The people that orchestrate this are the ones that control and police the laws of commerce and the banking system. What is important is that you simply get an appreciation for how commerce has been used for a long time and how it is the thread that binds nations and their people now.

## The Elegant Corporate Structure

There is still more to conclude this chapter of the story. Remember that the natural being had rights. The foreign bankers knew they could not control these real people with such a system of freedom. So they decided to design a fictional system, which looked like the real thing. But really it was not. You have noted that the commerce model of fictional entities they built to control freedoms of nations through banking is the same at a personal level.

The first thing that was done was to make an entity which looked and sounded like the federal republic entitled *'united States of America'*. Notice that the *'u'* in united is a small u. That's because it is an adjective, describing the States - a noun - of America. What if one capitalized the *'U'*, as in United States? This would be a name; or a *'title'* wouldn't it? So, now we have a *'title'* for the republic which was incorporated in England in 1871 as an English corporation.

This clearly shows that we are being ruled by a private foreign operated corporation, and not a government. Then in 1944, the Buck Act took the sovereignty away from the states so that the states could also have a title as in *'The State of Arizona'*. Then came the counties and municipalities, each had their own corporations which usurped the organic government. What we then had was an inverse relationship to the original organic republics.

So what they designed was a top down fictional model of corporate names to impose on nations all the way down to the biological Earthling – the only ones left to pay the bills. It appears very consistent. And this model was designed to control humankind, getting around the original rights and freedoms that took centuries to get.

If you look at how the hierarchy of authority is imposed using this model, you will see that there are three ways of identification. These are the authority, name and image or fiction. At the very bottom is you, also known as a sovereign or soveran, your name being upper and lower case letters with a fictional counterpart being the name on your birth certificate. Also in this hierarch is the Post Office which has a district called the POSTAL CODE. Next up is your neighborhood or area, identified with a fictional counterpart as a VOTING DISTRICT. Now you can follow this all the way up with township, municipality, county, state, country, and nation. These are all CORPORATIONS, each being a successive higher level above you. Each is subject to particular laws and legal acts. Thus the whole planet is divided into nations. And the glue that binds the major industrialized nations, all the way down to you, is the financial system backed by laws the Elite manipulate. So the model is consistent all the way down. But at the very bottom is the Earthling identified by NAME and BIRTH DATE.

On March 9, 1933 in the House 73rd Congress, Session I, Chapter I, page # 83, 1st paragraph, third sentence it states: *'Under the new law, the money is issued to the banks in return for government obligations, bills of exchange, drafts, notes, trade acceptances, and banker's acceptances. The money will be worth 100 cents on the dollar, because it is backed by the credit of the nation. It will represent a mortgage on all the homes and other property of all the people in the nation.'* The credit is you. You are the real creditor.

The commercial system of laws has been implemented through the Uniform Commercial Code, called a UCC in the U.S. That is hooked to every real being with original freedoms, into being a citizen under the 14th Amendment or a person a fictional overlay called a Strawman. The Bills of Exchange Act in Canada, for example is what commercial transactions are based on. If you look at the physical things on the planet and how these are proved to be owned or traded, there is typically another commercial counterpart describing it.

Take a vehicle for example. Proof of ownership is a bill of sale. The way this is identified is through title, name or number. In this case it is a Certificate of Title. Whether it is equipment, land, timber, mining, crops, animals, industry, or you, or whatever, there is something to represent it in the commercial system and there is a license that hooks you to the laws surrounding it. All the lands held in trust for the people were transferred to the Bureau of Land Management (BLM) and hypothecated by the UNITED STATES to help pay the artificial debt to the international bankers. Public lands are now in the hands of the BLM. You now have to register with the BLM in order to graze cattle on public land. It has nearly become so expensive to register and pay the BLM for grazing cattle that it is prohibitive. Trademarks are registered with the Patent Office as are bar codes. When you go to the grocery store, all food products are now registered by a bar code.

Everything is registered and owned through a holding vessel- a counterpart fictional entity called a corporation or trust. And then the counterpart has specific laws attached to it that the real thing is subjected to. Can you fly a plane through the air without a license? How about a plane registration and number? How about a radio or television station? Can you still get free air for your tires at any service station? Not really, Why? Because you also have joined yourself to the counterpart that is regulated some laws.

In addition to the fictional corporate structure, there is another imaginary system associated with all the material things. We are actually dealing paper representations of things in the form of titles or names. The real thing is not really the focus anymore. It is the paper representing the real thing like a receipt that is crucial to the commercial transaction.. When you buy things, it is the bill of exchange - the receipt - that is the crucial item to the commercial laws. This trade transaction is the item that binds us, not the item.

There is little of real value in the system any more. You used to be able to own gold, called a gold certificate. Now, a dollar bill is backed by another title – your credit. And that is simply an accounting record of debt.

## "Money" Is A Record Of Debt

So money is a record of debt. Your credit is being used by others. Fictional law, called statutes, even says you can't use the credit. Did you know your credit even has a title? It actually has many titles, but namely Federal Reserve Notes. There are many others also, including Federal Reserve Bills, Federal Reserve Bonds, Checks, Bills of Exchange, Trade Acceptances, Sight Drafts, Documentary Drafts, Judgments, and ANY AND EVERY BILL THAT YOU RECEIVE. Every bill that you receive is like a Federal Reserve Note. It is called a bill of exchange and falls under the Bills of Exchange Act. These *'bills'* are a record of the credit that has been accounted for against you.

That means under the bankruptcy deal, the nations had a free license to print what looks like money but is really like a line of credit drawing down more debt. The receiver and the system is there to make sure everything is accounted for in this imaginary fictional system of entities like the Strawmen and paper. It is like a parallel hologram. And like the top-down model of Strawmen, there is a fictional system of laws and money along with it.

And of course, we agree to buy into this model. But as a little diversion here, let us delve into how the local banking system works.

The local banking system has evolved in a similar fashion where the people have no idea of the nature of the deception that they perpetrate on people. The deception process is so ingrained that it is simply believed that they are following the law. The humor, if you can get a chuckle out of it, is that the deception goes so deep, the whole banking world we deal with think everything they do is legal, proper and above board. They believe the banks are doing you a huge favor with their loans, credit and services. Yet they are actually defrauding people, deceiving them and indulging in criminal activities.

Let's go through a typical real estate purchase and sale. Let us say you and a seller have signed the agreement of purchase and sale. You, the buyer, go to the bank because they lend money in accordance with their corporate charter. Does the bank tell you that they have assets or money to lend? Well, no. They are a bank. Why would you even ask? Right. But the truth is that it does not have any money to lend, and they are not permitted to use their depositors' money to lend to their borrowers. Do they tell you that? No, they are a bank you say regulated by laws of banking. You give your faith and trust out to them freely.

The bank makes you sign a mortgage loan application form which is essentially a promissory note. That means you promise to pay the bank for the money you are supposed to receive from the bank. You did this even before any value or consideration is received by you from the bank. This promissory note is an instant valuable consideration for them. It is a receivable and therefore an asset transferred from you to the bank. The bank can now enter this into its own asset account as a cash deposit.

After making sure that you have the ability to pay the required monthly payments, the bank agrees to lend you the money to pay the seller. But the bank has no money to lend, yet it gave you a promise to lend money by way of a commitment letter, loan approval letter, loan authorization or loan confirmation letter signed by a bank official.

It goes deeper. Anyway, they don't need it. It is an electronic entry on a balance sheet. Follow me here. Let us complete the transaction. The bank's acceptance of your promissory note made the bank liable to you for the full face value of the promissory note which is the agreed purchase price of the property, less any cash deposit or down payment money paid by you directly to the seller. It is important to note at this point that all real estate transactions require the property being sold to be conveyed by the seller to you free of all liens and encumbrances. This means that all liens such as existing mortgages and judgments must be paid before the property can be mortgaged by the buyer. The property is to be collateral to the mortgage loan which is yet to be received by the buyer pursuant to the promise made by the bank. So let me ask you this. How can the seller obtain clear title if he has not yet received any money from you? And how can you mortgage a property that does not yet belong to you?

This dilemma is solved using the bank's standard procedure. The bank, in concert with their lawyers cause all the liens and encumbrances to disappear by using a check drawn in the name of the bank backed by your promissory note and the agreement of purchase and sale. This check is deposited into the lawyer's trust account. In essence, the bank and its lawyers used your promissory note as the cash to enable the purchase agreement.

So it was your promissory note that made the conveyance possible. The bank caused the property to be conveyed to me from the seller with clear title, free and clear of all liens and encumbrances. Technically the property now belongs to you which makes it possible for you to mortgage the property to the bank. This means you paid for it using my own promissory note. It is because you are really the creditor.

The bank and its lawyers must perform another step in order to satisfy the seller's requirement to get paid or the whole deal is null and void. The seller does not even know that the property had been conveyed to your name in order for the seller to receive any money. Everything is in this La-La land in transition, right? The ensuing step is accomplished this way. You are made to sign another promissory note. The mortgage contract is attached to the bottom of the promissory note which makes you liable to pay the bank for the money or the loan which you have not yet or will never receive for up to twenty five years or more depending on the amortization term of the mortgage contract. This note is linked to the collateral through the mortgage contract and as such, it is valuable to the bank.

The bank then goes to the Bank of Canada or to another bank through its accomplice, the Canadian Payment Association, to pledge the deal that they have just gotten from you for credit. The Bank of Canada then gives the bank the so called credit. Remember, it is not the bank's credit, it's your credit. You promised to pay the bank if and when the money is received by you from the bank, payable for up to twenty-five years or more. What happened is basically a swap. This is a transaction all banks do to *'monetize'* security. In this case, the second promissory note that is linked to the mortgage contract and signed by you is a mortgage backed security.

The bank will then agree to pay the Bank of Canada a certain percentage of interest over prime. Thus your loan package goes to the Bank of Canada which credits the bank with the full amount of credit. This is the total amount of the money the bank is entitled to receive after twenty-five years, the amount of the principal plus all the interest payments you have promised to pay to the bank for twenty-five years or more. This is usually three times the amount of the money promised by the bank to you. By magic, the bank just enriched itself and got paid in advance, without using or risking its own money.

So now the bank's lawyer, who holds the check that is backed by my original promissory note, can cut a check to the seller as payment for the property. In effect, I paid the seller with my own money by virtue of the fact that it was my own money, namely the promissory note that made the purchase and sale possible. So they made a cool three hundred percent profit without using or risking any capital of their own. Neither was there any depositor's money deducted from the bank's asset account in this transaction.

What really happened was allegedly deception that if you tried, would land you in jail guilty of fraud and criminal conversion not to mention that the subject property would have been seized by the court. This would be an indictable crime if we issued a check with no funds. There would not be any deal and no purchase or sale agreement because there is no valuable consideration. In order to de-criminalize the transaction, we need the bank and their cohorts to make the deal happen. It is really a conspiracy of sorts but these *'persons'*, the banks, the lawyers, the land title offices and even the courts do not consider the transaction as fraudulent because the transactions happen all the time and all the monkeys accept this as the law; and the way it is done.

But think about this. Is it not so that such a contract is *void ab-initio* or void from the beginning, which means that the contract never took place in the first place? Moreover, the good faith and fair dealing requirement through full disclosure is non-existent which further voids the contract. The bank failed to disclose to me that it will not be giving me any valuable consideration and taking interest back as additional benefit to unjustly enrich the corporation. The bank also failed to disclose how much profit they are going to make on the deal.

The bank led you to believe that the money going to the seller would be coming from its own asset account. They lied because they knew or ought to have known that their own ledger would show that the bank does not have any money to lend and that their records will show that no such loan transaction ever took place. Their own books should show that there would be no debits from the bank's asset account at all and all that would show up are the two entries made when you gave the bank the first collateral or the promissory note. This enabled the bank to cut a check that made it possible to convey the property from seller to you free and clear of all liens or encumbrances as required by the agreement of purchase and sale entered into in writing between you and the seller. In reality, your promissory note was used by the bank and its lawyers and land title clerks to convey free title to you from the seller. So why do we need the mortgage contract?

It is because we have been led to believe this is the way things are done. And even though there are a lot of people that have become aware of it and are trying to do something about it, this is a pretty big dragon as it connects with some big guns, the Elite power group that controls banking. So who is going to take them on? There are many that are aware of this and there are many groups trying to do something but as of now, such has not been accomplished because you are playing against a very skilled stacked deck. If you oppose this you risk being pictured as radicals trying to beat the system for personal gain and the people believe it because the people have no information that paints a different picture. But the big picture that controls nations is not much different.

Yes, this may be a pretty dismal picture of how these Elite bankers have placed the chains around nations and people. The Elite bankers learned how to manipulate nations the same way. And now, with the way you can create so-called money with a keystroke, and everybody flocking to an even more imaginary hologram of money, it all plays into their hands.

So the debts incurred by nations are no different than a debt you could have with your local bank. Even though they have defrauded you, if you can't pay, they take since you are in their jurisdiction of contract law. If you can't pay, then the receiver is called in and you have to make a deal. You, like a nation, made a deal under the so called law; a contract in commerce, and you have to deal with the consequences.

You need to be aware of who you are. You need to understand what jurisdiction you fall under. Let us go back to the U.S. situation for a moment. In 1871, did *we the people* fall under the jurisdiction of this private government? No. Only those who lived in the jurisdiction of Washington, D.C., its territories and the 14$^{th}$ Amendment slaves did. This did not touch *we the people*. They were still enforcing the Original Jurisdiction and had the authority to do so. The original private corporate government back in 1789 was established on certain principles and rules, but as we've seen, it went through a bankruptcy almost right away, and with each stage of the bankruptcy there was reorganization. A reorganization creates a new set of circumstances, and probably a new set of creditors, masters and rules in order to discharge the old bankruptcy. Roughly every twenty years they had a re-organization to deal with and the banking system got entrenched. Each time they got different changes in the rules and regulations, and it just went on and on. The proprietors and creditors of that private law forum, as it goes into worse and worse bankruptcy, create tighter and tighter rules in order to raise the revenue to keep the thing going. That is what you see today.

## Relevance To Canada and Other Nations

Other nations are colonial holdings of the British Crown. The federal reserve banking system and the central banks are all a product of the 14th amendment, a breach of trust that began in America and has tainted the entire world. That is why this is a global event. Everyone can use this pass thru account to discharge debt all over the world. This is simply about redeeming your estate and returning it to solvency. That debt belongs to the federal reserve.

August 15, 1931, the United Kingdom of Great Britain and Ireland abrogated its power and authority over the Dominion of Canada as a British Colony by issuing the Statute of Westminster to Canada on that date. On October 1, 1949, King George VI executed by edict a Royal Proclamation of the Dominion of Canada to reclaim Canada as a British Colony. In this way the British recaptured the Dominion of Canada as their new colony and once again were able to re-exercise their original Power and Authority over the Dominion of Canada, as a British Colony. This is why the Bank of Canada to this day is still financially controlled by the Bank of England, a privately owned financial institution. So the private bankers of England actually recaptured Canada.

On October 11, 1949, King George VI cancelled the original Statute of Westminster of 1931, and re-established a new governor general in the Dominion of Canada within the new colony retroactive to October 1, 1949. King George used a little known International Salvage law to reclaim the Dominion of Canada because by this law he could pronounce that he had found the Dominion of Canada floating on the high seas of debt. Since no one objected or protested, Great Britain simply reacquired, by legal assumption, the Dominion of Canada as their new colony! It was all re-claimed unbeknown to people.

From this type of behavior it is very plain to understand what is implied by certain judges loyal to the crown of England when they say that '*We've got what it takes, to take what you've got*'. So this is why we are also actually slaves and the king or queen is today the master of our financial destiny in Canada.

And to carry this further, this is why Canada was the fifth most indebted nation on the planet. It was to the Bank of England. This is why Canada today as a debtor has already had the first step of foreclosure placed on her by her creditor, the International Monetary Fund during the 1995/6 federal fiscal year. And you know the IMF is a sister bank to the Bank of England.

So Canadians have hocked absolutely everything. But one cannot be so quick as to blame your current government as they are just as uninformed as you. The political systems in our countries play musical politics and there is no financial continuity, or responsibility between administrations. The debt is status quo and issues are always more of a local, petty nature. How would you like to change the board of directors and top management in your company every three years? Everybody is sleeping with regard to the bigger financial picture.

## Moving Higher In The Corporate Pyramid

Now, let us get back to move up in the pyramid. I mentioned this before but let me run through it again because it may make more sense to you now. The IRS, the receiver of the bankruptcy, is an agency of the IMF and the IMF is an agency of the UN. In Canada, as you have noted, you have a *'receiver'* of revenue. The U.S. has not had a treasury since 1921 because the U.S. treasury is now the IMF. The U.S. has operated under bankruptcy for over two hundred years. The FCC, CIA, FBI, NASA and all of the other alphabet gangs were never part of the United States government. They are the policing systems of the IMF, even though the U.S. government held shares of stock in the various agencies.

The U.S. social security numbers are issued by the UN through the IMF. According to the rules, you must have a social security number. The application for a social security number is the SS5 form issued by the Department of the Treasury that is really the IMF. There are no judicial courts in America and there has not been any since 1789. Judges do not enforce statutes and codes. Executive administrators enforce statutes and codes. There have not been any real judges in America since 1789. There have really been administrators.

The social security check comes directly from the IMF. You own no property because slaves can't own property. Read the deed to the property that you think is yours. You are listed as a tenant. America is a British colony, as is Canada. The UNITED STATES is a corporation not a land mass and it existed before the revolutionary war. Go and check these things out for yourself.

The real power is from outside of North America because we have not handled our financial affairs. The government has to conform to the bankruptcy agreement and the agencies like the FBI, IRS, CRA are the alien collectors that do not belong to the country. In truth they are responsible indirectly to the Jesuit Military Order. The law system is there to support them and the police force is there to enforce them. That is why the banks and agencies have so much power.

Britain is owned by the Vatican through the Treaty of 1213. The Pope can abolish any law in the United States. The Pope claims to own the entire planet through the laws of conquest and discovery. The Pope has ordered the genocide and enslavement of millions of people and the Pope's laws are obligatory on everyone. We have accepted being slaves and own absolutely nothing, not even our children. It is not the duty of the police to protect you. Their real job is to protect the corporation and arrest code breakers. We are human capital by Executive Order 13037. The UN has financed the operations of the United States government and now owns every man, women and child in America. The UN also holds all of the physical land in America in *'fee simple'*. And the binding threads are the system of commerce. Commerce is enacted through the Bank Act and the Bill of Exchange Act. These are the most powerful acts around.

Now we need to revisit the Crown temple and look at these Elite. The Crown Temple is not the Queen of England or the royal families of Britain. The Templar Church has been known for centuries by the world as the *'Crown'*. It is really a secret society for the Third Way Order. The Templars of the Crown is the domain of the black priests that are reflected in the black robes worn by our judges stemming from the days of Babylon. The crown, in reality, is the Crown Temple or Crown Templar. All three are synonymous. This is not the crown of England, or what we think is the queen. Indeed the queen is indeed part of this.

The Temple Church was built by the Knights Templar in two parts. The first part was the Round and the Chancel. The Round Church was consecrated in 1185 and modeled after the circular Church of the Holy Sepulcher in Jerusalem. The Chancel was built in 1240. The Temple Church serves both the Inner and Middle Temples and is located between Fleet Street and Victoria on the embankment at the Thames river. Its grounds also house the crown offices at Crown Office Row. This Temple Church is actually outside any canonical jurisdiction. The master of the temple is appointed and takes his place by sealed, non-public patent, without induction or institution.

The present queen of England is not the crown as you and everyone else thought, or have been led to believe. Rather, it is the bankers and attornies; you know them as attorneys, who are the actual crown or Crown Temple. The monarch aristocrats of England have not been ruling sovereigns since the reign of King John, around 1215. All royal sovereignty of the old British crown since that time has passed to the Crown Temple in Chancery. You know now that the U.S. and Canada are not the free and sovereign nations that our defacto federal governments tell us they are. Their fictional counterparts are part of the big corporate structure and the slaves comply with the laws on the structure. You know now that our federal governments are bankrupt corporations, pretending to serve the people, while they truly serve a different master, called the crown.

The banks rule the Temple Church and the attorners carry out their orders by controlling their victim's judiciary. Political minions to serve the banking cartel and the crown are chosen not elected. Since the first chancel of the Temple Church was built by the Knights Templar, this is not a new ruling system by any means.

The chancel, or chancery of the Crown Inner Temple Court was where King John was in January 1215 when the English barons demanded that he confirm the rights enshrined in the Magna Charta. This London temple was the headquarters of the Templar Knights in Great Britain where order and rule were first made and which became known as code. Here a manipulative body of Elite bankers and attorners from the independent city of London carved out the law of the world that imposes the legal, and a totally unlawful system of contracts, upon the real people of this planet. This is called the *'color of law'*, the fictional system that you are becoming familiar with.

It's very important to know how the British royal crown was placed into the hands of the Knights Templars, and how the Crown Templars became the fiscal and military agents for the Pope of the Roman Church. This all becomes very clear through the concession of England to the Pope on May 15, 1213. This charter was sworn in fealty by England's King John to Pope Innocent and the Roman Church. It was witnessed before the Crown Templars. King John stated upon sealing this: '*I myself bearing witness in the house of the Knights Templars*'. Pay particular attention to the words being used that we have defined below, especially charter, fealty, demur, and concession: '*We wish it to be known to all of you, through this our charter, furnished with our seal, not induced by force or compelled by fear, but of our own good and spontaneous will and by the common counsel of our barons, do offer and freely concede to God and His holy apostles Peter and Paul and to our mother the holy Roman church, and to our lord Pope Innocent and to his Catholic successors, the whole kingdom of England and the whole kingdom of Ireland, with all their rights and appurtenances. We perform and swear fealty for them to him our aforesaid lord Pope Innocent, and his Catholic successors and the Roman church. Binding our successors and our heirs by our life forever, in similar manner to perform fealty and show homage to him who shall be chief pontiff at that time, and to the Roman church without demur. As assign, we will and establish perpetual obligation and concession. From the proper and especial revenues of our aforesaid kingdoms. The Roman church shall receive yearly a thousand pounds sterling. Saving to us and to our heirs our rights, liberties and regalia; all of which things, as they have been described above, we wish to have perpetually valid and firm; and we bind ourselves and our successors not to act counter to them. And if we or any one of our successors shall presume to attempt this, whoever he be, unless being duly warned he come to his kingdom, and this senses, shall lose his right to the kingdom, and this charter of our obligation and concession shall always remain firm'.*

It is an oath of allegiance from feudal times. Most who have commented on this charter only emphasize the payments due the Pope and the Roman church. What should be emphasized is the fact that King John broke the terms of this charter by signing the Magna Charta on June 15, 1215. The penalty for breaking the 1213 agreement was the loss of the crown or right to the kingdom to the Pope and his Roman church. It says so quite plainly. To formally and lawfully take the crown from the royal monarchs of England by an act of declaration, on August 24, 1215, Pope Innocent III annulled the Magna Charta. Later in the year, he placed an interdict, meaning prohibition, on the entire British Empire. From that time until today, the English monarchy and the entire British crown belonged to the Pope. By swearing to the 1213 charter in fealty, King John declared that the British-English crown and its possessions at that time, including all future possessions, estates, trusts, charters, letters patent, and land, were forever bound to the Pope and the Roman church, the landlord.

Some five hundred years later, the New England colonies in America became a part of the crown as a possession and trust named the United States. By agreeing to the Magna Charta, King John had broken the agreement terms of his fealty with Rome and the Pope. What that means is that he lost all rights to the kingdom, and the royal English crown was turned over by default to the Pope and the Roman church. The Pope and his Roman church control the Crown Temple because his Knights established it under his orders. So also the Temple banks, the Templar attorneys, the corporate United States, the corporate British Commonwealth, the chartered Federal Reserve Bank and Bank of England. The list is pretty impressive. He who controls the gold controls the world. This is the Crown Temple today. Is it clearer now how the legal system and the attorneys are the unknowing spies for the system?

This is simply due to the fact that all Bar Associations throughout the world are signatories and franchises to the International Bar Association located at the *'Inns of Court'* at Crown Temple, which are physically located at Chancery Lane behind Fleet Street in London. Although they vehemently deny it, all BAR associations in the world, such as the American Bar Association, the Florida Bar, or California Bar Association, are franchises to the Crown. This would involve all Canadian Bar associations as well; indeed the world! The Inns of Court and The Four Inns of Court to the Crown Temple use the banking and judicial system of the city of London. It is a sovereign and independent territory which is not a part of Great Britain. This is Washington City, as DC was called in the 1800's, is not a part of the north American states, nor is it a state. It was done this way to administer and control the people. These Fleet Street bankers and lawyers work everywhere under the guise and *'color of law'*. They are known collectively as the crown. Their lawyers are actually Templar Bar attornies, not lawyers.

We are then actually dictated to by the Crown Temple through its bankers and attornies. We are all controlled and manipulated by this private foreign power and our federal government is their mechanism. The bankers and Bar attorneys of the world are franchises in oath and allegiance to the Crown at Chancery - the Crown Temple church and its Chancel located at Chancery Lane. So the legal system or judiciary of North America is controlled by the Crown Temple from the independent and sovereign City of London.

The private Federal Reserve System, which issues fiat U.S. Federal Reserve notes, is financially owned and controlled by the crown from Switzerland, the home and legal origin for the charters of the United Nations, the International Monetary Fund, the World Trade Organization, and most importantly, the Bank of International Settlements. The governmental and judicial systems within all public jurisdictions at federal, local and state/provincial levels are owned by the crown. Note that this is a privately owned corporate foreign power operating in defacto. All licensed Bar attorneys in the world owe their allegiance and give their solemn oath in pledge to the Crown Temple whether they realize this or not. Once again, look to the real meaning of words. Crown means imperial, regal power or dominion - sovereignty. There is a power behind the crown greater than the crown itself.

This is why we have crown land, land belonging to the crown, that is, to the sovereign, or Crown law, the law which governs criminal prosecutions, or Crown lawyer, one employed by the crown, as in criminal cases.

Associated with the Crown are the Four Inns of Court to the Temple. In England, the temples are two Inns of Court, being original dwellings of the Knights Templar. They are called the Inner and the Middle Temple. In England, there is a college of municipal or common law professors and students. Formerly the town-house of a nobleman, bishop or other distinguished personage, it was where they resided when they attended the court. The Inns of Court were colleges in which students of law reside and are instructed. The principals are the Inner Temple, the Middle Temple, Lincoln's Inn, and Gray's Inn. Inns of Chancery are colleges in which young students formerly began their law studies. These are now occupied chiefly by attorneys, solicitors, and the like. This is where the legalistic architecture is designed to promote the exclusive monopoly of the Temple Bar. These Inns/Temples are exclusive and private country clubs, occupied by secret societies of world power in commerce. They are well established, some having been founded in the early 1200's when the Templars rose to power. The Queen of England is a current member of both the Inner Temple and Middle Temple. Gray's Inn specializes in taxation legalities by rule and code for the Crown.

Lincoln's Inn received its name from the Third Earl of Lincoln around 1300. Just like all other franchise Bar Associations, none of the Four Inns of the Temple are incorporated, for a definite and purposeful reason. You can't make claim against a non-entity and a non-being. They are private societies without charters or statutes, and their so-called constitutions are based solely on custom and self-regulation. In other words, they exist as secret societies without a public front door unless you're a private member called to their Bar. While the Inner Temple holds the legal system franchise by license to steal from Canada and Great Britain, it is the Middle Temple that has legal license to steal from America. This comes about directly via their Bar Association franchises to the Honourable Society of the Middle Temple through the Crown Temple.

From the book **The History of the Inn** as written by the **Honorable Society of the Middle Temple**, we can see a direct tie to the Bar Association franchises and its crown signatories in America. A '*Call to the Bar*' or keeping terms in one of the four Inns is a pre-requisite to call at King's Inns until late in the 19th century. In the 17th and 18th centuries, students came from the American colonies and from many of the West Indian islands. The Inn's records would lead one to suppose that for a time there was hardly a young gentleman in Charleston who had not studied here.

You may think that Americans are pretty smart people so how did they get tricked way back then. By what authority has this crown suckered the natural sovereignty of the people? Is it acceptable that the supreme court decides on constitutional issues? How can it be considered in any manner as being constitutional when this same supreme court is appointed by (not elected) and paid by the '*defacto*' federal governments?

Well, to answer this you need to go back in time. Five of the signatories to the Declaration of Independence were Middle Templars, and notwithstanding it and its consequences, Americans continued to come here until the War of 1812. All Bar Association licensed attorneys must keep the terms of their oath to the Crown Temple in order to be accepted or be '*called to the Bar*' at any of the King's Inns. Their oath, pledge, and terms of allegiance are made to the Crown Temple. That is the way it is and the people are well conditioned to abide by this tradition. It's a real eye opener to know that the Middle Inn of the Crown Temple has publicly acknowledged there were at least five Templar Bar attornies, under solemn oath only to the Crown, who signed what was alleged to be an American Declaration of Independence. This simply means that both parties to the Declaration agreement were of the same origin, the Crown Temple. In case you don't understand the importance of this, there is no international agreement or treaty that will ever be honored, or will ever have lawful effect, when the same party signs as both the first and second parties. It's merely a worthless piece of paper with no lawful authority when both sides to any agreement are actually the same. In reality, the American Declaration of Independence and the Canadian Constitution Act and Bill of Rights are nothing more than an internal memo of the Crown Temple, made among its private members.

It means that the top Americans were fooled into believing that the legal crown colonies comprising New England were independent nation states, but they never were nor are today. They were and still are colonies of the Crown Temple, through letters patent and charters, who have no legal authority to be independent from the Rule and Order of the Crown Temple. That means neither the American people nor the queen of Britain own America. The Crown Temple owns America through the deception of those who have sworn their allegiance by oath to the Middle Templar Bar. The crown bankers and their Middle Templar attornies rule America through commerce, contracts, taxes, and contract documents of equity through debt. These are all strictly enforced by their orders, rules and codes of the Crown Temple Courts, our so-called judiciary in America. This is because the Crown Temple holds the land titles and estate deeds to all of North America.

But the highest or most comprehensive loss of status for humanity occurred when a human's condition was changed from one of freedom to one of bondage and became a slave. It swept away with it all rights of citizenship and all family rights. With the all capital names they converted everyone from the common lawful human of God into a fictional, legal, slave entity, subject to administration by State rules, orders and codes. People simply accepted being the corporations and accepting the liabilities and corporate charters. There is no law within any rule or code that applies to the lawful common human of the Lord. You know now that the human with inherent Godly law and rights must be converted into a legal person of fictional status in order for their legal - but completely unlawful - State Judiciary (Chancery Courts) to have authority over them.

This may seem like some more science fiction, but this is where this story ends about who the '*bad guys'* are. Really there are no bad guys because we all just simply allowed this to be by being outsmarted by accepting their game. Take a closer look at the one dollar private federal reserve system debt note that is part of a crown banking franchise. As stated before, there is no real money! There is only worthless fiat paper that the Federal Reserve can create or the U.S. government can create as a debt tally! Notice in the base of the pyramid the Roman date MDCCLXXVI written in Roman numerals for the year 1776. The words ANNUIT COEPTIS NOVUS ORDO SECLORUM are Roman Latin for ANNOUNCING

THE BIRTH OF THE NEW ORDER OF THE WORLD. The year 1776 signifies the birth of the New World Order under the Crown Temple. That's when the American crown colonies became the chartered governments called the United States. Since that date, the United Nations, another legal Crown Temple component by charter, rose up as a member. Note also that there are thirteen layers for the pyramid denoting the thirteen chartered colony-states and then there is he all seeing eye of Osirus. This was one of many Templar signs used, reflecting the Temple Illuminati or their Order of the Rose and Order of the Cross, names of the Elite controllers.

There is no mystery behind what some see as the current abomination of Babylon for those who study the Bible. It states in Revelation 17:5: *And upon her forehead was a name written, Mystery, Babylon the Great, the Mother of Harlots and Abominations of the Earth.* Looks like God reserved His judgment for this great idolatress. Rome was the chief seat of all idolatry that ruled over many nations with whom the kings have committed to the worship of her idols. What about the Pope and his purported church sitting on the temple throne at the Vatican, ruling the nations of the earth through the Crown Temple of ungodly deities? Does the rule and order of Babylon using the crown of Godlessness and the code of commerce carry on the tradition? If you want proof, look to the Bills of Exchange Act or the Uniform Commercial Code. They are the true bibles for the crown - and Babylon.

The Elite Rulers operate in the private domain through clubs and cults that can nowhere be mapped like any traditional organization. It, like the Matrix, is an invisible structure of that they abide by as heartless control freaks bound by initiation and bloodline. One may call the Elite rule of the world today by many names such as the New World Order, the Third Way, the Illuminati, Triad, Triangle, Trinity, Masonry, the United Nations, or many other names. However, they all point to one origin and one beginning. Many have traced this in history to the Crown Temple, the Temple Church created around 1200. The bloodline has been tracked even further back. But all world banking, judiciary, and rule of law has been under the Rule and Order of the Crown Temple since 1200. Because the various Popes created the Order of the Temple Knights and established their mighty Temple Church in the sovereign city of London, you can assume it is the Pope and his Roman followers who have a pretty serious interest in the control the world.

If there is any reason to bring further information into your mind, the most prolific and dedicated *'hunter'* of the Illuminati is a fellow named David Icke. You can find this impressive lad on **www.davidicke.com**. He has written many books on them and he is the world authority on this topic. All of what I have told you is clearly documented in his work. Another well known tracker is **Edward Griffin** who details how the Federal Reserve was created and who are behind it **www.realityzone.com** in a book "**The Creature from Jekyll Island – A Second look at the Federal Reserve'.**"

Let us go back to the whore of Babylon where it states "*And the woman was arrayed in purple and scarlet color, and decked with gold and precious stones and pearls, having a golden cup in her hand full of abominations and filthiness of her fornicatio*" in Revelation 17:4. This verse appears to be an accurate description of the Pope and his Bishops for the past seventeen hundred years. The idolatries of commerce in the world are all the gold and silver, the iron and soft metals, the money and coins and riches of the world. All of these are under the control of the Crown Temple. Here we have the Roman king and his false church, the throne of Babylon attended to by his Templar Knights, and all the wizards of abomination and idolatry.

And in conjunction with commerce is religion that has been anything but man's salvation and has been directly responsible for mass death and destruction. Take the 1611 King James Bible that you see everywhere. By the way, note that King James was a Crown Templar. This is not the entire canon of the early church. It has been edited. Guess who the editors were? There were other gospels and books that have been forbidden by the Papal Throne at Rome since the third century. Greek and Aramaic copies of the *'unapproved writings'* were sought after and destroyed by Rome. This in itself is no mystery as history records the existence and destruction of these early church writings, just as history has now proven their genuine authenticity with the appearance of the Dead Sea Scrolls and the Coptic library at Nag Hagmadi in Egypt, among many other recent Greek language discoveries within the past hundred years. The current Holy Bible quotes the Book of Enoch numerous times: *"By faith Enoch was taken away so that he did not see death, and was not found, because God had taken him; for before he was taken he had this testimony, that he pleased God."* This is in Hebrews 11:5. Now Enoch, the seventh from Adam, prophesied about these men also, saying, *"Behold, the Lord comes with ten thousands of His saints, to execute judgment on all, to convict all who are ungodly among them of all their ungodly deeds which they have committed in an ungodly way, and of all the harsh things which ungodly sinners have spoken against Him."* Check out Jude 1:14-15.

The Book of Enoch was considered scripture by most early Christians. The earliest literature of the so-called church fathers is filled with references to this mysterious book. The second century Epistle of Barnabus makes much use of the Book of Enoch. Second and third century church fathers, such as Justin Martyr, Irenaeus, Origin, and Clement of Alexandria, all make use of the Book of Enoch. Tertullian, around 160-230 BC, called the Book of Enoch a Holy Scripture. The Ethiopic Church included the Book of Enoch in its official canon. It was widely known and read the first three centuries after Christ. However, this and many other books became discredited after the Roman Council of Laodicea. They were under ban of the Roman papal authorities and afterwards they gradually passed out of circulation. At about the time of the Protestant Reformation, there was a renewed interest in the Book of Enoch, which had long since been lost to the modern world. By the late 1400's, rumors began to spread that a copy of the long lost Book of Enoch might still exist.

During the 1400's, many books arose claiming to be the lost book but were later found to be forgeries. The return of the Book of Enoch to the modern western world is credited to the famous explorer James Bruce, who in 1773 returned from six years in Abyssinia with three Ethiopic copies of the lost book. In 1821, Richard Laurence published the first English translation. The now famous R.H. Charles edition was first published by Oxford Press in 1912. In the following years, several portions of the Greek text also surfaced. Then, with the discovery of cave number four of the Dead Sea Scrolls, seven fragmentary copies of the Aramaic text were discovered. So you see, the Popes and their buddies have all through history created many other '*bibles*' and '*scriptures*' written to change the words or meaning to what *they* wanted to preach. What is coming out now is that the real stuff is very different. So all along, there has been an illusion of the spiritual box to keep the people powerless and subservient to God or at least their gods.

In fact, GOD is another fictional entity created by the Vatican to take possession of the Souls of humans. .

For everything created, there appears to be a fictitious imitation that looks like the genuine thing. There is the knowledge of good and the knowledge of evil. The problem is most believe they have the knowledge of God when what they really have is knowledge of world deceptions operating as Gods. Where there is the true Tabernacle or Temple of God, there are also the false Temples of unholy Gods. The only way to discern and begin to understand the Kingdom of Heaven is to seek the knowledge that comes only from God, not the knowledge of men who take their legal claim as earthly rulers and Gods. The false Crown Temple and its grand wizard knights have led the world to believe that they are of the lord God and hold the knowledge and keys to his kingdom. What they hold within their Temples are the opposite. They claim to be the holy church, but which holy church? The real one or the false one? Are the Pope and his Roman Church the Temple of God, or is this the unholy Temple of Babylon sitting upon the seven mountains? They use the same words but alter them to show the true meaning they have applied. The State is not a state. A Certificate is not a certification. The Roman Church is not the church (ekklesia). There is the Crown of the Lord and a Crown of that which is not of the Lord. There is the mark and seal of the Lord God and there are the Marks and Seals of the false Gods. All imitations appear to be the genuine article, but they are fakes. Which one are you now going to believe?

So the Popes have been pretty clever at overlaying another invisible deception that looks like the real thing. To really understand how the people have just followed it is because they deep down believe in God and want to be led. It is only when a new awareness is floods through us to become enlightened the same way and together and it is the intent of us all that will change this. We must not moan about deception because we accepted this fate.

If you reduce this down to simple terms, these guys at the top are just smart businessmen aren't they? They invented commerce so they are smarter. When the U.S. went bankrupt, they had the opportunity to take over and of course the guy who is bankrupt gets a crappy deal. But from then on, the spies and cronies are there to police their interests. So who is the bad guy? Is it the U.S. or Canadian government? Not really. The power is outside of the U.S. and the agencies of the IMF are the ones that really police their deal. And that is no different than the deal you would have to make if you went bankrupt personally and made a deal to pay off the debt.

And here is the bitter reality. The present wealth and power of all the world's gold, silver, tin, bronze, pearls, diamonds, gemstones, iron, and copper as belonged to the Babylon whore, are held in the treasuries of her Crown Templar banks and deep stony vaults. They have accumulated the hard treasures that once used to give real value to money. They control the real things and they control the fake things. Pretty good take-over strategy, wouldn't you say?

So this time something pretty major has to happen to break this. We can never pay off the debt so it's a pretty crappy deal but that's the way it is. Short of a world revolution, how can this be fixed? We all inherited it. Who is aware of it? And who cares? If you have food in your tummy and a place to sleep, who cares? As long as you believe you have money and can use this paper to get food and housing plus toys to play with, you probably don't care about it. So as they siphon your energy and essence, and keep you financially beholding, they continue to keep you from finding out who you are and what powers you have as a piece of God. But as you sit in front of the TV with your beer, drive off to work every day, deal with your creditors and feel *'whole'* are you not missing the point? What about being a part of God and co-creating your own destiny. What about building a life away from this Matrix that develops your full power and potential? What about this crippling debt that controls everyone?

Things become different because of the awareness. First is to realize the truth. If one of your creditors went bankrupt after owing you a lot of money and you made a deal that would continue to his children, would you or your inheritors of the deal enforce it? And what if you found out you got suckered into it? Would that change the picture? If you go through all I told you, which I think you now believe, you will find something to fight or move with. What is the choice? Those are questions you must answer for yourself. Then, are you happy about being fooled? Or did you fool yourself? Do you have a moral obligation? Are you content to live like you live now, in ignorance of a different "truth"? Now that you are aware of it, tell me how your gut feels about it?

The truth is that the Elite are marching to simply dominate the Empire and run things like a big corporation. Are they different than many corporations designed to fill the pockets of a few? Not really. Does it benefit you as a happier slave? And how did you get to be a slave? The story is not finished yet, now let us look at this corporate entity called a STRAWMAN that overlays the Eartling employees.

# 13

# THE FINAL CORPORATE OVERLAY: EARTHLINGS

And so it came to be that the process of capitalizing on the human capital to repay the debt of the nation had to be implemented. The corporate model of each Earthling as the fictional overlay was an appropriate way to do this. All that had to be done was that the human, like a nation under bankruptcy, needed to have a fictional counterpart that was subject to codes and laws that could be enforced. Once the humans accepted the rules and codes of the corporation as his responsibility, they would be subject to those codes of law. But how could this be done in a way that did not create rebellion? Here we will explain the story of the Strawman and how humanity, like the united states of America became subject to the corporate fiction UNITED STATES, accepted that responsibility without rebellion.

# Corporate Legal Fictions Overlay Real People

As has been discussed, Planet Earth has evolved kings and queens with their dynasties and kingdoms into the likes of CEO's and corporations. We have seen how this evolution has allowed those gods to retain their powers and we have eluded to the process of the same principle being applied to men and women. We see how a "citizen" and a "person" is not the real thing, only a representation of it. Such is a word. The word is not the real thing, it is a representation of it by a description of it. We have seen how "The Word" of a misrepresented God also represents intangible descriptions and rules than are attached to those who accept that word. This process has allowed the proliferation of a fictional world of corporations to flourish, and be accepted worldwide.

And so the evolution of the commercial system has involved the creation of "legal fictions". As we have already discussed, all one has to do is to look around to understand this more clearly; to think about a corporation or a business your work for, or have created yourself. The Name of the corporation like IBM, is a name only and it is not a living thing. It has real people within it that give it corporate life. Without the people it would be nothing. IBM, like any other corporation has purpose and a business charter, like the articles of incorporation which are its laws. It also has a conduct, purpose and code of behavior of the people that work within it. And as a CEO, Director, Founder of it, you may take on the responsibilities like the liabilities of it if you so agreed to. But you, outside of it have no liabilities and rules simply do not apply to you.

We have seen the elegant pyramid of corporate structures that overlay upon the real thing so as to make it look and feel the same. Yet it is not. We have seen how this structure of fictional entities has been deployed to effectively create a unity between the fiction and the real thing. And we have seen how this pyramid comes from the top Elite, down through the layers of nations, governments, states, districts, municipalities, towns, postal codes all the way down to you. How did you get caught in this process without knowing? It is the same as the 14th Amendment brought benefits to you as a "citizen". But that is not the whole of it because, remember, you are classified as "human capital". But how did these rules applied to these words get applied contractually to you? It is because of another fictional overlay classified as the Strawman.

What has evolved is the same system overlain upon each living individual. It works because we accept that this fictional corporation is us. And like Sole Proprietorship, we have assumed total responsibility for it. The difference is that the corporation is a Trust.

And so the story of the Strawman begins with the birth of a human. As the story goes, the Strawman is created with the hope that as the child grows up, he will be fooled into believing that he is actually the Strawman (which he most definitely is **not**) and pay all sorts of imaginary costs and liabilities which get attached to the Strawman.

Meriam-webster defines Strawman as a person set up as a cover for a usually questionable transaction. In Roman law, the word "persona" became used to refer to a role played in court, and it became established that it was the role rather than the actor that could have rights, powers, and duties, because different individuals could assume the same roles, the rights, powers, and duties followed the role rather than the actor, and each individual could act in more than one role, each a different "person" in law. Are you a person? Are you the live person? You can't be both any more than you can be a Trust or a Corporation.

In our current reality, the STRAWMAN is simply a corporation, trust or name given to a commercial entity for some purpose usually commercial. It is not live, it exists as a fictional tag which much like a corporation and the owner of it, the corporation has a set of rules and charters to abide by. How you as the owner, CEO, etc. decide to relate to those rules and liabilities is a choice, not a mandatory obligation. **So, what is a Strawman?** *A Strawman is a fictitious legal entity. But that is just another generic word, right? Well it is so but each of us has a personal Strawman, uniquely defined as our name and birthdate.*

As you have discovered, it was originally written into the Constitution that the jurisdiction of the federal government should be limited by making the people citizens of the state in which they were born or in which they lived. At this time the federal government only had jurisdiction over a person if they lived within Washington DC or any US territory. Taking on the regulations of your state or country is not exactly a big surprise, it's the same as taking on the rules of a corporation your work for to get a pay check.

It was after the Civil War that the 14th amendment was passed by the Federalists who took control of the government to protect "the former slaves." This amendment brought the former slaves under the jurisdiction of the Federal Government so that their constitutional rights could be protected by government. Many former slaves were receiving abuse from people as well as from local and state governments.

The 14th amendment might have protected these people from being oppressed by their neighbors but it gave them and us a new master the Federal Government. This amendment makes us citizens not only of our states but also it made us a citizen of the United States. This gave the Federal Government powers over the people that it had not known before. The 14th amendment also makes the debt of the Federal Government something we have no right to question. A citizen is a person owing loyalty to and entitled by birth or naturalization to the protection of a state or nation. Most people will receive their citizenship upon the acquisition of their Social Security card. But along with the Social Security Card came the obligation to pay Income Taxes.

We know this is true because of the necessity of a license, which is permission to break the law. If you were a FREE person why would you need a permission from any government to drive a vehicle, get married, start a business or even to do modifications to your home or property. You even need a license to hunt or fish as well.

## History Review Of The STRAWMAN

As we have come to know, the United States Of America has been completely bankrupt since 1933, and many times before but the "nail in the coffin" could be set at 1933. The Constitution requires the government to hold gold and silver as assets. That was taken away to be held by the private foreign corporations. The only actual producing asset left to the United States is its population. How does the country cover the costs of operation of the country?

What did the government come up with as a solution to this problem? The leaders were as a result of the forces of bankruptcy brought to a decision to collateralize the population for credit. How is this done? The people are registered in International Commerce, and the government sells bonds on them. The population becomes the security on the bond itself. The surety is the labour of the people which becomes payable as an undetermined future date. Instead of the people providing battery energy like in The Matrix movie, they provide the energy of capital. They are the human capital.

This makes the people the "utility for the transmission of energy". One could deduct that this results in a very sophisticated form of slavery that becomes our "birthright". The Constitution does not apply because the government, at every level becomes a part of international commerce, and this falls under the Uniform Commercial Code in which animals, in other words, humans and their offspring yet to be born become goods which are able to be sold in commerce. It is simply the way this has evolved because the leaders of nations have mismanaged their financial affairs the same way you or I if we mismanaged the affairs of our corporations would be at the mercy of the creditor assigned to the claim of bankruptcy. And in the game of bankruptcy are nations who have some very clever "creditors".

And so whenever a child is born into the jurisdiction of the UNITED STATES or CANADA, there is a birth certificate and a date that is registered with the Bureau of Vital Statistics in the state or province where the baby is born. When a child is registered it is thus registered into international commerce.

At the time that the birth certificate is registered, something else is created, a separate legal entity. It is a fictional entity called a Trust. It is identified by your name in CAPITAL LETTERS, also known as your Strawman. From now on this Trust will holds all titles to all assets while you the free born real human believes these are yours; but in reality, all you have is the limited right to use these things. They are limited because of the Laws, Statutes and acts that apply to the Corporation you are born under AND the laws that are applicable to the TRUST. How? It is because you have contracted this way, unknowingly perhaps, by way of your parents pledge. And so a new set of laws are applied to you because you accept this as so and you accept that the TRUST name and your name are the same.

When you, on behalf of your STRAWMAN break a law or violates a statute, like a traffic ticket the free born flesh and blood you have to appear at the arraignment. It is there that you are asked to accept the STRAWMAN's credit. This is so the real live you can provide the "energy surety" that is due in the way of fines and fees acquired while using the STRAWMAN.

This is why when before the court you are asked to voluntarily give up your name. The entity that is before the court is nothing more than a STRAWMAN. The real you is merely an offender on the offensive team until he agrees to join with the defense (the STRAWMAN) and becomes the defendant by acceptance.

When you were born your parents and the doctor became the pledgor of the birth certificate (Title) to the baby (YOU). The state becomes the owner of this pledge which is a pledge towards the future output (energy) of the child (YOU).

The state then converts this title of security document into a bond to be sold on open markets to cover the cost of government. The person who holds the bond becomes the secured party to receive the energy output of the child (YOU) in the future. The child (YOU) are merely the holder and possessor of the body only, you have no title. Your duty is to the secured party.

The existence and definition of a STRAWMAN should be obvious. It is nothing more than an artificial entity owned by the secured party who bought into the bond. The bonds are placed on the market by the Treasury of the United States.

You do not own your STRAWMAN. It is merely a front for the secured party in possession of the bond. Anything a STRAWMAN signs is to place title to property in the hands of the United States and the people who hold the bonds. A STRAWMAN is not set up so the child (You) can acquire property. That is because the child (YOU) do not hold the title to the STRAWMAN. All ownership of your STRAWMAN lies in the States and the bond owners.

The military government (democracy) has three tiers of leadership. First there is the Governor, followed by the

Secretary of State, and finally there is a Secretary of Treasury. It is the Secretary of State that retains the registration for the Democratic corporation. On the public side of registrations you have the "corporate filings" at the State and local levels. On the private side of filings you have the "Uniform Commercial Code filings" of the creditors to transactions.

The registration by the private creditor becomes the highest priority of recognition to a military state (Democracy). If there is not one registered then one is believed to be foreign with absolutely no rights public or private. The only rights you will have will be given by the military government in the form of Privileges.

Edward Mandell House had this to say in a private meeting with President Woodrow Wilson: ".... *soon, every American will be required to register their biological property in a national system designed to keep track of the people and that will operate under the ancient system of pledging. By such methodology, we can compel people to submit to our agenda, which will <u>effect</u> our security as a <u>chargeback</u> for our fiat paper currency. Every American will be forced to register or suffer being unable to work and earn a living. They will be our chattel, and we will hold the security interest over them forever, by operation of the law merchant under the scheme of secured transactions. Americans, by unknowingly or unwittingly delivering the bills of lading to us will be rendered bankrupt and insolvent, forever to remain economic slaves through taxation, secured by their pledges. They will be stripped of their rights and given a commercial value designed to make us a profit and they will be none the wiser, for not one man in a million could ever figure our plans and, if by accident one or two should figure it out, we have in our arsenal plausible deniability. After all, this is the only logical way to fund government, by floating liens and debt to the registrants in the form of benefits and privileges. This will inevitably reap to us huge profits beyond our wildest expectations and leave every American a contributor to* *this fraud which we will call "Social Insurance." Without realizing it, every American will insure us for any loss we may incur and in this manner, every American will unknowingly be our servant, however begrudgingly. The people will become helpless and without any hope for their redemption and, we will employ the high office of the President of our dummy corporation to foment this plot against America."*

## The Relation To The Constitution

The Constitution for the United States is a document of dual nature as it is a trust document, and it is the articles of incorporation and created a unique trust res and estate of inheritance. It is a tenant of law that in order to determine the intent of a writing one must look to the title, the Empowerment Clause in statute, which in the case of the Constitution is the Preamble. In writing the Constitution the founders followed the common law of England which stretches back some 1000 years. The Preamble fulfills the requirements necessary to establish a trust. It identifies the Grantor(s), Statement of Purpose, Grantee(s), Statement of Intent, Written Indenture, and the name of the entity being created and is written and constructed as a trust so that it would have the thrust of ageless law. Let us take a look:

*WE THE PEOPLE (Grantors) of the United States ( from or out of) in Order to form a more perfect union, establish justice, provide for the common defense, promote the general welfare and secure the Blessings of Liberty (statement of Purpose) to ourselves and our posterity (Grantees/heirs unnamed), Do Ordain and establish (Statement of Intent) this constitution (Written Indenture) for the United States of America ( name of the entity being created).*

The trust res is in the Articles of the Confederation and the Declaration of Independence. The intent of the constitution was to bequeath freedom, life, liberty and the pursuit of happiness to themselves and their posterity. The founders intended to secure and pass on the sovereignty of the people to the people of future generations of Americans, in perpetuity.

One's rights are derived from the land upon which one stands and your relation, or status, to that land. In America these rights originated with the Articles of Confederation and the Declaration of Independence and are attached to the land called America (The Laws of Real Property). Our status, or relation to that land, is determined by the laws of Descent and Distribution. The right to freedom, life, liberty and the pursuit of happiness are Our inheritance bequeathed to us via the Constitution of the United States of America.

The constitution granted the government the power and authority to administrate and to carry on corporate functions. Under the common law, inherent rights cannot devolve to a 'body politic' through a corporation. Rights only devolve to human beings is through and **by way of a trust.** Under the constitutional law, in order to determine the meaning of a written instrument the court must look to the title. In this case, once again, it is the Preamble. Pursuant to the laws of real property that have been existence from the beginning, the Preamble clearly shows a freehold in fee simple absolute in it. Freeholds in fee simple were instruments of trust, not corporate. "Our Posterity" cannot be speaking of a corporate entity as posterity can only mean a living man/woman, by birth/nativity.

The Articles of the Constitution are the Articles of Incorporation that established congress as Trustees of the Trust and defines their power and authority as well as their limitations. Annexed to the Constitutional Trust is a will like structure, the Amendments. The Trust and the trust res were already in existence when the will/codicil (Amendments) were added some four years later. The Amendments do not constitute the Trust in fact, they are annexed to the Trust as a codicil (a supplement or addition to the will, not necessarily disposing of the entire estate, but modifying, explaining or otherwise qualifying the will in some way.)

A Trust, once completed and in force cannot be amended or altered without the consent of the parties in interest except under reserved power of amendment and alteration. An amendment is ordinarily possible by parties in interest and against parties without vested interest. Prior to the $14^{th}$ Amendment the freeborn inhabitants, citizens of the states were the parties in interest. As we have seen, the $14^{th}$ Amendment created the $14^{th}$ Amendment legal fiction citizen who do not have a vested interest in the trust or the trust res.

The $14^{th}$ Amendment can be viewed as a codicil to the will that republished the constitution with new meaning, changed the intent behind it and turned it into a testamentary instrument with capabilities of being used against the free born inhabitants through a seemingly voluntary revocation.

We, the freeholders, as Beneficiaries to the trust have unknowingly accepted the Trustees words and procedures into Testifying against ourselves when we apply for an S.S. #, drivers permit, marriage license or when we sign an IRS 1040 form, which the Trustees have said and led us to believe are mandatory.

When one applies for a Social Security number, provide evidence of birth and claims to be a United States or Canadian citizen, a party with no vested interest in a freehold, the trust or the trust res, one literally **declared the free born inhabitant to be deceased**; the decedent retains no interest in the property and that you, in your dual capacity as a legal fiction citizen are now the **executor of the estate**.

The Trustees have in truth unknowingly breached the trust having amended the will for their own personal profit and gain at the expense of the true heirs. The freeholders/Beneficiary has unwittingly, without full disclosure, become the executor and the Trustees have thus allegedly become the Beneficiaries to the trust through the Laws of Donations, effectively stealing Our inheritance.

A breach of trust of fiduciary duty by a Trustee is a violation of correlative right of the Cestui Que Trust (explained later) and gives rise to the correlative cause of action on the part of the Beneficiary for any loss to the estate Trust. This rule is applicable in respect to both positive acts or negligence constituting a breach of fiduciary duty by the Trustee. A Trustee's breach of fiduciary duty falls within the maxim that "*equity will not aid one who comes into court with unclean hands*."

When the Trustee's breach is by an act of omission the beneficiary can question the propriety of the Trustee. The Beneficiary had to have full disclosure, full knowledge of the material facts and circumstances. A Beneficiary must have had knowledge of and understood their rights and have no obligation to search the public records to obtain said knowledge.

So it appears the Trustees have committed acts of omission, mis-representation, deceit and deception in order to mislead and coerce us into giving up our beneficial interest in the trust and the trust res. The Trustees have compelled the free born inhabitants, freeholders in fee simple, to accept the benefits "under the will" perverted by the $14^{th}$ Amendment, without freedom of choice for failure of full disclosure thereby precluding our enforcement of contractual rights in property bequeathed to us by the will. The Trustees are trying to repudiate the Trust, employing a lifetime of propaganda and programming and enforced through threats, violence and coercion, and failing to provide notice to the Beneficiaries of the repudiation which must be "brought home".

But here is the irony: They didn't even know they did it - or did they? And whatever it is, the process, the story of the five monkeys simply is accepted as the law, and the truth. So how could anyone prove this?

The Doctrine of Election in connection with testamentary instruments is the principle that one who is given a benefit "under the will" must choose between accepting the benefits and asserting some other claim against the testator's estate or against the property disposed of by the will. A Testamentary Beneficiaries right to elect whether to take "under the will" or "against the will" in case he has some inconsistent claim against the testator's estate, is personal to him; is a personal privilege which may be controlled by the creditors of the Beneficiary. They can claim no right or interest in the estate contrary to the debtor's election and may have no right of a legacy or devise to their debtor if he elected to take against the will.

Acceptance of benefits "under the will" constitutes an election which will preclude the devisee from enforcing contractual rights in property bequeathed the will. This rule is, of course, subject to the qualifications that acceptance of a benefit under the will when made in ignorance of the Beneficiaries rights or a mis-apprehension, mis-representation as to the condition of the Testator's estate does not constitute an election.

## The Creation Of Three Trusts

In the beginning God gave man dominion over all things, Beneficiaries of the Divine Trust. The Founding fathers of the United States of America created the constitution for the United States, an estate trust, to pass on sovereignty of the people to the people of future generations, in perpetuity.

In America and Canada today, as with many other nations under the kingdom of GREAT BRITAIN upon giving birth a mother is compelled, without full disclosure, to apply for the creation of the first Cestui Que Vie trust, creating a $14^{th}$ Amendment paper citizen of the United States. Upon receipt of the mother's application the Trustees establish a trust under the error of assumptions that the child has elected to accept the benefits bequeathed by the will, *under the will*. The Trustees further assume that the child is incompetent, a bankrupt and lost at sea and is presumed dead until the child re-appears and re-establishes his/her living status, challenges the assumption of his/her acceptance of the benefits *under the will* as being one of free choice and with full knowledge of the facts and redeems the estate.

Under the assumption that the child is a $14^{th}$ Amendment citizen, the child's print is placed on the birth certificate by the hospital creating a slave bond that is sold to the Federal Reserve, who converts the certificate into a negotiable instrument and establishes a second Cestui Que Vie trust. The child's parents are compelled to apply for a social security number for the child, unwittingly testifying that the child is a $14^{th}$ Amendment paper citizen of the United States, not a party in interest to the trust or the trust res, and assumed to be dead after 7 years, when the federal reserve cannot seize the child, they file for the issue of the salvage bond and the child is presumed dead.

When a child is Baptized by the church, the Baptismal certificate is forwarded to the Vatican who converts the certificate into a negotiable instrument and creates a third Cestui Que Vie trust. These three trusts represent the enslavement of the property, body and soul of the child.

The civil administration, UNITED STATES, continues to operate today under this triple crown based on this error of assumptions that we are $14^{th}$ Amendment citizens of the United States based on the breach of trust by the trustees.

So what has evolved here is that three trusts have unknowingly been created through the administrative process of governments.

# The Administrators Of The Strawman Fictions

Who are these unknowing administrators? As we have seen, in the early 1930's, when the Canadian and United States governments went bankrupt and could no longer pay back war financing, a new system of debt repayment began. The government pledged all its sentient people as collateral to secure the national debt, and everyone whose birth had been registered became *capitalized* as security. A process of registration of new capital came into being whereby the human born was unknowingly accepted as being a corporate entity (a STRAWMAN) as a copy representation of the sentient human. Over time, a system of exploitation developed where these birth registrations became used to secure the issuance of bonds that were, and still are today, traded internationally. Until just a few years ago you could actually take the bond tracking number from the back of a Canadian birth certificate and look up its value in the bond market. People are deceived into believing that the *capitalized* last-name-first name on the registration of their birth represents them, when in fact it represents a legal entity and a financial instrument created by the state — a *paper person* distinct from the living individual associated with it. The legal entity becomes synonymous with the real person, thus allowing the government and those behind government to *own* you like any other investment, with all the same rights and privileges.

It is important to remember that The "Crown" is the administrative corporation of the Pontiff of Rome owned City of London, the financial, legal and professional standards capitol of/for the Vatican, The City of London is a square mile area within Greater London, England, and is an independent city-state. In the USA, the administrative corporation for the Pontiff of Rome is the UNITED STATES, and that corporation administers the Vatican capitol, for, primarily, military purposes, called

Columbia, or the District of Columbia. The UNITED STATES also administers the 50 sub-corporate States of the United States of America, identified with the 2 cap letters – CA, OR, WA, etc.

All adult humans use the fiction name, as imprinted on the copy of the birth certificate you receive when ordering it from Provincial/State Vital Statistics, or to whatever the country upholds as the source you apply through. Although the birth certificate is of somewhat recent origin and used to formally offer "citizens" as chattel in bankruptcy to the Pope's Holy Roman Empire owned Rothschilds' Banking System, the false use of the family name goes back into the Middle Ages in England. Thus, it is with the family name made a primary, or surname, (example - Mister Jones), and the given names of the child (example - Peter) made a reference name to the primary name. This is the reverse or mirror image to reality. A "family name" is NOT a man's name - it is a name of a clan - a blood relationship. In truth then the given names would be Edward Alexander of the Rychkun clan or family.

By acceptance of the name EDWARD ALEXANDER RYCHKUN, I am then obliged to use that name in all commercial and Government dealings and communications. So, when I do use it, as 99.99% of the human inhabitants of North America (and most of the world) do, I voluntarily attach myself Edward Alexander, the free will adult human, to the Crown/State owned property, called the "legal identity name" as an accessory attached to property owned by another party. Think of a ship under tow by another ship. Which captain decides what route the ships will take? The legal name/Strawman is the tow rope, and the towing ship is the corporate (make-believe ship at sea) Crown of the City of London. As an attachment to the legal name owned by the Crown, you are the towed ship, and your vessel captain, your free will mind, is now a subservient crewmember to the captain of the Crown.

The State or Crown does not give us authority, grant, license, permission or leave to use the Crown or State owned legal identity name. Thus, our use of it as an adult free will man (male or female) is like a form of theft against a maritime jurisdiction entity (all incorporated bodies are "make-believe ships at sea"). In maritime law, the accused is guilty until proven innocent. This allows the Roman Law system, which we have, to impose "involuntary servitude" upon an adult man. Involuntary servitude simply means a slave stripped of granted rights of a slave called a citizen, subject or freeman. This stripped rights included "due process of law" - no jury trial, and charges where no harm has been done against another man, or his property with criminal intent.

We see this Roman Law within the US 13th Amendment (#2) instituted in the mid 1860's: *"Neither slavery nor involuntary servitude, except as a punishment for crime whereof the party shall have been duly convicted,"* The crime with which you have been convicted is *unauthorized use* of the State's or Crown's intellectual property - the legal identity name.

The Crown/State then invokes the legal maxim, accessio cedit principali, [an accessory attached to a principal becomes the property of the owner of the principal], where the principal is the legal identity name as "intellectual property". The owner is the corporation called the Crown/State, or UNITED STATES, and the accessory is the free will human who has volunteered himself to be "property by attachment" of the Crown/State. An adult human who is property is, and by any other name, of "slave status", be it citizen, subject or freeman.

As a slave, one's property in possession, including body and labour, belongs to the slave owner 100%. And, the property right is a bundle of rights - own, use, sell, gift, bequeath and hypothecate property. The process deployed, from Birth to Death is as below using CANADA as an example.

First of all, the Birth Certificate is a formal document which certifies as to the date and place of one's birth and a recitation of his or her parentage, as issued by an official in charge of such records. Note that a Birth Certificate is not a formal identity document but it is a negotiable instrument, a registered security, a stock certificate evidencing, or representing, the preferred stock of the corporation and against which you are the surety; it is a pedigree chattel document establishing the existence of our Strawman, a distinct artificial person with a fictitious name; it is a document of title to a Strawman; it is a warehouse receipt for your body; delivery receipt; industrial bond between you (flesh-and-blood man or woman) and the industrial society and corporate US or CANADA Government as an artificial person.

In Canada, the original birth certificate is generally created at the PROVINCIAL level (in rare instances city level) via birth documents from the hospital (for which the hospital receives $$$ from the PROVINCE for causing the registration of the birth) and passed to the Provincial and Federal levels, and likely elsewhere. Per the definition of "birth" below, the document references both the newborn and the straw man. Certified *copies* of the birth certificate may be obtained at the Vital Statistics Office. Your birth certificate is one of the kinds of security instrument used by the Government to obtain loans from its creditor, under which it is bankrupt.

The act of being born or wholly brought into separate existence. Black's $1^{st}$. Note: A man or a woman is *"born"*, Strawman are *"wholly brought into separate existence."* Each event qualifies as a *"birth"*. The birth certificate documents a muddied mixture of the two events that allows the system to both claim that it is *"your"* birth certificate yet also claim to hold title to (not ownership of) the corporately colored Strawman.

# The Detailed Story Of The STRAWMAN

### Marriage trust registration to create capital.

The first step in the administrative process is the MARRIAGE TRUST REGISTRATION TO CREATE CAPITAL. This occurs at the MUNICIPAL VITAL STATISTICS AGENCIES. Here a Mother and Father apply for a marriage and register to receive a Marriage Certificate in their STRAWMAN Names. As they marry they create a Trust which holds the estate of their progeny as human creations. The progeny becomes released to the title of the offspring to the Government for their use. It is noted that Registration" comes from Latin "Rex, Regis" etc. meaning regal. Thus what occurs is whatever is "registered" means to hand legal title over to the Crown. When you register anything with the public, it releases legal title to the government corporation and leaves you with only equitable title – the right to use, not own, and for that use you will pay a "use" tax, be it income, sin, sales, property, etc. as opposed to lawful taxes, excise and impost. In this way it doesn't *appear* that the government now owns the property which you have registered as they put it in a name which is a copy of You as a NAME owned by the government. If you choose rather to *record* your legal title to your property with the public, you maintain your status as Title Owner. This is one of the most important things you can ever learn for the sake of your commercial affairs.

If you examine older version of the marriage certificate or a birth certificate you will find a number in red ink that begins with a letter. On the small plastic card the number will appear on the back of the card. On the larger Birth Certificate printed on bank note paper the red number may be on the front. In the USA this bank note paper comes from the American Bank Note Company, in Canada it comes from the CANADIAN BANK NOTE COMPANY LIMITED. This information can be found along the lower left-hand edge of the note. If you are holding one of these you are holding a certified copy of a bank note in your name that has a value of well over $1,000,000 (one million dollars). The number in red ink is a Revenue Receipt in Canada and a bond number or a bond tracking number.

Let us follow this process in detail (some repetition). This process is done through the VITAL STATISTICS Agencies as a subsidiary of the department of HEALTH.

## Birth Of The Sentient Human In A Local Hospital

This step occurs with the birth of the sentient human in a local hospital. You, a real human are born as you are birthed (Berthed) through the mothers' water canal. This places the prime capital asset into the Trust holding equitable title of You. Your parents give you a Name that is accepted and taught as Upper and Lower case name. A certificate of Manifest is required as the vessel (Mother) and its cargo must be registered upon landing (born). A Registration of Birth is created and the Mother signs the Birth Certification as Trustee of You under your given name. An estate is therefore created for Your use and benefit so you become the GRANTOR of this estate as You will be placing items of value within it. Your parents are the creators of the estate as they created you. The BC refers to mother as an "informant". This process as in America and Canada today, as with many other nations under the kingdom of GREAT BRITAIN upon giving birth a mother is compelled, without full disclosure, to apply for the creation of the first Cestui Que Vie trust, creating a $14^{th}$ Amendment paper citizen of the United States.

Upon receipt of the mother's application the Trustees establish a trust under the error of assumptions that the child has elected to accept the benefits bequeathed by the will, "under the will". The Trustees further assume that the child is incompetent, a bankrupt and lost at sea and is presumed dead until the child re-appears and re-establishes his/her living status, challenges the assumption of his/her acceptance of the benefits 'under the will' as being one of free choice and with full knowledge of the facts and redeems the estate.

Under the assumption that the child is a $14^{th}$ Amendment citizen, the child's footprint is placed on the birth certificate by the hospital creating a slave bond that is sold to the federal reserve, who converts the certificate into a negotiable instrument and establishes a second Cestui Que Vie trust. The child's parents are compelled to apply for a social security number for the child, unwittingly testifying that the child is a $14^{th}$ Amendment paper citizen of the United States, not a party in interest to the trust or the trust res, and assumed to be dead after 7 years, when the federal reserve cannot seize the child, they file for the issue of the salvage bond and the child is presumed dead.

When a child is baptized by the church, the Baptismal certificate is forwarded to the Vatican who converts the certificate into a negotiable instrument and creates a *third Cestui Que Vie trust*. By the process of baptism, one then agrees to fall under the code of the VATICAN which is the Bible as written by them.

These three trusts represent the enslavement of the property, body and soul of the child. The civil administration of CANADA and UNITED STATES, continues to operate today under this triple crown of enslavement based on the error of assumptions that we are $14^{th}$ Amendment citizens of the United States based on the breach of trust by the trustees. So what has evolved here is that three trusts have unknowingly been created through the administrative process of governments. These three Cestui Que Vie Trusts represent the triple crown of enslavement and three claims against property, body and soul.

**Registration Of Capital**

Unknown to the administration of the Municipality, the Government at the Municipal level claims an interest in every child within its jurisdiction as a valuable asset as a human resource which if properly trained, can contribute valuable assets provided by its labour for many years. As You are to be pledged as "HUMAN CAPITAL RESOURCE," that can contribute to the welfare of the Municipality of origin every year, your 'registration places You as a 'ward of the Government'. Presented as a safeguard for the child and the parents, this allows the creation and registration of a commercial entity used for the purpose of exploitation.

**Birth Registration And Birth Of The Strawman**

The Birth Registration of the new cargo (child) creates an entry into the registry to create a Certificate of Birth in the NAME of the STRAWMAN as a fictional dead corporation which simulates a copy of You. As the Government creates this entity, it also owns it. As The number of the Birth Certificate becomes a reference in the Provincial Treasury to be like a certificate of Incorporation. It is also a descendant of You Note: A man or a woman is "born", straw men are *"wholly brought into separate existence."* Each event qualifies as a "birth". The birth certificate documents a muddied mixture of the two events that allows the system to both claim that it is "your" birth certificate yet also claim to hold title to (not ownership of) the corporately colored Strawman.

**Registration Of The Strawman As An Entity**

Now the registration of the STRAWMAN an entity (with the federal ministry of finance and the Secretary Treasurer is completed. The NAME now representing a new asset of You is registered in the Individual Master File as a Foreigner from a foreign jurisdiction as a Criminal with multiple criminal charges. This is registered into the MASTER FILE as a alien, resident of Puerto Rico. As a criminal the STRAWMAN has no rights and is guilty before proving innocence as it all fall under Maritime Law. This is opposite to the way it works in common law where the real human is innocent until proven guilty. The registration number is the Birth Certificate number. As the Government own this entity it can attach criminal violations or whatever history it deems necessary to keep the STRAWMAN in penal position.

The STRAWMAN Corporation is assigned a Municipal bond number by the Federal Ministry of Finance creating a negotiable instrument, a registered security, a stock certificate of the corporation against which You are the surety of this bond: a pedigree chattel document establishing the existence of the STRAWMAN in the name of STRAWMAN and gives authority to Provincial department to issue a Birth Certificate to the parents on your behalf. This number is the Treasury Direct number on the Birth Certificate (in Canada). The value of the bond is set at over 1 million dollars. The Birth Certificate is registered as a warehouse receipt for the body, a delivery receipt, an industrial bond between You and the Corporation (STRAWMAN) owned by the Government since they created it. This in earlier version of the Canadian Birth Certificates and Marriage Certificate is the red number stated as "Revenue Receipt XXXxXX for Treasury Use only" This security instrument sets the means for them to obtain loans from its creditor under which it, the Nation, is bankrupt.

**Delivery Of The Birth Certificate**

After creating the Birth Certificate on bank note paper (in USA this bank note paper comes from the American Bank Note Company, in Canada it comes from the CANADIAN BANK NOTE COMPANY LIMITED), a Certified Original Copy of The Birth Certificate is sent back to the parents who are Trustee for You. The original is retained by the Ministry of Finance on behalf of the provincial Treasury. This is a copy is an acknowledgement that You are born in the jurisdiction (landed cargo in Canada or US) and are an capital asset belonging to the Municipality where You were born.

**Registration Of Assets With Banking**

The registration of asset with banking (Bank of Canada, Federal Reserve Bank, IMF) now occurs. Since USA/CA have been bankrupt for decades, having no substance such as gold and silver to back it, the only asset it has is men and woman and their labour which was pledged to the IMF which is the private commercial entity that the bankruptcy/receivership deal was made with. The pledge of labour is registered as the collateral for the interest on the loan of the World Bank which the private banking entity associated with the IMF. Each Capital Asset allowed the treasury to issue the birth certificate and the bond which is registered within the Canadian and US banking systems. The Bond is registered with the World Bank and the Bank of Canada. This information can be found along the lower left-hand edge of the note. If you are holding one of these you are holding a certified copy of a bank note in Your name that has some set value of well over $1,000,000. The number in red ink is a bond number or a bond tracking number. The Bank of Canada can now issues debt instruments as paper which are assumed to be money as a draw against the IMF line of credit which is to paid off by You and your pledge.

**Registration With IMF System**

The bond is assigned an international; CUSIP 9 character number through CGS Municipal Issuer access through an authorized representative such as The Canadian Depository for Securities to cover a wide range of global financial instruments, including extensive equity and debt issues, derivatives, syndicated loans and U.S. listed equity options. This is done through CGS CUSIP GLOBAL SERVICES in New York (near DDTC) and MSRB Municipal Securities Rulemaking Board in Virginia.

The treasury issues a bond on the birth certificate and the bond is sold at a securities exchange and bought by the FRB/BoC, (Federal Reserve Bank/Bank of Canada) which then uses it as collateral to issue bank notes. The bond is held in trust for the Feds at the Depository Trust Corporation. We are the sureties on said bonds. Our labour/energy is then payable at some future date. Hence we become the "transmitting utility" for the transmission of energy.

The birth certificate created a FICTION (the name of the baby in upper case letters). The state/province sells the birth certificate to the Commerce Department of the corporations of USA/CA, which in turn places a bond on the birth certificate thereby making it a negotiable instrument, and placing the fiction, called a STRAWMAN, into the warehouse of the corporation of USA/CA. Representation for the created fiction was given to the BAR (British Accredited Registry/Regency), owned and operated by the Crown, for the purpose of contracting the fiction (which most of us think is ourselves) into a third party action. Do not underestimate the power behind this trick. It is to con us into contracting with the Feds so that they can 'legally' confiscate our property. All these contracts have only *our* signature on them because corporate fictions cannot contract (only natural beings have the right to contract – and the right *not* to contract). Because there is no full disclosure – we are never told that we have just signed away what we believe to be *our* property – these contracts are fraudulent, and hence, we are still the lawful owner and the profit earned by the Feds from stealing securities (our property) belongs to us and must go into a fund for our benefit, otherwise it would be fraud. Not wanting to be charged with fraud, the Feds had to create a remedy for us…and hope we wouldn't discover it.

### Bond Trading On World Markets

The World Bank, on behalf of the Ministry of Finance and the Bank of Canada lodges the bond with Fidelity Trust offshore in the Caribbean or other trading securities institutions for the purpose of trading it and deriving interest or profit from the activity. It is brokered as a security and traded on the exchanges such as New York stock exchange  You are the collateral for the interest on the loan of the World Bank. The bond is sold at a securities exchange and bought by the FRB/BoC, (Federal Reserve Bank/Bank of Canada) which then uses it as collateral to issue bank notes. Under the fractional reserve banking regulations, the original securities can be leveraged to create 10 such securities. As a result if the original bond value was 1 million, the value of securities to be traded on the worlds market would be $1 million.

## Monetary Enrichment And Holdings In Trust

The bond as a claim of capital is held in trust for Bank of Canada at the Depository Trust Corporation. You are the surety for this bond as the one who has the penal municipal bond against you and are the guarantee for the payment of it. It is through your labour/energy payable at some future date so it is held in trust. Hence You become the 'transmitting utility' for the transmission of energy. The bond is held in trust for the Government at the Depository Trust Corporation or DTC in New York but owned by the IMF as private agency. You become the unknowing the sureties on the bonds where labour/energy is then payable at some future date. Hence You become the 'transmitting utility' for the transmission of energy. The bond becomes part of the estate of You. At the same time the DTC in collaboration with the World Bank are free to use the original financial instrument as the Birth Certificate to trade on the market, so as to derive interest and enrichment as lodged into the DTC account under the Birth Registration number.

## Until The Age Of Maturity

Over time the estate is built through the efforts of You and the bonds as assets that are registered in the name of the Commercial Enterprise of the STRAWMAN. All commerce is transacted under this STRAWMAN NAME where the bond or any other assets that may have come into existence during the early life are registered against. The municipal bonds continue to generate revenue every year. As assets are registered, they are brought under the title of the STRAWMAN. If they are not, they remain as Your Estate.

**Application For Social Insurance**

At some age of maturity as an adult, You create an application for a Social Insurance Number (SIN) as a formal process. When one applies for a Social Security number, provide evidence of birth and claims to be a United States or Canadian citizen, a party with no vested interest in a freehold, the trust or the trust res, one literally declared the free born inhabitant to be deceased; the decedent retains no interest in the property and that you, in your dual capacity as a legal fiction citizen are now the executor of the estate. This is also the formalization of the pledge of future commercial output and Your consent to be taxed on that effort. As the application is done under the Crown/State owned STRAWMAN name, the name found on the birth certificate, and with that certificate being the pledged document to the bankruptcy creditor, that adult human, by attachment through application for registration, becomes a synonymous with it and becomes a ward or SLAVE owned by the corporate Crown of the City of London, and thus to the Vatican. All of the Slave's property, including his or her labour (100%) is claimed by the slave owner. (of the STRAWMAN Corporation). From that point on, all things you purchase, possess, and wages you earn are in the Crown/State owned name. The wages or earnings you get to keep for your own use and enjoyment is called a 'benefit' from the slave owner. Unknown to You, through the application of SIN or SSN this signals the equivalent wind up, cessation or death of You, the real sentient being. The STRAWMAN corporation and ESTATE which is available then provide the Government with the means to hold the estate which can be probated like a will.

**Issuance Of The SIN Number**

The issuance of the S.I.N. (or S.S.N.) is equivalent to a Certificate of Cessation, or Winding-Up of the company, or appropriately, a Death Certificate for the real You. The certification of the death provides the Government owned Strawman to create the Estate of that STRAWMAN in that name of that registered foreigner. At this age of maturity, or ability to work, You apply for a SIN as a Government requirement to account for the income created by Your efforts, all accumulated into the Your estate. It is registered with the Tax authority that remits this to the Receiver who acts as the receiver in bankruptcy for the IMF (all bankrupt treasuries and municipalities) to the Federal Ministry of Finance then the Bank of Canada. That residual revenues after tax is in fact Yours but the taxes form part of the Federal Transfer payments the federal government and the Bank of Canada are authorized to send to the provincial government every year--back to the local municipal level. The Federal Minister of Finance is acting as a fiduciary over that revenue and bond. Those funds are yours and they owe it to you as it is supported by Your secret pledge.

**Rollover Of The Estate Excecutorship**

With the cessation of You, only the shadow overlay of the criminal STRAWMAN registered in the IMF alien files exists. As you or your Father never claimed and position because neither were aware, You now fulfill automatically become the Executor in the Executor Office. You are an earthly estate walking around creating what you were to be beneficiary of. The Certificate of Birth or Live Birth Certificate is the Public Record of the Estate and that the Estate is Probated. A trust can only exist if there is already an Estate in existence. The address of the estate is the file number on the birth certificate. The estate resides at the file number. The estate is restricted to the file number; it cannot move anywhere else. Unknowingly You nor your Father do not step forward to claim the living position as Beneficiary and Grantor and hence the Government steps in through a change of Fiduciary to have the role of executor for the foreigners created estate assumed by You who by default abandoned it. The trustees thus become the Beneficiaries and You are effectively even as Grantor, judged incompetent at the age of maturity. Until you step up and correct this situation judges will treat you as a criminal since You have assumed the role of the DEAD MAN criminal, as registered in the IMF file you are incompetent to engage in the executor role.

**Probating The Estate**

At the point of probate, an living Executor is required. You are the legitimate Executor authorized to occupy the Executor Office because when You were born, You were sent the Executor Office (the Birth Certificate), and then only 3 people could get a copy of your Birth Certificate – You, Mom and Dad. Once you reached the age of maturity (21), you became the only one authorized until you come of age, your father has the authority to occupy the Executor Office of the Estate bearing your STRAWMAN provided he is aware. Upon attaining the age of majority (21), you may step into and assume your proper capacity in the Executor Office of Estate. As the grantor of the estate, You are the only one who can appoint the Executor or assign its duties to someone else. The Executor can appoint trustees but cannot authorize fictional entities to administrate the estate. By definition the *Executor is the authority that grants the power and duties and liabilities to each of the trustees, and to any beneficiaries. (A "grantor", is not equivalent to an Executor, and does not have or enjoy the Executor's powers, rights, or immunities. Through the process when You are declared diseased, a New Executor then assigns the STRAWMAN as trustee who has no claim of right. The executor must be a live human and that become you thus allowing the government to be the beneficiaries.*

**Taxes And Working Off The Debt**

As you work the efforts are recorded against the SIN and taxes are paid were the IRS and CRA administer and police the taxation. As the STRAWMAN belongs to the Government and they are the Executors of the estate, the tax proceeds are remitted towards the debt of the country, through CRA, the Ministry of Finance and the Bank of Canada to deposit in the World Bank for the account of the IMF. This is the payback that You pledged to uphold and the transfer payments are paid by the world bank as debt to the bankrupt operating company Canada. The administrative process of accounting within this receivership is the purpose of the Agencies created within the Country, such as the Bank of Canada, Federal Reserve Banks, and the CRA. The Ministries of the Country are there to administer and account for the payment and receipt of debt money.

**Banking And Loans Registration**

As you apply for loans, credit and mortgages, you as the energy and sole means of creating real money provide the authorization in the form of loan agreements, promissory notes on behalf of the STRAWMAN/TRUST that pledge your payments back. Similar to becoming the surety on the bonds created by them, your provide the signatures for them to create money for which you become the surety to pay it to them. The banks that cannot create money then create entries that simulate money being loaned to You. You pay them the amount and interest while they use these instruments to trade on the open market. They combine these into a bond of 100 million or greater and trade this to their benefit through the DTC CUSIP through the World Bank in association with the Bank of Canada who has the fiduciary duty of creation and monitoring this as a product of supporting the bankrupt nation. The amounts are registered in the DTC as they are accounted for within the registry Note that there are 20 Federal Reserve Banks listed in Canada including Montreal, Alberta Treasury, Scotia, HSBC, Credential Securities, CIBC and Bank of Canada as the Authority reporting to the Federal Reserve. The Bank of Canada, like the US Federal Reserve Bank are Central Banks.

You signed these contracts for SSN/SIN numbers, registrations and other licenses because you accepted this artificial CORPORATION was you and that you were obliged to sign. They did not tell you that by signing these contracts you were signing away your lawful *rights* and *freedoms* and giving the government total control of your life, property and labour. Today, the one simple fact that the World Bank does not want you to find out is that all these contracts could be deemed f*raudulent* and that because of that fact you have always had and still do, to this very moment, retain all your lawful *rights* and *freedoms*.

## Final Death Of The STRAWMAN

At the point of your death you will have accumulated three estates. One is the Constructive Trust that you abandoned, and the other contains the possessions that you have accumulated under your private affairs, except where you have registered into the commercial system under the name of the STRAWMAN. The other is the divine trust with the Vatican. In this case it is the title of the asset that is held as Your the right to use it, not the asset itself. This is deemed your benefit of tenancy and alleged ownership but allows you to trade and sell the use of what is not yours in a way that it so appears as the real thing. In reality it all belongs to the Government which is in tern owned by the IMF under the commercial laws of Bankruptcy. The true the power behind this that they can 'legally' confiscate the real property but as yet, have not taken this action which is the slaves benefit. When You die, a Registration of Death must be issued through the same Vital Statistics agency and the STRAWMAN along with You cease to exists (in actuality). The hidden estate of the STRAWMAN is now the property of the IMF (the supporter of the nations bankruptcy) and the gravestone and Death Certificate mark the termination of the STRAWMAN and You as one and the same. The birth certificate bonds and securities created cease to be of value as do the other assets within the STRAWMAN TRUST, however, this does not prevent the World Bank to do as they wish with it and the proceeds of enrichments. On the national level, the FICTION and the human cease to exist and do not contribute revenues and services. From the National warehouse of the corporation of USA/CA, the entries are deleted.

## All STRAWMEN Are Make-Believe Ships At Sea,

And so all STRAWMEN as corporate bodies are make-believe ships at sea, and are thus, internally, under maritime law, which will be explained later [incorrectly called admiralty law, unless applied to the military]. In maritime law, an accused is guilty unless proven innocent. This is why the STRAWMAN is automatically registered into existences as a criminal with a record of violations. Thus, a free will adult man who uses, without authority, the property of a corporate body is under maritime jurisdiction and assumed a criminal. This makes a free will man who uses a corporate Crown or corporate State owned legal identity name a 'convicted criminal', and thus subject to the imposition of slavery as in a prison, involuntary servitude.

You, as a child, were Crown or State property by way of the birth registry, and thus, you could use Crown or State property, the legal identity name. When you became an adult, as a vessel on the 'sea of life' as a sovereign captain/free will mind, you no longer had a right to use (as an 'identity' name) that Crown or State owned legal identity name.

However, under the "property right" of a slave owner in regard to property in the possession of an owned slave, a "demand" for the property by the slave owner, or the slave owner's agent (such as the IRS, or county tax collector, or for a court imposed fine), is all that is necessary, without regard to due process of law. Remember, ALL that a slave possesses belongs to the slave owner.

This does not mean you are a slave. It is that the Government, and its employees, judges and officers SEE you as a SLAVE. See sections 35, 46 and 78 of the "Bills of Exchange Act of Canada" regarding eligibility for use of the provisions of that Act. A bill can only be paid with money, and there is no money in Canada or the USA since the early 1930's. All that is left is some form of a "promissory note". In Canada, Parliament even converted the Canadian currency to pure Monopoly Game money by declaring that Canadian currency is no longer a promissory note nor bill of exchange. (Section 25(6) of the Bank of Canada Act).

When we are a child, we can have an identifying name because we are property, property that should belong to the natural parents, but by registry of live birth, where the parents identify themselves as being of slave status owned by the corporate Crown, the child becomes the property of the Corporate Crown. Because the child does not have a matured mind, it is a vessel under construction in "dry dock".

When the registry of live birth is performed, the Province, as an agent for the Crown, then changes the family name to a 'sur' or primary name, thus making the Crown owned legal name as intellectual property owned by the Crown. As the child grows up, the child is taught by society and the education system to identify him or herself by that legal name, an accept the idea that they have a 'surname'.

When the child reaches the age of majority, the human vessel is launched on the sea of life, and the mature moral thinking mind becomes the supreme commander of the human vessel. The supremacy of the captain of a vessel supersedes any claim of ownership when the vessel is on the high sea. This had to be overcome in the maritime world of corporate bodies, which are make-believe shops at sea.

So, what the Government, as agent for the corporate Crown devised, was to not give authorization for the adult man to identify him or herself by the legal name, even though they were taught to do so all their life as a child. Thus, a man, identifying him or herself as being one and the same as the legal name, the name one finds on the birth certificate, is an act of theft of intellectual property of another and triggers the legal maxim (requires no further proof) arising out of the property right - accessio cedit principali - an accessory attached (without authorization) to a principal becomes the property of the principal. Thus the supposed to be free will man, with the mind being the supreme commander of his human vessel/body, becomes like a ship under tow by another ship - a slave to the towing ship.

Even though the country was bankrupt the banks could not take away your *rights* and *freedoms*, under the terms of bankruptcy they forced the government to create an artificial CORPORATION (STRAWMAN) in your name. Then they had you sign fraudulent contracts to accept the *privileges* and *benefits* attached to this artificial CORPORATION. You only signed these contracts for SSN/SIN numbers, registrations and other licenses because you were led to believe this artificial CORPORATION was you and that you were obliged to sign. They did not tell you that by signing these contracts you were signing away your lawful *rights* and *freedoms* and giving the government total control of your life, property and labour.

## Who Became The Administrators Of The Trusts?

The local Vital statistics Agency is where this process starts. The Vital statistics agencies are tasked with birth, marriage and death. This is a subsidiary of the Ministry of Health.

| **CANADA** | **US** |
|---|---|
| CEO Vital Statistics Agency | Vital statistics Agency |
| Minster of Health | Rector Basilica of the National Shrine |
| Secretary of the Treasury Board | Secretary of State |
| Attorney General | Department of Justice |
| Governor General | American Inns of Court |

In any of these cases, those who administer simply do a job with a job description. The ones who may know some of the truth will be the ones who have signed non-disclosure and proprietary agreements that they violate at their peril. In looking at the lower structures of responsibilities, it is not usual that one department knows the whole picture, and as such all simply do a segment of the whole and never understand nor believe that this may be improper, fraud, or deception. And if this is "the law" or "way things are done" as policed by the code of laws, then that is the way it is supposed to be. Any attack on this becomes a radical fringe rebellion so enter this area at your peril!

Think about an analogy of a cage of five monkeys I told you about before. Inside, we hang bananas and place stairs under them. When a monkey attempts to climb the stairs, we spray the other four with cold water. They do not like cold water. If you repeat this when any monkey tries to climb to the bananas, soon the monkeys will prevent others from climbing. They kick up a fuss and even beat it. Now let us put the water away and replace one monkey. When the new one tries to climb, he gets attacked. So let us remove another original monkey and bring in another new one. It will get attacked if it tries climbing. If you do this until all five original monkeys are replaced, guess what? The monkeys that are beating the most recent one have no idea why they should not climb or why they should beat the others. After five are replaced, there is no water, no one is sprayed, yet no one climbs. Why? They know that's the way it has always been done. It's the law!

The **Cestui que** use and trust were rooted in medieval law, and became a legal method to avoid the feudal (medieval) incidents (payments) to an overlord, while leaving the land for the use of another, who owed nothing to the lord. The law of cestui que tended to defer jurisdiction to courts of equity as opposed to common law courts. The cestui que was often utilized by persons who might be absent from the kingdom for an extended time (as on a Crusade, or a business adventure), and who held tenancy to the land, and owed feudal incidents to a lord. The land could be left for the use of a third party, who did not owe the incidents to the lord. This legal status was also invented to circumvent the Statute of Mortmain. That statute was intended to end the relatively common practice of leaving real property to the Church at the time of the owner's death. Since the Church never died, the land never left the "dead hand" ("Mortmain" or Church). An alternative explanation of "mortmain" was that an owner from generations earlier was still dictating land use years after death, by leaving it to the Church. Hence the term "dead hand." Before the Statute of Mortmain, large amounts of land were bequeathed to the Church, which never relinquished it. This was in contradistinction to normal lands which could be inherited in a family line or revert to a lord or the Crown upon death of the tenant. Church land had been a source of contention between the Crown and the Church for centuries. Cestui que use allowed religious orders to inhabit land, while the title resided with a corporation of lawyers or other entities, who nominally had no relation to the Church.

There are multiple trusts and accounts created in this process and for decades, many people have tried to crack their way into these structures. It is virtually impossible because the process is so well a established that there is no question about it being something with questionable purposes.

In our next chapter, it is necessary to understand the real laws that bind us.

# 14

# MARITIME LAWS OF THE SEA

## UNITED STATES Corporation

*Ever wonder why some American flags, especially those in your courts of law, police stations, and even in the lobby of Walt Disney Corporation all have a gold fringe? It's not to make the flag look more regal, but to make sure that those who are governed by the law of that institution are NOT governed by the United States of America Constitution, but by the bylaws of the UNITED STATES OF AMERICA CORPORATION.*

For example, as researched on http://americankabuki.blogspot.ca/2013/08/united-states-of-america-inc-registered.html , SA INC Corporation registration in Delaware as a "Religious non-profit" corporation. Also includes the corporate registration of the CIA, IRS, US Treasury, Federal Land Acquisition Corp., and Social Security
File Number: **2193946**
Incorporation Date /Formation Date: **04/19/1989**

Entity Name: **UNITED STATES OF AMERICA, INC.**
Entity Kind: **CORPORATION**
Entity Type: **RELIGIOUS NONPROFIT**
Residency: **DOMESTIC**
State:**DEREGISTERED AGENT INFORMATION**
Name: **THE COMPANY CORPORATION**
Address: **2711 CENTERVILLE ROAD SUITE 400**
City: **WILMINGTON**
County:**NEW CASTLE**
State:**DE** Postal Code: **19808**
Phone: **(302)636-5440 (302)636-5440**

The Corporation is a headless fictional overlay of the real thing. It strives to create profit. Profit to a laymen is money. Profit to those who control the world is control. The gold fringe on any American flag is the greatest level of desecration one could have. This goes for state flags as well. It says to the legal world that you are under the law of the Corporation and NOT the country.

Ultimately when you walk into a court of law, you are being governed by the bylaws of a Corporation and not by your Constitution. There are courts that decide if a matter is Constitutional or Unconstitutional, but they are merely looking out of their legal domain and into ours, for we the people, are the only body or group that considers itself under the Constitution.

## What Is Maritime Law?

The gold fringe originates from something called **Maritime Law**. This was a technique that countries used back in the days of Naval fleets that needed to barter and or sign treaties between nations. Each ship flew a flag of its country to denote its legal domain. This flag was honored as the legal domain over that ship. If one were to step onto that ship, one was subject to the written and recorded laws of that flag's country.

The gold fringe on the United States flag is a legal holdover from these times. When one walks into the courtroom or any other institution with a gold fringe, one has surrendered to the bylaws of that Corporation and NOT the Constitution.

As you have come to learn, the UNITED STATES government is basically a corporate instrument of the international bankers. This means YOU as the corporate STRAWMAN are owned by the corporation from birth to death. The corporate UNITED STATES also holds ownership of all your assets, your property, and even your children. .

With the Act of 1871 and subsequent legislation such as the purportedly ratified 14th Amendment, our once-great nation of Sovereigns has been subverted from a Republic to a democracy. As is the case under Roman Civil Law, our ignorance of the facts has led to our silence. Our silence has been construed as our consent to become beneficiaries of a debt we did not incur. The Sovereign People have been deceived for hundreds of years into thinking they remain free and independent, when in actuality we continue to be slaves and servants of the corporation.

## Admiralty And Maritime Law

Everybody is familiar with these laws when they step onto a plane or a boat. Once you do, your action gives away many of your rights to be entrusted by the captain of the ship. He makes the life and death decisions and you are subject to a body of law called Admiralty Law. The terms "admiralty" and "maritime" are frequently used interchangeably. "Admiralty," refers to the body of law and procedures that govern matters related to the carriage of goods or passengers on the high seas and navigable inland waters. The term "maritime" however, is a far more general term. In effect, one as the head of the family is "captain of his ship" in the same way.

**Admiralty law** (also referred to as **maritime law**) is a distinct body of law which governs maritime questions and offenses. It is a body of both domestic law governing maritime activities, and private international law governing the relationships between private entities which operate vessels on the oceans. It deals with matters including marine commerce, marine navigation, shipping, sailors, and the transportation of passengers and goods by sea. Admiralty law also covers many commercial activities, although land based or occurring wholly on land, that are maritime in character. Admiralty law is distinguished from the Law of the Sea, which is a body of public international law dealing with navigational rights, mineral rights, jurisdiction over coastal waters and international law governing relationships between nations

The source of modern day admiralty law is hidden in the ancient past. It is thought by some scholars that it may be traced back as far as 900 B.C. to the island of Rhodes in the eastern Mediterranean. Whatever its origin, it is very old indeed, and doctrines clearly recognizable to today's admiralty practitioner may be found in several medieval maritime codes. Special courts arose in the Mediterranean, Atlantic, and Baltic trading states to enforce what was accepted by these states as a form of international law arising from the longstanding customs of the sea. Of particular interest to us is the system established in England where courts set up under the cognizance of the Lord High Admiral were, in the latter part of the 14th century, given jurisdiction to hear civil cases limited to "a thing done upon the sea." This system of separate Courts of Admiralty was still in existence throughout the time England colonized North America. Colonial courts were set up under the Vice-Admiralty in British North America and given expanded jurisdiction to hear criminal and civil matters involving colonists. Following the Revolutionary War, the newly formed United States incorporated the English judicial system.

The US constitution together with the Judiciary Act of 1789, give the federal judiciary cognizance of matters which were within the jurisdiction of the British Admiralty. The system of separate admiralty courts with separate procedures was continued in the United States until 1966, when the courts were unified. Even though they are now unified, separate and distinct admiralty procedures are still available and the substantive law applied to decide cases, whether in state or federal court is the body of federal admiralty law.

According to Wikipedia, Seaborne transport was one of the earliest channels of commerce, and rules for resolving disputes involving maritime trade were developed early in recorded history. Early historical records of these laws include the Rhodian law (Nomos Rhodion Nautikos) (of which no primary written specimen has survived, but which is alluded to in other legal texts: Roman and Byzantine legal codes) and later the customs of the Hanseatic League. In southern Italy the Ordinamenta et consuetudo maris (1063) at Trani and the Amalfian Laws were in effect from an early date.

Islamic law also made major contributions to international admiralty law, departing from the previous Roman and Byzantine maritime laws in several ways. These included Muslim sailors being paid a fixed wage "in advance" with an understanding that they would owe money in the event of desertion or malfeasance, in keeping with Islamic conventions in which contracts should specify "a known fee for a known duration." (In contrast, Roman and Byzantine sailors were "stakeholders in a maritime venture, inasmuch as captain and crew, with few exceptions, were paid proportional divisions of a sea venture's profit, with shares allotted by rank, only after a voyage's successful conclusion.") Muslim jurists also distinguished between "coastal navigation, or *cabotage*", and voyages on the "high seas", and they made shippers "liable for freight in most cases except the seizure of both a ship and its cargo". Islamic law "departed from Justinian's *Digest* and the *Nomos Rhodion Nautikos* in condemning slave jettison", and the Islamic *Qirad* was a precursor to the European *commenda* limited partnership. The "Islamic influence on the development of an international law of the sea" can thus be discerned alongside that of the Roman influence.

Admiralty law was introduced into England by Eleanor of Aquitaine while she was acting as regent for her son, King Richard the Lionheart. She had earlier established admiralty law on the island of Oleron (where it was published as the *Rolls of Oleron*) in her own lands (although she is often referred to in admiralty law books as "Eleanor of Guyenne"), having learned about it in the eastern Mediterranean while on a Crusade with her first husband, King Louis VII of France. In England, special *admiralty courts* handle all admiralty cases. These courts do not use the common law of England, but are civil law courts largely based upon the Corpus Juris Civilis of Justinian.

Admiralty courts were a prominent feature in the prelude to the American Revolution. For example, the phrase in the Declaration of Independence "For depriving us in many cases, of the benefits of Trial by Jury" refers to the practice of Parliament giving the Admiralty Courts jurisdiction to enforce The Stamp Act in the American Colonies. Because the Stamp Act was unpopular, a colonial jury was unlikely to convict a colonist of its violation. However, because admiralty courts did not (as is true today) grant trial by jury, a colonist accused of violating the Stamp Act could be more easily convicted by the Crown.

Admiralty law became part of the law of the United States as it was gradually introduced through admiralty cases arising after the adoption of the U.S. Constitution in 1789. Many American lawyers who were prominent in the American Revolution were admiralty and maritime lawyers in their private lives. Those included are Alexander Hamilton in New York and John Adams in Massachusetts.

In 1787 Thomas Jefferson, who was then ambassador to France, wrote to James Madison proposing that the U.S. Constitution, then under consideration by the States, be amended to include "trial by jury in all matters of fact triable by the laws of the land [as opposed the law of admiralty] and not by the laws of Nations [i.e. not by the law of admiralty]". The result was the Seventh Amendment to the U.S. Constitution. Alexander Hamilton and John Adams were both admiralty lawyers and Adams represented John Hancock in an admiralty case in colonial Boston involving seizure of one of Hancock's ships for violations of Customs regulations. In the more modern era, Supreme Court Justice Oliver Wendell Holmes was an admiralty lawyer before ascending to the federal bench.

This interesting history of admiralty law has very real consequences to those who find themselves pressing claims within the admiralty jurisdiction. The criminal and civil law with which we are most familiar is derived from the English common law. The law of admiralty, however, having had its origin in the Mediterranean and European sea trade, more closely resembles the European civil law system than the English common law. One significant difference which proved an irritant to our colonial forefathers given the expanded jurisdiction of the British Admiralty Court in the American colonies is the lack of jury under admiralty procedures.

## The Flag Shows Substantive Law Of Admiralty

Maritime law is a legal body that regulates ships and shipping. As sea-borne transportation is one of the most ancient channels of commerce, rules for maritime and trade disputes developed very early in recorded history. In England, special admiralty courts handle all admiralty cases. The courts do not use the common law of England. Admiralty or maritime law is distinct from standard land-based laws even today and even within another country's claimed waters, admiralty law states that a ship's flag dictates the law. This means that a Canadian ship in American waters would be subject to Canadian law and crimes committed on board that ship would stand trial in Canada. In the United States the Supreme Court is the highest court of appeals for admiralty cases, though they rarely progress beyond the state level. United States, admiralty law is of limited jurisdiction, so it is up to the judges to assign verdicts based on a combination of admiralty and specific state law.

At first you wonder what does this have to do with land. Don't be thrown by the fact this process is related to the sea, and that it doesn't apply to land. Admiralty law has come on land. Note the court cases below:

*"Pursuant to the Law of the Flag, a military flag does result in jurisdictional implication when flown. The Plaintiff cites the following: Under what is called international law, the law of the flag, a shipowner who sends his vessel into a foreign port gives notice by his flag to all who enter into contracts with the shipmaster that he intends the law of the flag to regulate those contracts with the shipmaster that he either submit to its operation or not contract with him or his agent at all."* - **Ruhstrat v. People**, 57 N.E. 41, 45, 185 ILL. 133, 49 LRA 181, 76 AM.

When you walk into a court and see this flag you are put on notice that you are in a Admiralty Court and that the king is in control. Also, if there is a king the people are no longer sovereign. Admiralty law is for the sea, maritime law governs contracts between parties that trade over the sea. That's what our fore-fathers intended. However, in 1845 Congress passed an act saying Admiralty law could come on land. The bill may be traced in Cong. Globe, 28th Cong., 2d. Sess. 43, 320, 328, 337, 345(1844-45), no opposition to the Act is reported. Congress held a committee on this subject in 1850 and they said:

*"The committee also alluded to 'the great force' of the great constitutional question as to the power of Congress to extend maritime jurisdiction beyond the ground occupied by it at the adoption of the Constitution...." -* ***Ibid****. H.R. Rep. No. 72 31st Cong., 1st Sess. 2 (1850)*

It was up to the Supreme Court to stop Congress and say no as the Constitution did not give you that power, nor was it intended. But no, the courts began a long sequence of abuses. Here are some excerpts from a few court cases.

*"This power is as extensive upon land as upon water. The Constitution makes no distinction in that respect. And if the admiralty jurisdiction, in matters of contract and tort which the courts of the United States may lawfully exercise on the high seas, can be extended to the lakes under the power to regulate commerce, it can with the same propriety and upon the same construction, be extended to contracts and torts on land when the commerce is between different States. And it may embrace also the vehicles and persons engaged in carrying it on. It would be in the power of Congress to confer admiralty jurisdiction upon its courts, over the cars engaged in transporting passengers or merchandise from one State to another, and over the persons engaged in conducting them, and deny to the parties the trial by jury. Now the judicial power in cases of admiralty and maritime jurisdiction, has never been supposed to extend to contracts made on land and to be executed on land. But if the power of regulating commerce can be made the foundation of jurisdiction in its courts, and a new and extended admiralty jurisdiction beyond its heretofore known and admitted limits, may be created*

*on water under that authority, the same reason would justify the same exercise of power on land."* -- **Propeller Genessee** Chief et al. v. Fitzhugh et al. 12 How. 443 (U.S. 1851)

And all the way back, before the U.S. Constitution John Adams talking about his state's Constitution, said:

*"Next to revenue (taxes) itself, the late extensions of the jurisdiction of the admiralty are our greatest grievance. The American Courts of Admiralty seem to be forming by degrees into a system that is to overturn our Constitution and to deprive us of our best inheritance, the laws of the land. It would be thought in England a dangerous innovation if the trial, of any matter on land was given to the admiralty."* -- **Jackson v. Magnolia**, 20 How. 296 315, 342 (U.S. 1852)

This began the most dangerous precedent of all the Insular Cases. This is where Congress took a boundless field of power. When legislating for the states, they are bound by the Constitution, when legislating for their insular possessions they are not restricted in any way by the Constitution. Read the following quote from the Harvard law review of AMERICAN INS. CO. v. 356 BALES OF COTTON, 26 U.S. 511, 546 (1828), relative to our insular possessions:

*"These courts, then, are not constitutional courts in which the judicial power conferred by the Constitution on the general government can be deposited. They are incapable of receiving it. They are legislative courts, created in virtue of the general right of sovereignty which exists in the government, or in virtue of that clause which enables Congress to make all needful rules and regulations respecting the territory belonging to the united States. The jurisdiction with which they are invested is not a part of that judicial power which is conferred in the third article of the Constitution, but is conferred by Congress in the execution of those general powers which that body possesses over the territories of*

*the United States."* -- **Harvard Law Review**, Our New Possessions. page 481.

Here are some Court cases that make it even clearer:

*"...[T]he United States may acquire territory by conquest or by treaty, and may govern it through the exercise of the power of Congress conferred by Section 3 of Article IV of the Constitution... In exercising this power, Congress is not subject to the same constitutional limitations, as when it is legislating for the United States. ...And in general the guaranties of the Constitution, save as they are limitations upon the exercise of executive and legislative power when exerted for or over our insular possessions, extend to them only as Congress, in the exercise of its legislative power over territory belonging to the United States, has made those guarantees applicable."* -- **Hooven & Allison & Co. vs Evatt,** 324 U.S. 652 (1945)

## How Admiralty Happened

With reference to ***www.stopthepirates.blogspot.ca/ Jack Anderson*** explains:
Around the time of the war between the United States and the southern states of the American union, the United States was busy putting together a plan that would increase the jurisdiction of the United States. This plan was necessary because the United States had no subjects and only the land ceded to it from the states, i.e. the District which was only ten miles square and such land as was necessary for forts, magazines, arsenals, etc.

Between the 1860's and the early 1900's, banking and taxing mechanisms were changing through legislation. Cunning people closely associated with the powers in England had great influence on the legislation being passed in the United States. Of course such legislation did not apply to the states or to the people in the states, but making the distinction was not deemed to be a necessary duty of the legislators. It was the responsibility of the people to understand their relationship to the United States and to the laws that were being passed by the legislature. This distinction between the United States and the states was taught in the homes and the schools and churches. The early admiralty courts did not interpret legislation as broadly at that time because the people knew when the courts were overstepping their jurisdiction. The people were in control because they knew who they were and where they were standing in relation to the United States.

In 1913 the United States added numerous private laws to its books that facilitated the increase of subjects and property for the United States. The 14th Amendment provided for a new class of citizens – United States citizens, that had not formerly been recognized. Until the 14th Amendment in 1868, there were no persons born or naturalized in the United States. They had all been born or naturalized in one of the several states. United States citizenship was a result of state citizenship. After the Civil War, a new class was recognized, and was the beginning of the democracy sited in the District of Columbia. The American people in the republic sited in the several states, could choose to benefit as one of these new United States citizens BY CHOICE. The new class of citizens was given the right to vote in the democracy in 1870 by the 15th Amendment. All it required was an application. Benefits came with this new citizenship, but with the benefits, came duties and responsibilities that were totally regulated by the legislature for the District of Columbia. Edward Mandell House is attributed with giving a very detailed outline of the plans to be implemented to enslave the American people. The 13th Amendment in 1865 opened the way for the people to volunteer into the equivalent of slavery to accept the benefits offered by the United States. Whether House actually spoke the words or not, is really irrelevant because the scenario detailed in the statement attributed to him has clearly been implemented. Central banking for the United States was legislated with the Federal Reserve Act in 1913. The ability to decrease the currency in circulation through taxation was legislated with the 16th Amendment in 1913. Support for the presumption that the American people had volunteered to participate in the United States democracy was legislated with the 17th Amendment in 1913. The path was provided for the control of the courts, with the creation of the American Bar Association in 1913.

In 1917 the United States legislature passed the Trading with the Enemy Act and the Emergency War Powers Act, opening the doors for the United States to suspend limitations otherwise mandated in the Constitution. Even in times of peace, every contrived and created social, political, or financial emergency was sufficient authority for the officers of the United States to overstep its peace time powers and implement volumes of "law" that would increase the coffers of the United States. There is always a declared emergency in the United States and its States, but it only applies to their subjects.

In the 1920's the States accelerated the push for mothers to register their babies. Life was good and people were not paying attention to what was happening in government. The stock market crashed, and those who were not on the inside were not warned to take their money out before they lost everything.

## Plausible Deniability: The Background Plan

In the 1930's federal legislation provided for registration of babies through applications for birth certificates, so government workers could get maternity leave with pay. The States pushed for registration of cars through applications for certificates of title, and for registration of land through registration of deeds of trust. Constructive trusts secretly were created as each of the people blindly walked into the United States democracy, thereby agreeing to be sureties for the debts of the United States. The great depression supplied the diversion to keep the people's attention off what government was doing. The Social Security program was implemented, along with numerous other United States programs that invited the American people to volunteer to be the sureties behind the United States' new registered property and adhesion contracts through the new United States subjects.

The plan was well on its path by 1933. Massive registration of property through United States agencies assuring the United States and its officers would get rich beyond their wildest expectations, as predicted by Mendall House. All of this was done without disclosure of the material facts that accompanied each application for registration – fraud. The fraud was a sufficient reason to charge all the United States officers with treason, UNLESS a remedy could be supplied for the people to recoup their property and collect for the damages they suffered as a result of the fraud.

If a remedy were available, and the people chose not to or failed to use their remedy, no charge of fraud could be sustained even in a common law court. The United States only needed to provide the remedy. It was not required to explain it or even tell the people where the remedy could be found. The attorneys did not even have to be taught about the remedy. That gave them plausible deniability when the people struggled to understand the new laws. The legislators did not have to have the intricate details of the law explained to them regarding the bills they were passing. That gave them plausible deniability. If the people failed to use their remedy, the United States came out the winner every time. If the people did discover their remedy, the United States had to honour it and release the registered property back to the people, but only if the people knew they had a remedy, and only if they requested it in the proper manner. It was a great plan.

With plausible deniability, even when the people knew they had a remedy and pursued it, the attorneys, judges, and legislators could act like they did not understand the people's claims. In fact, it is true, they are not trained to understand. Requiring the public schools to teach civics, government, and history classes out of approved politically correct text books also assured the people would not find the remedy for a long time. Passing new State and Federal laws that appeared to subject the people to rules and regulations, added another level of protection against the people finding their remedy. The public media was molded to report politically correct, though substantially incorrect, news day after day, until few people would even think there could be a remedy available to them. The people could be separated from their money and their time to pursue the remedy long enough for the solutions to be lost in the pages of millions of books in huge law libraries across the country. So many people know there is something wrong with all the conflicts in the laws with the "facts" taught in the schools. How can the American people be free and subject to a sovereign governments whims at the same time? Who would ever have thought the people would be resourceful enough to actually find the remedy?

In 1933 the United States put its insurance policy into place with House Joint Resolution 192 (2) and recorded it in the Congressional Record. It was not required to be promulgated in the Federal Register. An Executive Order issued on April 5, 1933 paving the way for the withdrawal of gold in the United States. Representative Louis T. McFadden brought formal charges on May 23, 1933 against the Board of Governors of the Federal Reserve Bank system, the Comptroller of the Currency, and the Secretary of the United States Treasury (Congressional Record May 23, 1933 page 4055-4058). HJR 192 passed on June 3, 1933. Mr. McFadden claimed on June 10, 1933: "Mr. Chairman, we have in this country one of the most corrupt institutions the world has ever known. Refer to the Federal Reserve Board and the Federal Reserve Banks..." HJR 192 is the insurance policy that protects the legislators from conviction for fraud and treason against the American people. It also protects the American people from damages caused by the actions of the United States.

HJR 192 provided that the one with the gold paid the bills. It removed the requirement that the United States subjects and employees had to pay their debts with gold. It actually prohibited the inclusion of a clause in all subsequent contracts that would require payment in gold. It also cancelled the clause in every contract written prior to June 5, 1933, that required an obligation to be paid in gold – retroactively. It provided that the United States subjects and employees could use any type of coin and currency to discharge a public debt as long as it was in use in the normal course of business in the United States. For a time, United States Notes were the currency used to discharge debts, but later the Federal Reserve and the United States provided a new medium of exchange through paper notes, and debt instruments that could be passed on to a debtor's creditors to discharge the debtor's debts. That same currency is available to us to use to discharge public debts.

# 15

# THE LAWS OF THE LAND

## The Uniform Commercial Code Laws

In the 1950's the Uniform Commercial Code was presented to the States as a means of unifying the generally accepted procedures for handling the new legal system of dealing with commercial fictions as though they were real. Security instruments replaced substance as collateral for debts. Security instruments could be supported by presumptive contracts. Debt instruments with collateral, and accommodating parties, could be used instead of money. Money and the need for money was disappearing, and a uniform system of laws had to be put in place to allow the courts to uphold the security instruments that depended on commercial fictions as a basis for compelling payment or performance. All this was accomplished by the mid 1960's.

The commercial code is merely a codification of accepted and required procedures all people engaged in commercial activities must follow. The basic principles of commerce had been settled thousands of years ago, but were refined as commerce become more sophisticated over the years. In the 1900's the age-old principles of commerce shifted from substance to form. Presumption became a big part of the law. Without giving a degree of force to presumption, the new direction in enforcing commercial claims could not be supported in courts. If the claimants were required to produce their claims every time they tried to collect money or time from the people, they would seldom be successful. The principles expressed in the code combine the means of dealing with substantive commercial activities with the means of dealing with presumptive commercial activities. These principles work as well for the people as they do for the deceivers. The rules do not respect persons.

Those who enticed the people to register their things with the United States and its sub- divisions, gained control of the substance through the registrations. The United States became the Holder of the titles to many things. The definition of "property" is the interest one has in a thing. The thing is the principal. The property is the interest in the thing. Profits (interest) made from the property of another, belong to the owner of the thing. Profits were made by the deceivers by pledging the registered property in commercial markets, but the profits do not belong to the deceivers. The profits belong to the owners of the things. That is always the people. The corporation only shows ownership of paper – titles to things. The substance cannot appear in the fiction. [[Watch the movie Last Action Hero and watch the confusion created when they try to mix substance and fiction.]] Sometimes the fiction is made to look very much like substance, but fiction can never become substance. It is an impossibility.

The profits from all the registered things had to be put into trust (constructive) for the benefit of the owners. If the profits were put into the general fund of the United States and not into separate trusts for the owners, the scheme would represent fraud. The profits for each owner could not be commingled. If the owner failed to use his available remedy (fictional credits held in a constructive trust account, fund, or financial ledger) to benefit from the profits, it would not be the fault of the deceivers. If the owner failed to learn the law that would open the door to his remedy, it would not be the fault of the deceivers. The owner is responsible for learning the law, so he understands that the profits from his things are available for him to discharge debts or charges brought against his public person by the United States.

If the United States has the "gold", the United States pays the bills (from the trust account, fund, or financial ledger). The definition of "fund" is money set aside to pay a debt. The fund is there to discharge the public debts attributed to the United States subjects, but ultimately back to the accommodating parties – the American people. The national debt that is owed is to the owners of the registered things – the American people, as well as to other creditors.

If the United States owes a debt to the owner of the thing, and the owner is presumed (by accommodation) to owe a public debt to the United States, the logical thing is to ask the United States to discharge that public debt from the trust fund. The way for the United States to get around having to pay the public debts for the people is to claim the owner cannot be an owner if he agreed to be the accommodating party for a debtor person. If the people are truly the principle, then they know how to handle their financial and political affairs, UNLESS they have never been taught. If the owner admits by his actions out of ignorance, that he is an accommodating party, he has taken on the debtor's liabilities without getting consideration in exchange. Here lies the fiction again. The owner of the thing does not have to knowingly agree to be the accommodating party for the debtor person; he just has to act like he agreed. That is easy if he has a choice of going to jail or signing for the debtor person. The presumption that he is the accommodating party is strong enough for the courts to hold the owner of the thing liable for a tax on the thing he actually owns.

Debtors may have the use of certain things, but the things belong to the creditors. The creditor is the master. The debtor is the servant. The Uniform Commercial Code is very specific about the duties and responsibilities a debtor has. If the owner of the thing is presumed to be a debtor because of his previous admissions and adhesion contracts, he is going to have a difficult time convincing the United States that it has a duty to discharge public debts for him. In addition, the courts are staffed with loyal judges who will look for every mistake the people make when trying to use their remedy.

## Uniform Commercial Code: The Law Of The Land

The **Uniform Commercial Code** (**UCC** or the Code), first published in 1952, is one of a number of uniform acts that have been promulgated in conjunction with efforts to harmonize the law of sales and other commercial transactions in all 50 states within the United States of America.

The UCC is the longest and most elaborate of the uniform acts. The Code has been a long-term, joint project of the National Conference of Commissioners on Uniform State Laws (NCCUSL) and the American Law Institute (ALI), who began drafting its first version in 1942. Judge Herbert F. Goodrich was the Chairman of the Editorial Board of the original 1952 edition, and the Code itself was drafted by some of the top legal scholars in the United States, including Karl N. Llewellyn, William A. Schnader, Soia Mentschikoff, and Grant Gilmore.

In one or another of its several revisions, the UCC has been enacted in all of the 50 states, as well as in the

District of Columbia, the Commonwealth of Puerto Rico, Guam and the U.S. Virgin Islands. Louisiana has enacted most provisions of the UCC, with the exception of Article 2, preferring to maintain its own civil law tradition for governing the sale of goods.

The Uniform Commercial Code also attempts to make commercial paper transactions, such as the processing of checks, less complicated. It differentiates the difference between merchants, who are knowledgeable of business transactions, and consumers, who are not.

What the UCC is supposed to accomplish is to conduct transactions without it being necessary to involve lawyers in the trade it administers. The affairs which are addressed with the eleven articles of the **Uniform Commercial Code** includes the sale of goods, all bank and negotiable instruments, letters of credit, bills of receipts, bulk transfers, investment securities, and secured transactions.

As you have learned, your Birth Certificate is traded on the Stock Market Under UCC. The **Uniform Commercial Code**, is the most discussed and implemented of many Uniform Acts which is sponsored by the National Conference of Commissioners on Uniform State Laws, which originated in 1892. Some of the other Uniform Acts include the **Uniform Child Custody Jurisdiction Action** as well as the **Uniform Foreign Money Claims Act**.

The **NCCUSL** is a combination of lawyers and business professionals, which are chosen by the States and territories, these people discuss exactly which laws should be uniform throughout the country. The reason for the American Law Institute, which was established in 1923, is to formulate the **American Common Law** according to the diversified social needs. The ALI and NCCUSL both are authorized to maintain and revise the **Uniform Commercial Code (UCC)**.

The Uniform Commercial Code (UCC) is a set of suggested laws relating to commercial transactions. The UCC was one of many uniform codes that grew out of a late nineteenth-century movement toward uniformity among state laws. In 1890 the American Bar Association, an association of lawyers, proposed that states identify areas of law that could be made uniform throughout the nation, prepare lists of such areas, and suggest appropriate legislative changes. In 1892 the National Conference of Commissioners on Uniform State Laws (NCCUSL) met for the first time in Saratoga, New York. Only seven states sent representatives to the meeting.

In 1986 the NCCUSL offered up its first act, the Uniform Negotiable Instruments Act. The NCCUSL drafted a variety of other Uniform Acts. Some of these dealt with commerce, including the Uniform Conditional Sales Act and the Uniform Trust Receipts Act. The uniform acts on commercial issues were fragmented by the 1930s and in 1940, the NCCUSL proposed revising the commerce-oriented uniform codes and combining them into one uniform set of model laws. In 1941 the American Law Institute (ALI) joined the discussion, and over the next several years lawyers, judges, and professors in the ALI and NCCUSL prepared a number of drafts of the Uniform Commercial Code.

In September 1951 a final draft of the UCC was completed and approved by the American Law Institute (ALI) and the NCCUSL, and then by the House of Delegates of the American Bar Association. After some additional amendments and changes, the official edition, with explanatory comments, was published in 1952. Pennsylvania was the first state to adopt the UCC, followed by Massachusetts. By 1967 the District of Columbia and all the states, with the exception of Louisiana, had adopted the UCC in whole or in part. Louisiana eventually adopted all the articles in the UCC except articles 2 and 2A.

The UCC is divided into nine articles, each containing provisions that relate to a specific area of Commercial Law:

Article 1, General Provisions, provides definitions and general principles that apply to the entire code.
Article 2, Covers the sale of goods.
Article 3, Commercial Paper, addresses negotiable instruments, such as promissory notes and checks.
Article 4 deals with banks and their handling of checks and other financial documents.
Article 5 provides model laws on letters of credit, which are promises by a bank or some other party to pay the purchases of a buyer without delay and without reference to the buyer's financial solvency.
Article 6, on bulk transfers, imposes an obligation on buyers who order the major part of the inventory for certain types of businesses. Most notably Article 6 provisions require that such buyers notify creditors of the seller of the inventory so that creditors can take steps to see that the seller pays her debts when she receives payments from the buyer.
Article 7 offers rules on the relationships between buyers and sellers and any transporters of goods, called carriers. These rules primarily cover the issuance and transfer of warehouse receipts and bills of lading. A bill of lading is a document showing that the carrier has delivered an item to a buyer.
Article 8 contains rules on the issuance and transfer of stocks, bonds, and other investment Securities.
Article 9, Secured Transactions, covers security interests in real property. A security interest is a partial or total claim to a piece of property to secure the performance of some obligation, usually the payment of a debt. This article identifies when and how a secured interest may be created and the rights of the creditor to foreclose on the property if the debtor defaults on his obligation. The article also establishes which creditors can collect first from a defaulting debtor.

The ALI and the NCCUSL periodically review and revise the UCC. Since the code was originally devised, the House of Delegates of the American Bar Association has approved two additional articles:

Article 2A on Personal Property leases. Article 2A establishes model rules for the leasing or renting of personal property (as opposed to real property, such as houses and apartments), and
Article 4A on fund transfers. Article 4A covers transfers of funds from one party to another party through a bank. This article is intended to address the issues that arise with the use of new technologies for handling money.

Most states have adopted at least some of the provisions in the UCC. The least popular article has been article 6 on bulk transfers. These provisions require the reporting of payments made, which many legislators consider an unnecessary intrusion on commercial relationships.

If you have ever heard the statement "*The constitution has NO place in the courts and your life?*" consider this: When one argues a "Constitutional" position whether in the courts or society that position will NOT prevail. Why? We grew up with the concept of personal freedom and constitutional rights. Yet, even to the most casual observer America is NOT free, not when your work for PLANET EARTH by agreement (even though you're were not aware of it). The Constitution is NOT in effect in the courts of this land. Ask any judge, he will quickly tell you the constitution is not permitted in his courtroom.

Every company, corporate entity or any organization is governed by a charter, by-laws, or some sort of 'constitution' that will legally dictate and control the operation. Ever stop to consider that if the Constitution is NOT the charter for the Federal government and society what is the "law" of that society?

Then what is the law and "constitution" of the federal government and society in which we live? It is The Uniform Commercial Code!

Today the majority of Americans pay taxes because when they get a job their employer requests that they fill out an Internal Revenue Service Form W-4, which, as a direct result, withholds taxes from their paychecks for their labour. The majority doesn't have a clue as to why they are paying these taxes in the first place. It has been affirmed that labour is a fundamental, unalienable right, protected by the United States Constitution. This fundamental right is not supposed to be taxed. It is presumed that everyone is expected to know the law. It has been long held that, ignorance of the Law is not an excuse or a defense. The well established maxim that: *"He who fails to assert his rights - HAS NONE!"*, unequivocally establishes that just as a closed mouth never gets fed, *"a matter must be expressed to be resolved."* When it comes to dealing with lawyers, government, and the Internal Revenue Service (which is not an agency of the United States Government, but a private foreign-owned corporation) withholding and keeping knowledge from the people is nothing new. It is a common business tactic that has been going on from the beginning of its inception. It will, most likely continue as long as we rely upon lawyers and government to do that which we ourselves should be doing.

In order to find the answer as to why your labour is being taxed, when the Constitution says it is not supposed to be, it is necessary to understand how government exists and operates. To accomplish this requires a quick review back in history to the time of the War Between the States. The People of this Nation lost their true Republican form of government. On March 27, 1861 seven southern States walked out of Congress leaving the entire legislative Branch of Government without quorum. The Congress of the Constitution was dissolved for inability to disband or re-convene. The

Republican form of Government, which the People were guaranteed - ceased to exist. Out of necessity to operate the Government, President Lincoln issued Executive Order No. 2. in April 1861, reconvening the Congress at gunpoint in Executive, emergency, martial-law-rule jurisdiction. Since that time there has been no "de jure" (sanctioned by law) Congress. Everything functions under "color of law" (the appearance or semblance, without substance, of legal right.) Through Executive Orders under authority of the War Powers, (i.e. emergency, i.e. the law of necessity) the "law of necessity" means no law whatsoever, as per such maxims of law as: "Necessity knows no law" (the law of forbidding killing is voided when done in self-defence). *"In time of war laws are silent."* **Cicero**.

To establish the underlying debt of the Government to the Bankers, to create corporate entities that are legally subject to the jurisdiction which they exist, and to create the jurisdiction itself correctly, the so-called (fraudulent and unratified) Fourteenth Amendment was proclaimed and passed in 1868. This was a cestui que trust (operation in law) incorporated in a military, private, International, commercial, de facto (jurisdiction created by, and belonging to, the Money Power, existing within the emergency of the War Powers, the only operational jurisdiction since the dissolution of Congress in 1861. Through the 14th Amendment, an artificial person-corporate entity-franchise entitled "citizen of the United States" was born into private, corporate limited liability. Section 4 of the 14th Amendment states: "The validity of the Public Debt of the United States (to the Bankers) ... shall not be questioned."

Within the above-referenced private jurisdiction of the International Bankers, the private and foreign owned "Congress" formed a corporation, commercial agency, and Government for the "District of Columbia" on February 21, 1871, Chapter 62, 16 Stat. 419. This corporation was reorganized June 11, 1878, Chapter 180, 20 Stat. 102, and re-named "United States

Government." This corporation privately trade marked the names: "United States," "U.S.," "US," "U.S.A.," "USA" and "America."

When the United States declared itself a municipal corporation, it also created what is known as a **cestui que trust** (a trust where one party receives benefits and use while legal title rests in another covered later in detail) to function under by implementing the Federal Constitution of 1871, and incorporating the previous United States Constitutions of 1787 and 1791 as amended, as by-laws. Naturally, as the grantor of the trust, this empowered the United States Government to change the terms of the trust at will. As evidenced under the Federal Constitution of 1871, the 14th Amendment, the People of the United States without their consent, were declared "Citizens" and granted "Civil Rights." These so-called civil rights are nothing more than mere privileges. Privileges which government licenses, regulates, and can re-interpret to suit it's purposes at any time for any reason. The Federal Corporate Government also conveniently somehow forgot to disclose to the People that the term "Citizen" with which they have made every living and breathing inhabitant a "subject", was defined in law as a "Vessel" engaged in commerce, hence falling under admiralty Law.

In 1912, when the bonds, that were keeping the US Government afloat, and, were owned by the Bankers, came due, the Bankers refused to re-finance the debt, and the colorable, martial-law-rule Congress was compelled to pass, the Federal Reserve Act of 1913. This Act surrendered constitutional authority to create, control, and manage the entire money supply of the United States to a handful of private, mostly foreign, bankers. This placed exclusive creation and control of the money within the private, commercial, foreign, and military jurisdiction of 1861, into corporate limited liability.

America converted from United States Notes to Federal Reserve Notes, beginning with the passage of The Federal Reserve Act of 1913. Federal Reserve Banks were incorporated in 1914, and, in 1916, began to circulate their private, corporate Federal Reserve Notes as "money" alongside the nations "de jure" (according to law) currency, the United States Notes. The United States Notes were actually warehouse receipts for deposits of gold and silver in a warehouse (bank), thus representing wealth (substance, portable land; the money of sovereigns), the new flat money (Federal Reserve Notes) amounted to "bills for that which was yet to be paid," i.e. for what was owed! For the new "benefit" of being able to carry around U.S. Government debt instruments (Federal Reserve Notes) in our wallets instead of Gold Certificates or Silver Certificates, we agreed to redeem the newly issued Federal Reserve Notes in gold and also to pay interest for their use in gold ONLY! Essentially, the Fed issued paper with pretty green ink on it and we agreed to give them gold in exchange for the "privilege" of using it. Such was the bargain. And those that made the deal knew what they were doing!

Through paying interest to the Federal Reserve Corporation in gold, the US Treasury became progressively depleted of its gold. America's gold certificates, coin, and bullion were continually shipped off to the coffers of various European Banks and Power Elite. In 1933, when the Treasury was drained and the debt was larger than ever (a financial condition known as "insolvency"), President Roosevelt proclaimed the bankruptcy of the United States. Every 14th Amendment "citizen of the United States" was pledged as an asset to finance the Chapter 11 re-organization expenses and pay interest in perpetuity to the CREDITORS (Federal Reserve Bankers) and the "national debt", ("which shall not be questioned").

On March 9, 1933, Congress passed the Amendatory Act (also known as the Emergency Banking Relief Act) to the

Trading with the Enemy Act (originally passed on October 6, 1917) at a time when the United States was not in a shooting war with any foreign foe and included the People of the United States as the enemy.

At the conference of Governors held on March 6, 1933, the Governors of the 48 States of the Union accommodated the Federal Bankruptcy of the United States Corporation by pledging the faith and credit of their State to the aid of the National Government.

Senate Document 43 of the 73rd Congress, 1st Session (1933) did declare that ownership of ALL PROPERTY is in the STATE and individual so-called ownership is only by virtue of government, i.e. law amounting to "mere-user" only; and individual use of all property is subordinate to the necessities of the United States Government.

Under House Joint Resolution 192 of June 5, 1933, Senate Report No. 93549, and Executive Orders 6072, 6012 and 6246, the Congress and President Roosevelt officially declared bankruptcy of the United States Government.

Regardless of the cause or reason, what many American's either do not understand and/or have failed to seriously grasp, is that by the use of Federal Reserve Notes; (which is not Constitutional Money defined under Article I Section 10 of the United States Constitution)), the People of the United States since 1933, have not had any Constitutionally lawful way to pay their debts. They therefore have not had any way to buy or own property. The People, for the benefits granted to them by a bankrupt corporate Government, discharge their debts with limited liability using Federal Reserve Notes. They have surrendered, by way of an unconscionable contract, their individual Rights under the Constitution, in exchange for mere privileges!

A review of countless United States Supreme Court decisions since the 1938, landmark case, Erie Railroad v.

Tompkins, (304 U.S. 64-92) clearly establishes that only the State has Constitutional Rights, not the People. The People have been pledged to the bankruptcy of 1933. The federal law administered in and by the United States is the private commercial "law" of the CREDITORS. That, due to the bankruptcy, every "citizen of the United States" is pledged as an asset to support the bankruptcy, must work to pay the insurance premiums on the underwriting necessary to keep the bankrupt government in operation under Chapter II Bankruptcy (Reorganization). That upon the declared Bankruptcy, Americans could operate and function only through their corporate colored, State created, ALL-CAPITAL-LETTERS-NAME, - that has no access to sovereignty, substance, rights, and standing in law. The Supreme Court also held the "general (Universal) common law" no longer is accessible and in operation in the federal courts based on the 1933, bankruptcy, which placed everything into the realm of private, colorable law merchant of the Federal Reserve CREDITORS. To take this to a different level and not only explain why you pay taxes, but also why you do not own the house you live in, the car you drive, or own anything else you think you've bought and paid for etc. The State Government and its CREDITORS own it all. If you think you own your home just because you believe you paid it using those Federal Reserve Notes, just like everything else you possess by permission of Government, simply stop paying your taxes, (user-fees), (licenses) and see just how long Government and the CREDITORS allow you to keep it before they come to take it away from you.

How can all this really be? Why haven't you been told all of this before now? Ignorance of the law is no excuse they say is your problem. It's like the satanic belief structure that says the Dummies are there to be taken advantage of! . Every man is deemed (required) to know the law. Government expects you to know the law, and holds you fully accountable for doing so. and, in truth, as we have repeated over and over: *It is hidden in plain sight*. Ignoring these facts will not protect you. The majority of American's have been given a Public Education to teach them only what the Public, i.e. government (CREDITORS) wants them to know. It is and always has been each individual's personal responsibility, duty and obligation to learn and know the law.

What this breaks down to is this: Back in 1933, when the United States went into bankruptcy because it could no longer pay its debts it pledged the American People themselves without their consent as the asset to keep the government afloat and operating. Because government no longer had any way to pay its debts with substance, was bankrupt, it lost its sovereignty and standing in law. Outside and separate from Constitutional Government, to continue to function and operate, it created an artificial world consisting of artificial entities. This was accomplished by taking everyone's proper birth given name and creating what is called a "fiction in law," by way of an acronym, i.e. a name written in ALL-CAPITAL-LETTERS to interact with. As we have detailed, a name written in ALL-CAPITAL-LETTERS is not a sentient, flesh and blood human being. It is a corporation, fiction or deceased person. Government as well as all corporations, including the Internal Revenue Service cannot deal interact with you or interact with you via your proper name given you at birth, only through your ALL-CAPITAL-LETTERS-NAME! Another little tidbit of knowledge, which has been conveniently kept from the People is this: When the Several united States signed the treaty with Great Britain ending the Revolutionary War, it was a concession that ALL COMMERCE would be regulated and contracted through British Attorney's known as Esquires only.

This condition and concession still exists today. No attorney or lawyer in the United States of America has ever been "licensed" to practice law (they've exempted themselves) as they are a legal fiction "person" and only an "ADMITTED MEMBER" to practice in the private franchise club called the BAR (which is itself an acronym for the British or Barrister Aristocratic or Accreditation Regency), as such are un-registered foreign agents, and so they are traitors. Esquires (Unconstitutional Title of honour and nobility = Esquires), foreign non-citizens (aliens) who are specifically prohibited from ever holding any elected Public Office of trust whatsoever! Article I, Section 9, clause 8, states: "*No Title of Nobility shall be granted by the United States: And no Person holding any Office of Profit or Trust under them, shall, without the Consent of the Congress, accept any present, Emolument, Office, or Title, of any kind whatsoever, from any King, Prince, or foreign State.*"

Like said before, as a direct result, attorneys and lawyers cannot and do not represent you in your proper birth or given name. Attorneys and lawyers re-present corporations, artificial persons, and fictions in law - ONLY! What the majority in this country fail to recognize is this: because of the bankruptcy and having been pledged as an asset to the National Government's debt, this makes all citizens DEBTORS under Chapter 11. DEBTORS in bankruptcy having lost their solvency - - have NO RIGHTS nor STANDING IN LAW and are at the mercy of the CREDITORS.

All courts today sit and operate as Non-Constitutional, Non-Article Three Legislative Tribunals administering the bankruptcy via their "statutes," ("codes."). All Courts are Title 11 Bankruptcy Courts where these statutes are, in reality, "commercial obligations" being applied for the "benefit" or "privilege" of discharging debts with limited liability of the Federal Reserve-monopoly, colorable-money Federal Reserve Notes (debt Instruments). This means every time you end up before a court - not only do you NOT have any standing in law to state a claim upon which relief can be granted, YOU HAVE NO CONSTITUTIONAL RIGHTS! Why? Because you are a DEBTOR under the bankruptcy and in addition to having contracted away your rights in exchange for benefits and privileges; you do not have one single shred of evidence to establish otherwise. In bankruptcy ONLY CREDITORS have rights!

In a nutshell, as a DEBTOR, it is impossible for you to access Constitutional Rights, they are reduced to mere privileges which are licensed, regulated, and can be altered, amended and changed to meet whatever the particular or special needs of government for whatever whim. If taking away your home, your car, taxing your labour, or locking you up for violating any of the Sixty MILLION plus legislatively created DEBTOR codes and statutes they have on the books today happens to meet the needs of government? It really doesn't take a rocket scientist to realize who the loser will be!

## Everything Is Commerce

Through the contents of this book, you may come to a legal understanding of how/why you have become a slave to the society (democracy) around you. Then you will understand how to regain your freedom and 'constitutional' rights.

The only thing prohibiting your freedom is legal awareness and lack of information. ALL; i.e., EVERY thing or action you do is "commercial" even religions. Even God's (god's) words in the bible laid out a commercial plan as you have seen. You can NOT function except through a "commercial contract". It is well established that a legal fiction (corporation, government, etc) cannot directly approach a "private" individual. When government, court, tax, and corporate agents approach you in person, via the mail, over the phone, etc., they are soliciting your consent for "voluntarily" entering into a commercial contract and "doing business." The controlling law for these contracts is the Uniform Commercial Code.

All governments are corporate, for-profit operations. The U.S. [federal] Government and its administrative agencies bring suits against people and other government entities every day. In the legal system there is no difference between civil and criminal jurisdictions; each is commercial. All crime (including murder) is commercial, i.e. has a monetary value affixed thereto. 27 CAR 72.11 spells this out in unequivocal terms. Nowadays it is common for both artificial and flesh-and-blood entities to settle criminal charges out of court, i.e. via payment. Note: committing a crime is a physical impossibility for an artificial person/corporation, but such are charged criminally almost every day.

## The Uniform Commercial Code at Article 1, §103 it states: § 1-103. Supplementary General Principles of Law Applicable.

Unless displaced by the particular provisions of this Act, the principles of law and equity, including the law merchant and the law relative to capacity to contract, principal and agent, estoppel, fraud, misrepresentation, duress, coercion, mistake, Bankruptcy, or other validating or invalidating cause shall supplement its provisions. What they're telling us is that all other law - common, constitutional, equity, bankruptcy, etc. - is only supplemental to the supreme law of the land - the Uniform Commercial Code. If we don't proceed on the basis upon which they proceed, then we will lose due to failure to procedure, not substance.

The entire hierarchy of the court system is a model identical to the Catholic Church. Here as you have learned, the Pope holds title and lien secured party to everything in "The United States of America" and the Bank of England and the Queen is the administrator for the collection of the tribute, see the Treaty of Paris of 1783 (see Yale University Diana Project) wherein Prince George, King of England, refers to himself as the "arch-treasurer of the United States." Each of us has more contracts and applications that force us into a taxpayer/fiduciary obligation that there are far too many of them to even consider revoking all ab initio. You must get control of the artificial person and capture the value of the bond that was created by the Vatican who operate the illusion so that you can discharge debt. All money must first be predicated upon the creation of an instrument of debt based upon a promise to pay usury sometime in the future.

So who creates the money with which to pay the interest? No one. That is why there were bankruptcy courts created to handle the redistribution of the assets the fiduciary generated and leave the fiduciary enough assets to get started generating wealth again for the trust. The debt creation side first is a rule of the Generally Accepted Accounting Procedures' (GAAP) double entry balance sheet deception. The trusts are in Puerto Rico. All of the things done to us that look like crimes are actually perfectly legal and lawful due to our breach of fiduciary duty, and the foundation for what is done to us has been laid over the past 150 years by the lawmakers who were influenced by the spawn of the "gods" who operate the banks.

## Precepts And Maxims Of Commercial Law

For many people it might come as a surprise (in many cases a pleasant one) if they were informed that essentially all of the law of the world is founded on, derived from, and is a function of ten simple, essential, and fundamental Commercial Maxims seven (7) basic ones plus three (3) corollaries. These foundational principles/axioms underlie all of man's law. Notwithstanding the vastness and complexity of the law today, it is safe to say that all of the world's law is fundamentally a function of the ten Commercial Maxims. Although the dazzling complexity and ever-changing forms, parameters, and labels obfuscate this fact, the essence of the matter remains intact.

The Commercial Maxims constitute the basic rules involved in preventing and resolving disputes, including relating in life and commercial affairs as if disputes might arise and written proof of one's position, in time and content, must be securely established. Although commerce is usually thought of as "buying, selling, and trading," all of man's interactions with his fellow man are considered as being "commerce." Commerce encompasses all relationships between people.

Black's Law Dictionary, Fifth Edition, for instance, defines "commerce" as follows:

*Commerce. "The exchange of goods, productions, or property of any kind; the buying, selling, and exchanging of articles…. Intercourse by way of trade and traffic between different peoples or states…including not only the purchase, sale, and exchange of commodities, but also the instrumentalities and agencies by which it is promoted and the means and appliances by which it is carried on, and transportation of persons as well as of goods, both by land and sea…. Also interchange of ideas, sentiments, etc., as between man and man."*

The Commercial Maxims codify the fundamental principles/maxims of law and commerce upon which man's law and governments have operated on this planet for at least the past 4-6 thousand years. They constitute, as it were, the rules of the game. Part of the grief of mankind today is that the vast, overwhelming percentage of the populace does not know the basic rules of the game they are playing and are hence incapable of playing it. It should not be surprising to know the origins back to Sumeria when the "gods" reigned and prospered.

If one who does not know the rules of a game is playing that game with others who are masters of the rules, the outcome is a foregone conclusion: the one who knows the rules wins the game while the one who does not know the rules necessarily loses. Such is the state of the world. This is PLANET EARTH Inc. and its pyramid structure--all operating under the rules of commerce.

Elucidating the underlying, fundamental rules so that one understands what is going on helps greatly in "leveling the playing field." These rules, therefore, are set forth below with the understanding that they operate within the context and setting of the universal Underlying Principles. The Commercial Maxims are the most basic, enduring, and minimalist codification of universal, real law extant on earth.

They are very simple, largely self-evident, and based on common sense. The Jews, for instance, have studied, analyzed, practiced, and refined Commercial Law, founded on these Maxims, for thousands of years. This continuous, relentless, single-minded absorption in the law over millennia has "worked the bugs out." Every angle, facet, ramification, application, and nuance of practice of Commercial Law has been seasoned over time, and is deeply and thoroughly known by those who "own, run, and rule the world."

When you look at the "Elite" and their "New World Order" with PLANET EARTH INC, they are precisely where they are because they do know this fundamental law, because it is real, that it must work, always works, and it is impossible for it not to work, since it is grounded in natural law. They created the codes and laws. And the Earthling's preoccupation with a perception of freedom allowed this to infuse into the system without question. Those who do not know and use the law by which everything functions necessarily and always lose. This esoteric truth must be obscured and concealed from the "masses" by every means possible. Otherwise, those who would rule mankind would have no way of obtaining their positions of power, privilege, and plunder (all of which are frauds). By knowing and using the law themselves and keeping the knowledge of such law from the masses, the people are deliberately rendered defenseless, confused, emasculated, dependent, helpless "sheeple," considered as existing for the purpose of being exploited, herded, sheered, gelded, and slaughtered at will.

The Elite Powers thus achieve and operate their monopoly on "law" (the very thought is absurd, like stating one has a monopoly on light or life), by propagandizing the lie that law is so complex, esoteric, obtuse, vast, and confusing that only they and their hatchet men called "attorneys" and "judges" can administer it. The law is "mystified," made into some kind of quasi-religious cult, operated by a high priesthood that alone has the knowledge and authority for operating the resulting "legal system" that rules the life of man. Law must be transformed into a "closed union shop" such as the Bar Association, into whose hands the people must entrust their "lives, fortunes, and sacred honor" without availability of alternative sources of remedy and redress of grievances. Where can one go for relief when the fox guards the henhouse? If the so-called "Rulers of the World" did not withhold from general understanding the knowledge that the foundational principles of real law are few in number and easily mastered by everyone, and that all of the documents and instruments used in all law and commerce are likewise few in number and comprehensible to laymen, such con men would have to abandon their aristocratic "titles of nobility" and find real jobs based on genuine productivity, contribution, and "win-win" interactions with their fellow man.

It is empowering and exhilarating to understand that the ever-changing, monstrous vastness of "law" can be distilled into a handful of universal principles that can be contained on a 3" X 5" card, and that all of the legal documents and instruments functioning today can be mastered by nearly anyone. Attorneys and Judges deliberately conceal the fact that the only significance inhering in court cases and statutes consists of the simple and universal principles of commercial law codified by the Maxims.

All legal documents, proceedings, and processes are obscured by re-naming and mislabeling said documents and processes in accordance with whatever degrees of multiplicity and complexity are needed for preserving its inaccessible aloofness. Law is made diffuse, enormously complex, and allegedly far beyond the ken of regular folks. With knowledge of the truth underlying all of that misdirection and deception, i.e. seeing through the Wizard's Light Show, you can understand what is happening and place yourself in a position of mastery of the situation instead of being relegated to the status of a confused, helpless victim forever in the dark and at the mercy of those who exploit your ignorance of the rules and processes by which law (i.e. organized, deadly force) operates.

In short, "*Know the truth and the truth shall make you free.*" The problem is there may some serious consequences in trying.

As mentioned above, the word "commerce" encompasses all interactions and interchanges between people, including exchanges of such "noncommercial" things as "ideas, sentiments, etc." The fundamental principles and precepts of universal commercial law that have for millennia formed the underpinnings of civilized law on this planet are both biblical and non-biblical, i.e. their truth and validity is a function of themselves and the long-accepted usage and practice by many cultures and peoples, in diverse forms, throughout the world for thousands of years. These fundamental Maxims of Commerce, which underlie all commercial documents, instruments, and processes, are enumerated herewith (with biblical references in parenthesis):

### 1. A workman is worthy of his hire
(Exodus 20:15; Lev. 19:13; Matt. 10:10; Luke 10:7; II Tim. 2:6. Legal maxim: "It is against equity for freemen not to have the free disposal of their own property").

### 2. All are equal under the Law

(God's Law--Ethical and Natural Law). (Exodus 21:23-25;
Lev. 24:17-21; Deut. 1:17, 19:21; Matt., 22:36-40; Luke
10:17; Col. 3:25. Legal maxims: "No one is above the law.", "Commerce, by the law of nations, ought to be common, and not to be converted into a monopoly and the private gain of a few.").

### 3. In Commerce truth is sovereign
(Exodus 20:16; Ps. 117:2; Matt. 6:33, John 8:32; II Cor.
13:8. Legal maxim: "To lie is to go against the mind."

### 4. Truth is expressed by means of an affidavit
(Lev. 5:4-5; Lev. 6:3-5; Lev 19:11-13; Num. 30:2; Matt.
5:33; James 5:12).

### 5. An unrebutted affidavit stands as the truth in Commerce
(1 Pet. 1:25; Heb. 6:13-15. Legal maxim: "He who does not deny, admits.").

### 6. An unrebutted affidavit becomes the judgment in Commerce
(Heb. 6:16-17. Any proceeding in a court, tribunal, or arbitration forum consists of a contest, or "duel," of commercial affidavits wherein the points remaining unrebutted in the end stand as the truth and the matters to which the judgment of the law is applied.).

### 7. A matter must be expressed to be resolved
(Heb. 4:16; Phil. 4:6; Eph. 6:19-21. Legal maxim: "He who fails to assert his rights has none.").

### 8. He who leaves the field of battle first loses by default
(Book of Job; Matt. 10:22. Legal maxim: "He who does not repel a wrong when he can, occasions it.").

**9. Sacrifice is the measure of credibility**
(One who is not damaged, put at risk, or willing to swear an oath that he consents to claim against his commercial liability in the event that any of his statements or actions is groundless or unlawful, has no basis to assert claims or charges and forfeits all credibility and right to claim authority.)
(Acts 7, life/death of Stephen, maxim: "He who bears the burden ought also to derive the benefit.").

**10. A lien or claim can be satisfied only through rebuttal by Counter-affidavit point-for-point, resolution by jury, or payment**
(Gen. 2-3; Matt. 4; Revelation. Legal maxim: "If the plaintiff does not prove his case, the defendant is absolved.").

All law in Canada and United States can be reduced to the above ten listed maxims.

# The Ten Commandments

When Jesus spoke the Truth to his accusers, he would justify himself by quoting **Law**. First, he would quote God's Law, and after quoting God's Law He would often quote the accuser's law and use that against them as well. For example, Jesus would say, *"Did ye never read in the **scriptures**..."* and then **quote God's Law**. Then he would turn around and say, "Is it not written in **your law**..." and **quote their own law**! His accusers would have no answer, they could not overcome Him. How could anyone overcome somebody who is obeying both God's Law and man's law!? If a man made law is just, it will be in harmony with God's Law.

These maxims are the foundation and principles of the laws that man passes today. Unfortunately, men enforce their own will more than they enforce law. So, this is why, in addition to knowing God's Law, it is also important to know man's law, because man's law is based upon God's Law. And when you are accused of "breaking the law," you can do what Jesus did, and use both God's Law and man's law to justify your lawful acts, for this is the only thing that will excuse you.

It is important to distinguish between commercial law and maxims of law, when quoting from their law. We should never, ever quote their codes, rules, regulations, ordinances, statutes, common law, merchant law, public policies, constitutions, etc., because these are commercial in nature, and if we use their commercial law, they can presume we are engaged in commerce (which means we are of the world), which will nullify our witness (because we are not of the world). Maxims of law are not commercial law, but are mostly based upon scripture and truth.

Many insist on using the "common law" to defend themselves. The reason we should not is because, first and foremost, you do not see the term "common law" in scripture. Bondservants of Christ are only to use God's Law. Secondly, the common law is a commercial law today, created by merchants, influenced by Roman Law, and used for commercial purposes. The following definitions are taken from "***A Dictionary of Law,*** *by* ***William C. Anderson****, 1893.*"

**Custom of merchants:** A system of customs, originating among merchants, and allowed for the benefit of trade as part of the common law. *Page 303.*
**Law-merchant; law of merchants:** The rules applicable to commercial paper were transplanted into the common law from the law merchant. They had their origin in the customs and course of business of merchants and bankers, and are now recognized by the courts because they are demanded by the wants and conveniences of the mercantile world. *Pages 670-671.*
**Roman Law:** The common law of England has been largely influenced by the Roman law, in several respects: Through the development of commercial law. *Page 910.*
All of man's laws, except for many maxims of law, are commercial in nature.

The following are the definitions of "maxims," and then the relevant maxims of law will be listed.

**Maxim** (*Bouvier's Law Dictionary, 1856*): An established principle or proposition. A principle of law universally admitted, as being just and consonant with reason. Maxims in law are somewhat like axioms in geometry. *1 Bl. Com. 68*. They are principles and authorities, and part of the general customs or common law of the land; and are of the same strength as acts of parliament, when the judges have determined what is a maxim; which belongs to the judges and not the jury. *Terms do Ley; Doct. & Stud. Dial. 1, c. 8*. Maxims of the law are holden for law, and all other cases that may be applied to them shall be taken for granted. *1 Inst. 11. 67; 4 Rep. See 1 Com. c. 68; Plowd. 27, b.*

Finally, here are the Catholic Ten Commandments:

1. I am the LORD your God. You shall worship the Lord your God and Him only shall you serve.
2. You shall not take the name of the Lord your God in vain.
3. Remember to keep holy the Sabbath day.
4. Honor your father and your mother.
5. You shall not kill.
6. You shall not commit adultery.
7. You shall not steal.
8. You shall not bear false witness against your neighbor.
9. You shall not covet your neighbor's wife.
10. You shall not covet your neighbor's goods.

The Ten Commandments are a description of the basic freedom from sin that is necessary to live as a Christian. They are a minimum level of living, below which we must not go. The Ten Commandments and Catholicism have been bound together since the time of Christ. In the Bible which is written as the Commercial Code of GOD and Articles of Incorporation for PLANET EARTH

INC, is executed through the Vatican and the corporate VATICAN. When you willfully accept the religion, you willfully accept the Code as your Law.

It's important to note that each Commandment is simply a **summary** of a whole category of actions. Don't be legalistic, searching for a way around them because their wording doesn't fit you perfectly! For example, "bearing false witness against your neighbor" covers any kind of falsehood: perjury, lying, slander, detraction, rash judgment, etc.

The Catholic Ten Commandments are linked together to form a coherent whole. If you break one of them, you're guilty of breaking all of them (*Catechism*, #2069). The Commandments express man's **fundamental duties** to God and neighbour. As such, they represent *grave* obligations. To violate them knowingly & willingly in a significant way is to commit mortal sin. (See *Catechism*, #2702-3) and then the god of vengeance and the greatest love will reap upon you serious mortal repercussions.

# 16

# THE TRUST AS A PRIME CORPORATE VEHICLE

For banking purposes, there is very little difference between a Corporation and a Trust. All organizations include what is required to open a banking or brokerage account. Generally, the corporations are used for business profit purposes, such as security trading, banking, international commerce, real estate property, etc.

Foundations are more commonly used for non-profit activities such as charities, give or receive donations, grants, etc., but also they may be used for "holding" purposes, as to keep the property of corporations or any other type of goods. Most of our clients use the foundations for confidentiality purposes to keep the ownership of their corporations and asset protection.

Trusts are generally used as "holding" of a corporation property or to keep assets as real estate.

PLANET EARTH is a private business enterprise serving those gods who carefully crafted it. It is not a formal registered organization. It is a fictional entity that I have created. It is a concept but rest assured that there exists some pacts, secret agreements, vows, or other connective means of purpose that is overseen by a fear of death and destruction. Over centuries, the evolution of commerce has required the creation of fictional entities called corporations to act as the vessels. There are many different types. Of particular interest now is the business enterprise vessel which is called a Trust which is a very old concept of holding titles to what are thought as assets. Here we will learn more about the origins and implementations of these trusts as they relate to the vessel which is you, the human, and to that which it holds titles to as Beneficiary, your Estate.

Let us look more closely at this vehicle of commerce called a Trust.

## The History Of Trusts

Trusts date back to ancient Egypt, circa 4000 B.C., when the equivalent of today's trust officers were charged with holding, managing, and caring for other people's property. Various prototypes of trust institutions were later developed in second-century Rome, some of which involved the use of property for charitable purposes. Trusts began to evolve into their present form during the eighth century, when English clergymen acted as executors of wills and trusts. Throughout the Middle Ages and into the 17th century, trusts developed under English common law to resemble their current legal structure in the United States.

Roman law had a well-developed concept of the trust (*fideicommissum*) in terms of "testamentary trusts" created by wills but never developed the concept of the "inter vivos trust" that applied while the creator was still alive. This was created by later common law jurisdictions. Personal trust law developed in England at the time of the Crusades, during the 12th and 13th centuries.

At the time, land ownership in England was based on the feudal system. When a landowner left England to fight in the Crusades, he needed someone to run his estate in his absence, often to pay and receive feudal dues. To achieve this, he would convey ownership of his lands to an acquaintance, on the understanding that the ownership would be conveyed back on his return. However, Crusaders would often return to find the legal owners' refusal to hand over the property.

Unfortunately for the Crusader, English common law did not recognize his claim. As far as the King's courts were concerned, the land belonged to the trustee, who was under no obligation to return it. The Crusader had no legal claim. The disgruntled Crusader would then petition the king, who would refer the matter to his Lord Chancellor. The Lord Chancellor could do what was "just" and "equitable", and had the power to decide a case according to his conscience. At this time, the principle of equity was born.

The Lord Chancellor would consider it "unconscionable" that the legal owner could go back on his word and deny the claims of the Crusader (the "true" owner). Therefore, he would find in favor of the returning Crusader. Over time, it became known that the Lord Chancellor's court (the Court of Chancery) would continually recognize the claim of a returning Crusader. The legal owner would hold the land for the benefit of the original owner, and would be compelled to convey it back to him when requested. The Crusader was the "beneficiary" and the acquaintance the "trustee". The term *use of land* was coined, and in time developed into what we now know as a *trust*.

Also, the Primogeniture system could be considered as a form of trust. In Primogeniture system, the first born male inherited all the property and *"usually assumes the responsibility of trusteeship of the property and of adjudicating attendant disputes."*

The Waqf (***http://en.wikipedia.org/wiki/Waqf***) meaning confinement and prohibition is an equivalent institution in Islamic law, restricted to charitable trusts.

Antitrust law emerged in the 19th century when industries created monopolistic trusts by entrusting their shares to a board of trustees in exchange for shares of equal value with dividend rights; these boards could then enforce a monopoly. However, trusts were used in this case because a corporation could not own other companies' stock and thereby become a holding company without a "special act of the legislature". Holding companies were used after the restriction on owning other companies' shares was lifted.

The trust is widely considered to be the most innovative contribution to the English legal system. Today, trusts play a significant role in most common law systems, and their success has led some civil law jurisdictions to incorporate trusts into their civil codes. France, for example, recently added a similar, though not quite comparable, notion to its own law with *la fiducie*, which was modified in 2009; *la fiducie*, unlike the trust, is a contract. Trusts are widely used internationally, especially in countries within the English law sphere of influence, and whilst most civil law jurisdictions do not generally contain the concept of a trust within their legal systems, they do recognize the concept under the Hague Convention on the Law Applicable to Trusts and on their Recognition (to the extent that they are signatories thereto). The Hague Convention on the Law Applicable to Trusts and on their Recognition also regulates conflict of trusts.

Although trusts are often associated with intrafamily wealth transfers, they have become very important in American capital markets, particularly through pension funds (essentially always trusts) and mutual funds (often trusts).

## Setting Up A Trust: The Mechanics

**Basic principles of a Trust** Property of any sort may be held on trust, but growth assets are more commonly placed into trust (for tax and estate planning benefits). The uses of trusts are many and varied. Trusts may be created during a person's life (usually by a trust instrument) or after death in a will. In a relevant sense, a trust can be viewed as a generic form of a corporation where the settlors (investors) are also the beneficiaries. This is particularly evident in the Delaware business trust, which could theoretically, with the language in the "governing instrument", be organized as a cooperative corporation, limited liability corporation, or perhaps even a nonprofit corporation. One of the most significant aspects of trusts is the ability to partition and shield assets from the trustee, multiple beneficiaries, and their respective creditors (particularly the trustee's creditors), making it "bankruptcy remote", and leading to its use in pensions, mutual funds, and asset securitization.

**Creation of a Trust** Trusts may be created by the expressed intentions of the settlor (express trusts) or they may be created by operation of law known as implied trusts. An implied trust is one created by a court of equity because of acts or situations of the parties. Implied trusts are divided into two categories resulting and constructive. A resulting trust is implied by the law to work out the presumed intentions of the parties, but it does not take into consideration their expressed intent. A constructive trust is a trust implied by law to work out justice between the parties, regardless of their intentions.

Typically a trust can be created in the following ways:

1. a written trust instrument created by the settlor and signed by both the settlor and the trustees (often referred to as an *inter vivos* or "living trust");
2. an oral declaration;
3. the will of a decedent, usually called a testamentary trust;
4. a court order as for example in family proceedings.

In some jurisdictions certain types of assets may not be the subject of a trust without a written document.

**Formalities of a Trust** Generally, a trust requires three certainties:
1. **Intention**. There must be a clear intention to create a trust
2. **Subject Matter**. The property subject to the trust must be clearly identified One may not, for example, settle "the majority of my estate", as the precise extent cannot be ascertained. Trust property may be any form of specific property, be it real or personal, tangible or intangible. It is often, for example, real estate, shares or cash.
3. **Objects**. The beneficiaries of the trust must be clearly identified, or at least be ascertainable. In the case of discretionary trusts, where the trustees have power to decide who the beneficiaries will be, the settlor must have described a clear **class** of beneficiaries. Beneficiaries may include people not born at the date of the trust (for example, "my future grandchildren"). Alternatively, the object of a trust could be a charitable purpose rather than specific beneficiaries.

**Trustees** The trustee may be either a person or a legal entity such as a company. A trust may have one or multiple trustees. A trustee has many rights and responsibilities; these vary from trust to trust depending on the type of the trust. A trust generally will not fail solely for want of a trustee. Where a trust is absent any trustees, a court may appoint a trustee, or in Ireland the trustee may be any administrator of a charity to which the trust is related. Trustees are usually appointed in the document (instrument) which creates the trust.

A trustee may be held personally liable for certain problems which arise with the trust. For example, if a trustee does not properly invest trust monies to expand the trust fund, he or she may be liable for the difference. There are two main types of trustees, professional and non-professional. Liability is different for the two types.

The trustees are the legal owners of the trust's property. The trustees administer the affairs attendant to the trust. The trust's affairs may include investing the assets of the trust, ensuring trust property is preserved and productive for the beneficiaries, accounting for and reporting periodically to the beneficiaries concerning all transactions associated with trust property, filing any required tax returns on behalf of the trust, and other duties. In some cases, the trustees must make decisions as to whether beneficiaries should receive trust assets for their benefit. The circumstances in which this discretionary authority is exercised by trustees is usually provided for under the terms of the trust instrument. The trustee's duty is to determine in the specific instance of a beneficiary request whether to provide any funds and in what manner.

By default, being a trustee is an unpaid job. In modern times trustees are often lawyers, bankers or other professionals who will not work for free. Therefore, often a trust document will state specifically that trustees are entitled to reasonable payment for their work.

Trusts are often confused with legal persons, but are mere *relationships*, not entities. Thus, they have no legal existence independent from the trustee and his or her ownership of the subject matter of the trust. In order to sue a trust, one must sue the trustee in his or her capacity as trustee for a specific trust; conversely, if the trust needs to sue someone, the lawsuit must be brought by the trustee in his or her capacity as such.

**Beneficiaries** The beneficiaries are beneficial (or **equitable**) owners of the trust property. Either immediately or eventually, the beneficiaries will receive income from the trust property, or they will receive the property itself. The extent of a beneficiary's interest depends on the wording of the trust document. One beneficiary may be entitled to income (for example, interest from a bank account), whereas another may be entitled to the entirety of the trust property when he attains the age of twenty-five years. The settlor has much discretion when creating the trust, subject to some limitations imposed by law.

**Implied and Express Trust** An implied trust, as distinct from an express trust, is created where some of the legal requirements for an express trust are not met, but an intention on behalf of the parties to create a trust can be presumed to exist. A resulting trust may be deemed to be present where a trust instrument is not properly drafted and a portion of the equitable title has not been provided for. In such a case, the law may raise a resulting trust for the benefit of the grantor (the creator of the trust). In other words, the grantor may be deemed to be a beneficiary of the portion of the equitable title that was not properly provided for in the trust document.

## Vatican & State Cestui Que Trusts

In 1666, in London, during the black plague, and great fires of London Parliament enacted an act, behind closed doors, called Cestui Que Vie Act 1666. The act being debated the Cestui Qui act was to subrogate the rights of men and women, meaning all men and women were declared dead, lost at sea/beyond the sea. (back then operating in admiralty law, the law of the sea, so lost at sea).

When a child is Baptized by the church, the Baptismal certificate is forwarded to the Vatican who converts the certificate into a negotiable instrument and creates a third Cestui Que Vie trust. These as I have stated before are apparently appropriate to reflect a purpose of the enslavement of the property, body and soul of the child.

The civil administration, UNITED STATES, continues to operate today under this triple crown of enslavement based on the error of assumptions that we are 14$^{th}$ Amendment citizens of the United States based on the breach of trust by the trustees.

## Cestui Que As A Method Of Fraud

***Cestui que*** (also ***cestuy que***) (is a shortened version of *cestui a que use le feoffment fuit fait,* literally, *"The person for whose use the feoffment was made."* It is a Law French phrase of medieval English invention, which appears in the legal phrases *cestui que trust*, *cestui que use*, or *cestui que vie*. In contemporary English the phrase is also commonly pronounced "setty-kay" (/ˈsɛtikeɪ/) or "sesty-kay" (/ˈsɛstikeɪ/). According to Roebuck, *Cestui que use* is pronounced "setticky yuce" (/ˌsɛtikiˈjuːs/). *Cestui que use* and *cestui que trust* are more or less interchangeable terms. In some medieval materials, the phrase is seen as **cestui a que**.

The *cestui que use* is the person for whose benefit the trust is created. The *cestui que trust* is the person entitled to an equitable, as opposed to a legal, estate.

Thus, if land is granted to the use of A in trust for B, B is cestui que trust, and A trustee, or use. The term, principally owing to its cumbersome nature], has been virtually superseded in modern law by that of "beneficiary", and general law of trusts.

By the fifteenth century, *cestui que use* was a vehicle to defraud creditors. The main use was to leave land, or parts of land to members of the family other than the primary heir. This was a way to avoid primogeniture inheritance. While the use was intact, the occupant of the land could take advantage of the *cestui que use* to avoid the feudal payments and duties (incidents). Incidents such as wardship, marriage penalties and other gifts, taxes, fines, fees, and knight service were onerous. Common law did not recognize *cestui que uses* as such, and there was difficulty fitting these cases into the existing writs and case law. The incidents could not be enforced against a person who was on a Crusade, or other war, or business adventure. They were not present in the kingdom to be enforced to perform. Since the feudal oath was to the person, and not the land, there could be no lien against the land. A hallmark of medieval feudalism was the person to person oath of allegiance. The feudal incidents could not be enforced upon the beneficiaries of the *cestui que use*, since these were not the owners of the land. The users had not sworn an oath to the lord. Therefore, they owed the lord nothing. The *cestui que use* had no estate. They had no seisin, nor a trespass, and therefore, ejectment could not be effected. These required possession. Assumpsit was of no avail. In 1402, the Commons had petitioned the king for a remedy against dishonest feoffees to uses, apparently with no result. *Cestui que use* became a new kind of property and property use.

# Cestui Que A Medieval Invention

Many reasons have been given for the invention of the cestui que use as a legal device. During the Crusades, and other wars on the Continent, landowners might be gone for long periods of time. Others might be absent because of business adventures or religious pilgrimages. There was no assurance they would ever return home. The *cestui que use* allowed them to leave a trusted friend or relative with the sort of powers, discretions and they hoped, the duties. Today, this power would be called the "power of attorney". Religious orders such as Franciscans, Cistercians, Benedictines and other mendicant orders took vows of poverty, yet retained the use of donated property. *Cestui que use* allowed them the benefits of land without legal ownership. Besides the obvious limitations placed on cestui que by the Statute of Mortmain, Statute of Uses and the Statute of Wills, its legality was shaped indirectly by provisions within the Magna Carta and Quia Emptores.

Concerted efforts were made under Henry VII of England to reform cestui que. A change in the laws made feoffees the absolute owners of the property of which they had been enfeoffed, and they became subject to all the liabilities of ownership. They were the only ones who could take proceedings against those who interfered with their ownership. If a trespass had been committed with the license of the *cestui que use* they could take proceedings against him, for he was at law only a tenant at sufferance. Similarly, feoffees were the only ones who could take the proceedings against tenants of the land to compel them to perform their obligations. If a debt was brought for rent by a *cestui que use*, and the defendant pleaded "nihil habuit tempore dimissions", the plaintiff would have lost his action if he had not made a special replication setting out the facts. The purpose of these changes was to make *cestui que* in general, and *cestui que use trusts* more cumbersome and economically unattractive.

Henry VIII sought to end all cestui que uses and regain the incidents (fees and payments) that had been deprived him. Thomas Cromwell and Audley who succeeded Thomas More vigorously crushed cestui que uses in the courts, persuading judges to declare them illegal or void.[ By 1538-39, over 800 religious land holdings had been returned to the Crown. Many of these were subsequently sold, converted to private dwellings, given to loyal supporters of the English Reformation, dismantled for building materials, or abandoned and allowed to degenerate into ruins. Claims of religious corruption were frequently used to justify reclamation by the Crown. Since many of these religious orders provided charity, much of the local medical and social services were left in disarray.

The Statute of Uses was enacted in 1535, and was intended to end the "abuses" which had incurred in *cestui que use*. It declared that any holder of a cestui que use became the holder of the legal title of the ownership in fee simple. This voided the advantages of a cestui que use. The feoffee to uses was bypassed. The *cestui que use* had seisin. Henry VIII of England got his incidences back. The land owner lost the ability to will the land to heirs other than those in direct lineage. There could be no bypassing of heirs with a cestui que. This condition was modified in the Statute of Wills (1540). One of the effects of the Statute of Uses in executing the use, was to make a mere sale of land without feoffment (the formal public transfer) effective to pass the legal estate. The buyer became the owner by operation of the statute. It necessitated a public announcement of the intended sale to determine if the land had been surreptitiously sold to someone else. The Statute of Uses required a public registry of sale of land, later called the Statute of Enrollments.

Lawyers quickly determined that adding the words to a conveyance "land to Leonard and his heirs, to the use of John and his heirs, to the use of Kenneth and his heirs." For a time, this device defeated the intent of the Statute of Uses. Lord Hardwicke wrote that the Statute had no real effect other than to add, at most three words, to a conveyance. He was referring to the doctrine that had become settled before his time: that the old use might still be effected despite the Statute, by a "use on a use". The Statute of Uses had been considered a great failure. It did not wipe out double ownership, legal and equitable, which has survived into the modern system of trusts. The preamble of the Statute went far in enumerating the abuses the system of uses had brought into play. The Statute did not, as had previously been suggested, try to remedy these abuses by declaring any uses void. It merely declared that the possession should be transferred to the use and that the cestui que use should have the possession after such manner and form as he had before the use.

**History in German and Roman Law** It is the opinion of William Holdsworth quoting such scholars as Gilbert, Sanders, Blackstone, Spence and Digby, that cestui que in English law had a Roman origin. An analogy exists between cestui que uses and a usufructus (usufruct) or the bequest of a fideicommissum. These all tended to create a feoffement to one person for the use of another. Gilbert writes, (also seen in Blackstone): *"that they answer more to the fideicommissum than the usufructus of the civil law." These were transplanted into England from Roman Civil Law about the close of the reign of Edward III of England by means of foreign ecclesiastics* *who introduced them to evade the Statute of Mortmain. Others argue that the comparison between cestui que and Roman law is merely superficial. The transfer of land for the use of one person for certain purposes to be carried out either in the lifetime or after the death of the person conveying it has its basis in Germanic law. It was popularly held that land could be transferred for the use from one person to another in local custom. The formal English or Saxon law didn't always recognize this custom. The practice was called Salman or Treuhand. "Sala" is German for "transfer".[5] It is related to the Old English "sellen", "to sell".*

The earliest appearance of cestui que in the medieval period was the feoffee to uses, which like the Salman, held on account of another. This was called the cestui que use. It was because the feoffor could impose on him many various duties that landowners acquired through his instrumentality the power to do many things with their land. This was a to avoid the rigidity of medieval common law of land and its uses. Germanic law was familiar with the idea that a man who holds property on account of, or to the use of another is bound to fulfill his trust. Frankish formulas from the Merovingian period describe property given to a church "ad opus sancti illius." Mercian books in the ninth century convey land "ad opus monachorum". The Doomsday Book refers to geld or money, sac and soc held in "ad opus regus", or in "reginae" or "vicecomitis". The laws of William I of England speak of the sheriff holding money "al os le rei" ("for the use of the king").

Others state that the *cestui que use trust* was the product of Roman Law. In England it was the invention of ecclesiastics who wanted to escape the Statute of Mortmain. The goal was to obtain a conveyance of an estate to a friendly person or corporation, with the intent that the use of the estate would reside with the original owner.

Pollock and Maitland describe *cestui que use* as the first step toward the law of agency. They note that the word "use" as it was employed in medieval English law was not from the Latin "usus", but rather from the Latin word "opus", meaning "work". From this came the Old French words "os" or "oes". Although with time the Latin document for conveying land to the use of John would be written "ad opus Johannis" which was interchangeable with "ad usum Johannis", or the fuller formula, "ad opus et ad usum", the earliest history suggests the term "use" evolved from "ad opus".

## Significance Of The Cestui Que Vie Trust

In 1666, in London, during the black plague, and great fires of London Parliament enacted an act, behind closed doors, called Cestui Que Vie Act 1666. The act being debated the Cestui Qui act was to subrogate the rights of men and women, meaning all men and women were declared dead, lost at sea/beyond the sea. (back then operating in admiralty law, the law of the sea, so lost at sea).

The state (of London) took custody of everybody and their property into a trust, the state became the trustee/husband holding all titles to the people and property, until a living man comes back to reclaim those titles and can also claim damages. The rule of the use of CAPITAL LETTERS used in a NAME: when CAPITAL letters are used anywhere in a NAME this always refers to a LEGAL ENTITY/FICTION, COMPANY or CORPORATION no exceptions. e.g. John DOE or Doe: JANE (PASSPORT,

DRIVER LICENSE, MARRIAGE CERTIFICATE and BIRTH CERTIFICATE)

CEST TUI QUE TRUST: (pronounced setakay) common term in NEW ZEALAND and AUSTRALIA or STRAWMAN common term in USA or CANADA is a LEGAL ENTITY/FICTION created and owned by the GOVERNMENT whom created it. Legally, we are considered to be a FICTION, a concept or idea expressed as a NAME, a symbol. That LEGAL PERSON has no consciousness; it is a juristic PERSON, ENS LEGIS, a NAME/word written on a piece of paper.

This traces back to 1666, London is a state, just like Vatican is a state, just like Washington DC is a state. The Crown is an unincorporated association. Why unincorporated, its private, the temple bar is in London, every lawyer called to the "bar" swears allegiance to the temple bar. You can't get called, without swearing this allegiance. The Crown already owns North America and everything in it. Your only way out is to reclaim your dead entity (Strawman) that the Crown created, become the trustee of the cest tui qui trust and remove yourself from the admiralty law that holds you in custody.

When London burned the subrogation of men's and woman's rights occurred. The responsible act passed... CQV act 1666 meant all men and women of UK were declared dead and lost beyond the seas. The state took everybody and everybody's property into trust. The state takes control until a living man or woman comes back and claims their titles by proving they are alive and claims for damages can be made.

This is why you always need representation when involved in legal matters, because you're dead. The legal fiction is a construct on paper, an estate in trust. When you get a bill or summons from court it is always in capital letters, similar to tomb stones in grave yards. Capital letters signify death. They are writing to the dead legal fiction. A legal fiction was created when someone informed the government that there was a new vessel in town, based upon your birth. Birth certificates are issued at birth, just as ships are given berth certificates.

Your mother has a birth canal, just like a ship. All this information relates to how the general public are still legally tied. Through admiralty law, through this ancient legal construct we can be easily controlled. Learning about your legal fiction helps you to unlock yourself. Otherwise you are just a vessel floating on the sea of commerce. It is possible to be free from financial stress and debt.

Parents are tricked into registering the birth of their babies. In about 1837 the Births, Deaths and Marriages act was formed in UK and the post of registrar general was established. His job was to collect all the data from the churches which held the records of birth.

Regis - from queen or crown. All people are seen to be in custody of," The Crown". This allows people to function in commerce and to accept the benefits provided by state.

So we are in custody. Worldwide - under the IMF the majority of people are fed, sheltered and provided for, however now it is the system that is benefitting while many are suffering, are poorly fed, housed and water is contaminated. Many people are now getting sick and dying as a result - not to mention that as people evolve, they now seek to be independent of any system that seeks to control or oppress and harms the earth that this is all taking place on.

We have legally elected representatives. We have to understand who we are as men and women and how we can relate in the system.

The City of London is a centre for markets, where merchants work. Then there is mercantile law. It comes from Admiralty. Look at the symbols in the City of London that relate to Admiralty.

Our national banks are not our banks. The private shareholders from the private banks own the banks. It is all private, not public as we are led to believe. "OF" also means "without", eg. The bank without England. Private banks issue private currency.

With WWI a change happened where money was not backed by gold or silver anymore, it is now based on peoples labour. People are now pledged to the IMF as the surety to pay back the creditors in the global bankruptcy. Men and women are not bankrupt, they are the only source of credit. The public is bankrupt.

Regarding the currency that gets issued at the Bank of England, people are the gold or the treasure. The government issues bonds or treasury bills that are bought by investors. The money goes back into the economy in order to pay for the people to build things, e.g. an Olympic Stadium. However, the people are paying taxes for the privilege of using someone else's currency and paying back the principal and the interest on the original loan that was given against the treasury bonds, bills and notes. It is a private corporation that will own the Olympic stadium, be responsible for running it, be able to sell commercial rights, yet the people are actually the ones who own it and should be profiting from it. However, principal and interest is coming through the people in order to raise the money.

So where you have commerce and money, you also have "justice". You need to understand the bankruptcy before you can understand the judiciary. You need to accept the bankruptcy. We have accepted the claim to accept the summons. There is an obligation to accept any liability which has been created. All you can do is accept the bankruptcy. We are operating in admiralty. A not guilty plea dishonours the bankruptcy. The Strawman, aka legal fiction is always guilty. It needs to be accepted for value. Barristers and solicitors make a living out of creating controversy. By creating a controversy you become liable for the case.

Are you in honour and dishonour? To remain in honour you have to accept a claim and settle it. Then you add conditions. I accept on proof of claim and proof of loss. This gives the liability back to them. The legal fiction is always guilty. Only in the high courts, can the real man or woman appear. Games are played on courts; hence the name court is a game with actors (acting on acts). It has to be treated as a game and just business. Court room dramas are misinformation. In the public, we are operating in bankruptcy and you receive benefits. It takes a lot of time, effort and study to use these tools. You have to be prepared to go fully through the process, get the right tool out of your toolbox at the right time. People need to learn how to act as creditors. In summary:

- Money is backed by labour.
- We cannot exchange it fairly for gold or silver.
- Capitalization of "name" means a dead entity, a legal fiction.

- Know who you are, you are not your Strawman or dead fictitious entity.
- Learn how to become a creditor in commerce.

So in summary, when in 1666 an act of parliament created during the black plague, and great fires of London , behind closed doors, it was called Cestui Que Vie Act 1666. (see end of chapter)

The act being debated was the Cestui Qui act which was to subrogate the rights of men and women, meaning all men and women were declared dead, lost at sea/beyond the sea. This was done during a crisis. The state took custody of everybody and their property into a trust, the Cestui Qui trust, the state became the trustee/husband holding all titles to the people and property, until a living man comes back to reclaim those titles and can also claim damages.

The Cestui Qui act or Trust created is an ALL-CAPITALIZED NAME, a 'dead entity' who had all his belongings put into a trust. This act still exists, and this trust still exists. This is how it started. If you were born on Earth, if you have a birth certificate, this applies to you. The only way to claim your trust and get free from admiralty law, is to understand who you really are, and that admiralty law does not apply to you, but in order to get free you must do some homework, file forms and know how commerce applies to you.

Finally, you may ask what is the significance today? Include a letter posted on the Internet from: Hughes, Paul (Civil Law) Ministry of Justice 18 February 2011. It was a response from a letter sent by a Mr. Bolwell which asked about the Cetui Que trust:

"Dear Mr. Bolwell, Thank you for your e-mail of 19 December 2010 to the Data Access and Compliance Unit in which you ask for information about the Cestui que Vie Act 1666. You ask what the Act is about and whether or not it is still in effect. Your e-mail has been passed to me for reply as I work in the part of the department responsible for issues relating to the presumption of death. Your e-mail is not being dealt with under the Freedom of Information Act 2000. I am sorry for the delay in sending you a reply. The Cestui que Vie Act 1666 is still in force but parts of it have been amended or repealed over the years. Specifically:

The preamble was amended by the Statute Law Revision Act 1948; Section 2 was repealed by the Statute Law Revision Act 1948; Section 3 was repealed by the Statute Law Revision Act 1863; and Section 4 was amended by the Statute Law Revision Act 1888. The Act provides for the recovery of a lease where the life tenant has disappeared for seven or more years and there is no proof that the person is still alive. In this situation, the Act gives the court the power to declare the life tenant dead. There are very few references to the statute in the textbooks I have checked, suggesting it is little used. The following extract was taken from Halsbury's Statute Volume 20 (2009 reissue).

In the normal form of a strict settlement (which by virtue of the [1]Trusts of Land and Appointment of Trustees Act 1996, s 2, cannot in general be created on or after 1 January 1997) a limitation to a life tenant invariably precedes one to a tenant in tail in order to restrict the tenant in tail's power to bar the entail. Save where there is a trust for sale, the land will fall within the [2]Settled Land Act 1925 (see s 1 of that Act) and, if the life tenant is of full age, he will be the statutory tenant for life under s 19 of that Act, in whom the fee simple should be vested in trust for himself and the remainder men. The Cestui que Vie Acts 1666 and 1707 help to ascertain whether a life tenant is still alive.

If you have a problem to which the Act relates I can only recommend that you take independent legal advice. If you do not have an adviser your local Citizens Advice Bureau or Community Legal Advice Centre may be able to help him find one. Information about Community Legal Advice can also be found on its website: [3]www.communitylegaladvice.org.uk or by telephoning 0845 345 4345. I hope you find this information helpful."

Yours sincerely, Kirsty Milliam
Ministry of Justice
102 Petty France
London SW1H 9AJ Tel: 020 3334 3207

## A Final Word of Advice

As a final conclusion, I wish to enforce the thesis of this book is to provide education towards determining truth, NOT for taking on the system. Although there are many researchers and antagonists who will promise a fast means to wealth by conflicting with the "system", they are yet to prove they are right and that their processes really work or are "lawful". So user beware because many have gone to jail and many have attained financial ruin by following these unorthodox "STRAWMAN" theories. It is granted that change can occur and these myths and truth do have the potential of eventually being the "rule of law" but that time is not yet. So for that reason, this book can only be considered as pseudo-fiction... a fictional story with some facts thrown in.

339